LIBRARIES, IMMIGRANTS, AND THE AMERICAN EXPERIENCE

Recent Titles in
Contributions in Librarianship and Information Science

LIBRARIES, IMMIGRANTS, AND THE AMERICAN EXPERIENCE

Plummer Alston Jones, Jr.

Contributions in Librarianship and Information Science, Number 92

GREENWOOD PRESS
Westport, Connecticut • London

Library of Congress Cataloging-in-Publication Data

Jones, Plummer Alston.
    Libraries, immigrants, and the American experience / Plummer
Alston Jones, Jr.
       p.   cm.—(Contributions in librarianship and information
science, ISSN 0084–9243 ; no. 92)
    Includes bibliographical references (p.   ) and index.
    ISBN 0–313–30769–5 (alk. paper)
    1. Public libraries—Services to immigrants—United States—
History—19th century.   2. Public libraries—Services to
immigrants—United States—History—20th century.   I. Title.
II. Series.
Z711.8.J66   1999
027.6—dc21   98–26439

British Library Cataloguing in Publication Data is available.

Library of Congress Catalog Card Number: 98–26439
ISBN: 0–313–30769–5
ISSN: 0084–9243

First published in 1999

Greenwood Press, 88 Post Road West, Westport, CT 06881
An imprint of Greenwood Publishing Group, Inc.

Printed in the United States of America

The paper used in this book complies with the
Permanent Paper Standard issued by the National
Information Standards Organization (Z39.48–1984).

10 9 8 7 6 5 4 3 2 1

Every reasonable effort has been made to trace the owners of copyright materials in this book, but in some instances this has proven impossible. The author and publisher will be glad to receive information leading to more complete acknowledgments in subsequent printings of the book and in the meantime extend their apologies for any omissions.

Copyright Acknowledgments

The author and publisher gratefully acknowledge permission for use of the following material:

Extracts from Edna Phillips's correspondence and memorandum on behalf of the ALA Committee on Work with the Foreign Born, contained in file folder of records of the ALA Committee on Work with the Foreign Born (1918–1948). Courtesy American Library Association Archives, University of Illinois at Urbana-Champaign. Used with permission.

Extracts from Eleanor (Edwards) Ledbetter Papers. Courtesy of Cleveland Public Library Archives. Used with permission.

Extracts from Annual reports, correspondence, and miscellaneous publications of the Massachusetts Free Public Library Commission relating to Jane Maud Campbell and Edna Phillips, librarians, who worked as Secretaries of Work with the Foreign Born, 1913–1932. Courtesy of Massachusetts Board of Library Commissioners. Used with permission.

Extracts from Papers of Governor Edward Casper Stokes: correspondence and miscellaneous documents relating to Stokes's appointment of Jane Maud Campbell to the New Jersey Immigration Commission, 1906–1907. Courtesy of New Jersey State Archives, Department of State. Used with permission.

Extracts from John Foster Carr Papers. Courtesy of The New York Public Library, Manuscripts and Archives Division, Astor, Lenox and Tilden Foundations. Used with permission.

Extracts from Jane Maud Campbell Papers and Elizabeth Lowell Putnam Papers. Courtesy of Schlesinger Library, Radcliffe College, Cambridge, MA. Used with permission.

In loving memory of my parents,

Plummer Alston Jones, Sr. (1920–1987)

Elva Lucille (Pridgen Wright) Jones (1925–1972)

Contents

NO list of illus.: pp. 1, 4, 38, 47, 68, 96, 130, 149, 166, 181, 194

Acknowledgments

For permission to quote and reprint photographs, I acknowledge the assistance of the New York Public Library, the Cleveland Public Library, the New Jersey Archives, the Arthur and Elizabeth Schlesinger Library on the History of Women in America at Radcliffe College, the Massachusetts Board of Library Commissioners, and the Morrill Memorial Library (Norwood, MA).

For moral support, photographs, and her gracious hospitality, I thank Fay Campbell (Reed) Kaynor, the great-niece of Jane Maud Campbell, one of the protagonists and certainly the original inspiration for this work.

For guidance and sharing his own special gift for library historical writing, I will always be grateful to Dr. Edward G. Holley, Kenan Professor Emeritus of the School of Information and Library Science at the University of North Carolina at Chapel Hill.

For her help in preparing this manuscript for publishing, I am indebted as always to my friend Gayle Fishel and to my production editor at Greenwood Press, David Palmer.

For my family, friends, colleagues, and students, I offer my thanks for your encouragement and for your forbearance when I launched into yet another seemingly interminable paean to my hero and heroines.

Now, finally, the lives and accomplishments of John Foster Carr, Jane Maud Campbell, Eleanor (Edwards) Ledbetter, and Edna Phillips have been recorded for posterity, and in the process the sterling reputation of American public library service to immigrants has been polished once again.

Abbreviations

The following abbreviations are used extensively throughout the text, notes, and bibliography.

ALA	American Library Association
AR	Annual Report
CAB	*Cleveland Americanization Bulletin*
Campbell Papers	Jane Maud Campbell Papers
Carr Papers	John Foster Carr Papers
CPL	Cleveland Public Library
CPL/BB	Cleveland Public Library, Broadway Branch
CWFB	Committee on Work with the Foreign Born
DAR	Daughters of the American Revolution
GPO	Government Printing Office
Ledbetter Papers	Eleanor (Edwards) Ledbetter Papers
LJ	*Library Journal*
MFPLC	Massachusetts Free Public Library Commission
MLC	Massachusetts Library Club
MLCB	*Massachusetts Library Club Bulletin*
NACLI	North American Civic League for Immigrants
NEA	National Education Association
Phillips Papers	Edna Phillips Papers
Putnam Papers	Elizabeth (Lowell) Putnam Papers
Stokes Papers	Governor Edward Casper Stokes Papers
WLB	*Wilson Library Bulletin*

LIBRARIES, IMMIGRANTS, AND THE AMERICAN EXPERIENCE

Immigrant children during story time at an immigrant branch of the Boston Public Library, circa 1915, when Jane Maud Campbell was Secretary for Work with the Foreign Born of the Massachusetts Free Public Library Commission. Photo courtesy Boston Public Library, Public Relations Department.

1

Introduction

After years of research and noting issues and trends in American immigration, British historian Maldwyn Allen Jones concluded that "immigration, which was America's historic *raison d'être*, has been the most persistent and the most pervasive influence in her development."[1] His finely crafted sentence comprised the subliminal message underlying the festivities that attended the Statue of Liberty celebration held in New York during the summer of 1986.

Scheduled concurrently with the American Library Association annual conference, this event brought together librarians, historians, and enthusiasts from across the United States and throughout the world. All were invited to a champagne reception and treated to a dazzlingly magnificent exhibition of memorabilia in the New York Public Library assembled in honor of "Miss Liberty," the most enduring and endearing symbol of the vast migratory phenomenon that has shaped our national destiny.[2]

Of all the delights of the eye spread before the throng of visitors, the most poignant, perhaps even the most significant, display was tucked away on a third-floor gallery. Appropriately titled "The Ellis Island Experience," the exhibit featured photographs by renowned photographers Augustus Francis Sherman and Lewis Wickes Hine. These hauntingly beautiful photographic portraits captured the bewildered visages of immigrants—Armenian Jews, Serbian Gypsies, Dutch children, women from Guadaloupe—all meeting and returning the equally amazed and curious stares of the spectators.

As if these priceless photographs were not enough to evoke the very essence of America's immigration history, an even more lasting impression was made by the contents of a simple glass case. Here were displayed copies of John Foster Carr's *Guide to the United States* in its various editions and translations. Here were artifacts from the era of free immigration to America—guidebooks, which were written to acquaint Yiddish-, Italian-, Polish-, and English-speaking immigrants with the realities and, alas, the vagaries of life in America.[3] These guidebooks represented tangible reminders of how one individual, an admirer of immigrants and a lover of libraries, had provided the basic information to introduce newcomers to the New World and to accomplish their assimilation.

Notwithstanding the marvelous displays and exhibits depicting our nation's continued fascination with its immigrant origins and pride in its free public libraries, something incredibly fundamental was missing from the New York Public Library's splendid collection. Ironically, an in-depth history of how American public libraries and librarians have interacted with the immigrant community had not been written.

An abundance of secondary sources on American immigration exist. None are as remarkable, however, as those of Marcus Hansen, Oscar Handlin, Maldwyn Allen Jones, and, most recently, John Bodnar.[4] Secondary sources on American public library history are also available. Phyllis Dain's history of the New York Public Library treats library service to immigrants in a local context. Wayne Wiegand's history of public libraries during World War I places services to immigrants in a national context. Both are worthy examples, respectively, of histories of individual public libraries and histories of public libraries during specific time periods.[5]

The purpose of this work is to document the history of American public library service to immigrants from the beginning of librarianship as a profession in 1876 through World War II. This history will focus on the interaction between American public libraries and the immigrant community. It will integrate the societal and political contexts of immigration as a national phenomenon with the history of library service to immigrants.

The American library profession's stance on library service to immigrants will be explored further to answer fundamental questions. Was librarianship as a profession reflective of the opinions and attitudes of the Congress or the country as a whole? Did library service during the period of free immigration, from 1876 to 1924, change in content and focus during the period of restricted immigration, from 1924 to 1948? Was the library profession content to maintain the status quo, or did it seek new groups to serve?

The lives of individual library leaders in work with immigrants and their attitudes toward their immigrant clienteles will be examined closely. Their views on the Americanization, or assimilation, process itself will be discovered through their correspondence, publications, and speeches. Which theory of assimilation did they incorporate into their work—Angloconformity, melting pot, or cultural pluralism?

This history will focus on the immigrants themselves—their dreams and their potentialities—and how the public library empowered them to make their homes in America. Did immigrant groups have similar or different needs for the library to fill? Did they come to America to change their lives, as did the Russian Jews? Did they come to America to continue the patterns of life of the Old World, as did the Italians? Or did they bring with them to America a pragmatism that called forth their innate abilities to find their particular niches in the New World?

Finally, what were the attitudes of immigrants themselves toward the public library? Did the library help some immigrant groups more than others? Were some immigrant groups more predisposed to benefit from the services of a free public library? Did immigrants desire to Americanized?

During the twentieth century, the United States was transformed from a nation that credited immigrants as an asset to a nation that debited them as a liability. Will America remain a viable option for immigrants from troubled lands in the twenty-first century? Will American public libraries continue to lend a helping hand to immigrants whose languages and worldviews are different?

At the turn of the century as at the beginning, Americans are still debating the place of immigrants in American society. When the Statue of Liberty was erected and when John Foster Carr was publishing his immigrant guides, the Congress and state legislatures were troubled by the hordes of legal immigrants coming to American shores from Europe and Asia. Nowadays, politicians, particularly in the Southwest, California, and Florida, are elected or defeated according to their positions on the status of legal and an increasing number of illegal immigrants from Mexico, Central America, Cuba, and other Western Hemisphere countries.

Ironically, librarians are now, as they were then, going about their duties and responsibilities of providing advice and materials to help immigrants, legal and illegal, to cope with everyday life in America. The American public library has remained the sovereign alchemist, turning the base metal of immigrant potentialities into the gold of American realities.

NOTES

1. Maldwyn Allen Jones, *American Immigration* (Chicago: University of Chicago Press, 1960), 1.

2. *Gala Champagne Reception* [brochure], distributed to members of the American Library Association who attended the reception and exhibit entitled *A Birthday Party for Ms. Liberty*, held Saturday, 28 June 1986, 7:00–9:00 P.M., at the New York Public Library headquarters at 42nd Street and Fifth Avenue.

3. See, for example, Carr's *Guide to the United States for the Immigrant Italian; A Nearly Literal Translation of the Italian Version*, published under the auspices of the Connecticut Daughters of the American Revolution (Garden City, NY: Doubleday, Page, 1911).

4. Marcus Lee Hansen, *The Immigrant in American History*, edited with a foreword by Arthur M. Schlesinger (New York: Harper and Row, 1964, copr. 1940); Oscar Handlin, *The Uprooted: The Epic Story of the Great Migrations that Made the American People* (Boston: Little, Brown, 1951); Jones, *American Immigration*; and John Bodnar, *The Transplanted: A History of Immigrants in Urban America* (Bloomington: Indiana University Press, 1985).

5. Phyllis Dain, *The New York Public Library: A History of Its Founding and Early Years* (New York: New York Public Library, Astor, Lenox and Tilden Foundations, 1972); and Wayne Wiegand, *"An Active Instrument for Propaganda": The American Public Library during World War I*, foreword by Edward G. Holley, Beta Phi Mu Monograph no. 1 (Westport, CT: Greenwood Press, 1989).

"Serbian Gypsies." Photograph courtesy William Williams Papers, Manuscripts and Archives Division, The New Public Library, Astor, Lenox and Tilden Foundations.

2

Libraries, Immigrants, and Free Immigration, 1876–1924

Ironies abounded during the turbulent half century from 1876 to 1924. Due in no small measure to the over 26 million emigrants who came to the United States during this period, the nation was transformed from a mainly rural and agricultural society into a society increasingly urban and industrial. Rather than being recognized for their contributions toward the overall prosperity accompanying this national transformation, these newly arrived American immigrants were more often blamed for the social and political upheavals associated with the phenomenal economic and industrial growth.[1]

FREE IMMIGRATION AND THE NATION

Americans as a nation still cherished the ideal of the United States as the asylum for the oppressed, the haven for the homeless, the refuge for the persecuted, and, above all, the land of unlimited opportunity for the ambitious. Many native-born Americans, however, had no qualms with erecting barriers, in the form of regulatory exceptions or exclusions, to the entrance of immigrants whose moral, medical, or financial circumstances rendered them undesirable.

Most Americans were reluctant to acknowledge openly their racial prejudices as justification for the exclusion of immigrant groups. Nevertheless, racial considerations also determined American immigration policy to a great extent, particularly with regard to the Chinese and Japanese, whose immigration was suspended respectively by the Chinese Exclusion Act of 1882 and the Gentlemen's Agreement of 1907–1908 with Japan. Both treaties set the precedent for future legislation, which would regulate in theory, while in practice would severely limit, Oriental immigration.[2]

National Attitudes toward Immigration

These, then, were the conflicting stances of native-born Americans on the controversial issue of immigration at the beginning of the 1870s. Conservative Americans, usually labeled nativists, lobbied vigorously and unabashedly for the enforcement of even more stringent measures to stem the immigrant tide. Liberal Americans, usually labeled progressives, in keeping with an avowed belief in the asylum concept, advocated a laissez-faire attitude toward immigration, at least the "old" immigration originating from the British Isles and northern and western Europe, whose presence did not threaten Anglo-Saxon hegemony. The old immigration had consisted primarily of Germans, who fled from political upheavals in Germany; the Irish, who fled the potato famines in Ireland; and other western Europeans and Scandinavians, who, for a myriad of political, religious, and economic reasons, came to America during the 1840s, 1850s, and 1860s to start a new life.[3]

The 1870s witnessed a marked change in the complexion of the "new" immigration, which, in contrast to the "old," began to stream from southern and eastern Europe and the Middle East. Ironically, the new immigrants came to America for essentially the same reasons as the old. They included Jews from czarist Russia and Armenians from Turkish-ruled Armenia, who risked almost certain annihilation if they remained in their homelands, and Italian and Slavic immigrants, who fled agricultural reforms and manufacturing revolutions, which threatened their livelihoods as small farmers and craftsmen. Nevertheless, the presence of the new immigrants in ever-increasing numbers in overcrowded ghettos in large urban centers, primarily on the East and West Coasts and in the Midwest, caused native-born Americans, both conservatives and liberals, to question whether these immigrants could be assimilated as easily as the earlier immigrants had been.

The related phenomenon of return migration, or the repatriation of immigrants when their circumstances did not improve in America, not only earned for many of the new immigrants, especially the Italians, the disparaging epithet "birds of passage," but also affirmed nativists' suspicions that immigrants were disloyal. Thus, coincidental with the new immigration beginning in the 1870s came not only a rededication of nativists to their restrictionist cause, but also a movement by the progressive majority away from a strictly laissez-faire attitude toward immigration.[4]

The Movement for Restricted Immigration

The fears of nativists were fanned and, from their perspectives, justified by the involvement of immigrants in violent labor disputes, including the Molly Maguire coalfield strikes in Pennsylvania in the early 1870s and the railroad strikes of 1877, and political demonstrations, notably the infamous Haymarket Affair of 1886 in Chicago. With the support of politicians, labor leaders, economists, and eugenicists, whose pseudoscientific theories purportedly affirmed the racial superiority of Americans of Anglo-Saxon stock, nativists began a relentless crusade for the restriction of American immigration.

The first federal immigration law, passed in 1882, took regulatory control of immigration out of the hands of the individual seaboard states and placed it in the hands of the federal government. Enacted ironically just four years before the dedication in 1886 of the Statue of Liberty, this Act of 1882 and subsequent Acts of 1891, 1903, and 1907 gave the weight of federal sanction to restrictions formerly imposed by state authorities. These restrictions had forbidden the entry of immigrants with certain diseases, criminal records, no capital, or radical political opinions.

Labor union leaders argued convincingly that the employment of immigrants was jeopardizing the livelihood of American laborers. Although the employment opportunities and low wages available to unskilled immigrant laborers were in no way attractive to skilled native-born American laborers, trade union officials nevertheless felt duly compensated for their lobbying efforts by the passage of the Foran Act of 1885, which forbade the importation of unskilled laborers under contract.[5]

Buoyed by their successes in achieving the legal exclusion of immigrants from China and Japan as well as immigrant laborers under contract, nativists focused their energies on the passage of bills to exclude illiterate immigrants, those who could not read in their own or any other language. Lobbying efforts for a literacy test, which were aimed primarily at reducing the flow of the new immigration, emanated from various nativist organizations, but none was more effective than the Immigration Restriction League, founded in 1894 by Boston blue bloods, aided by their congressional spokesman, Henry Cabot Lodge of Massachusetts. Congress passed bills calling for a literacy test for immigrants in 1897, 1913, and 1915, only to be vetoed by Presidents Cleveland, Taft, and Wilson.

Eventually, legislation in support of a literacy test for immigrants was enacted over Wilson's veto in February of 1917, due, to a great extent, to the voluminous recommendations published in 1911 by the Dillingham Commission, which had been charged by Congress earlier in 1907 to study the new immigration as a preliminary to the framing of more stringent immigration legislation. Scarcely three months later, in April 1917, the United States joined its European allies and adversaries in the "war to end all wars."[6]

World War I and Its Aftermath

Rather than causing the movement toward immigration restriction, World War I merely accelerated it. Long before the entrance of the United States into World War I, native-born Americans, of widely divergent opinions concerning immigration had cooperated in projects and programs geared toward the assimilation or Americanization of the foreign-born unnaturalized immigrants already residing in the United States. World War I, by drawing the nation's attention to the "strangers within our gates," imbued a vast array of philanthropic, patriotic, and educational organizations with a profound sense of urgency to ensure the loyalty of the foreign born. Their collective mission be-

WWI as ebb in tide

came to teach immigrants to speak and read English and to encourage them to become citizens.[7]

The flow of immigration into the United States lessened considerably during World War I, but after the signing of the armistice in 1918 and continuing into the early 1920s, immigration began to resume its prewar proportions. Along with this renewed immigration, a new concern was added to the nativists' list of reasons for restriction.

The period from 1918 to 1920, later referred to as the Red Scare, was an era dominated by the irrational fear that Bolshevism was being imported by immigrants fleeing the aftermath of the Russian Revolution of 1917. During the Red Scare, Americanization efforts were intensified. The deportation of hundreds of immigrant radicals, who were arrested during the infamous Palmer raids of 1919–1920, drove home the message that immigrants already in the United States were not safe from governmental intervention until they were Americanized, naturalized citizens.[8]

National Origins Act of 1924

By 1921, the Congress, responding to this groundswell of support for immigration restriction, passed, as an emergency measure, the first in a series of legislation to limit the actual numbers of immigrants coming annually into the United States. Between 1921 and 1924 an elaborate immigration quota system was devised.

The effect of the resultant National Origins Act of 1924 was to encourage immigration from northern and western Europe as well as all countries in the Western Hemisphere, while discouraging immigration from southern and eastern Europe, the Middle East, Asia, and other parts of the Eastern Hemisphere. Thus, America, the asylum for all immigrants before 1924, would be transformed after 1924 into the haven for a select few.[9]

FREE IMMIGRATION AND PUBLIC LIBRARIES

The most extreme irony was that this shift in national thinking on immigration was occurring when America's major public libraries were being founded and when American librarians, through the founding of the American Library Association in 1876, were gaining recognition as a profession. Libraries and librarians joined other social organizations and professionals in the collective quest to make America's vast resources—cultural, educational, and material—available on an equal basis to all citizens and residents of the United States.

Attitudes of Librarians toward Free Immigration

Librarians did not turn inwardly within their newly organized profession, but instead turned outwardly to the American society for direction in their quest to be of service to the American populace. They, like the social workers and educators they emulated, found in the immigrant a client or patron who could benefit not only from their advocacy, but also from the resources and services available in the public library. Although individual librarians in their personal lives and, particularly, in the voting booths, may have supported nativist policies on immigration, as professionals they evinced a genuine commitment, notwithstanding varying degrees of condescension and paternalism, to serving the immigrants within their respective communities.

While nativists clamored for immigration restriction and progressives pled for the melting pot to work its special magic on the immigrant masses, the library profession seems never to have questioned immigration policy, as it was or even as it was evolving to be. Rather, librarians lent a hand in the movement to Americanize the immigrants already in the United States.

Beginnings of Library Service to Immigrants

It is impossible to document when immigrants first began to use American public libraries as their principal source for informational and recreational reading or even when American librarians first identified immigrants as the targets for library service. It is clear, however, that immigrants themselves assigned access to libraries and library materials as a high priority. Many immigrant groups established their own social libraries long before the establishment of free, tax-supported public libraries.

The contents of these immigrant social libraries formed the nuclei of the foreign language collections of the major public libraries, which eventually incorporated them. This pattern was witnessed in Buffalo, where in 1907 the collection of the Deutsche Jungmaenner Gesellschaft (German Young Men's Association), established earlier in 1841, became the nucleus of the German collection. Also, in Brooklyn in 1905, the Brownsville Branch incorporated not only the collection of but also the physical structure housing the Hebrew Educational Association.[10]

Foreign language materials were amassed through other channels as well. In 1914, the beneficence of immigrant cultural societies, notably the Dante Alighieri Society and the Polish National Alliance, resulted in the gifts of Italian and Polish books respectively to the foreign language collections of the public libraries in New York and Cleveland. Renowned special collections of foreign language materials were established around the gifts and continuing philanthropy of prominent citizens. Jacob H. Schiff's gifts in the Slavic and Semitic languages formed respectively the cores of the great Slavonic and Jewish Divisions of the New York Public Library. John G. White's gifts of Arabic folklore and other Orientalia formed the nucleus of the great collection of the Cleveland Public Library, which bears his name. Finally, librarians acknowledged with gratitude the donations and loans from foreign governments, notably the Swedish government, whose gifts of Swedish books and loans of King Oscar's traveling libraries were obtained by the public libraries in San Francisco in 1905, Providence in 1908, and Denver in 1912.[11]

Community Service with Immigrants: The Missionary Spirit

Librarians in Buffalo in 1914 and Boston in 1920, who identified themselves, along with their colleagues in social and public health work, as community leaders, were convinced that library work with immigrants occurred within a framework of community service. A case in point involved a Cleveland librarian, who decided in 1907 to live in the midst of the immigrant neighborhood her library served, believing that Americanization work with immigrants required a "missionary spirit." With surprising uniformity of opinion, librarians and library boards throughout the country thus revealed their acceptance of Americanization as an appropriate social and educational mission of the public library.[12]

In the immigrant neighborhoods of Brooklyn at the beginning of the twentieth century, in 1901, the library was perceived as one of the "civilizing influences." This perception was shared in Cleveland, where the public library in 1910 served as a "potent factor in linking the old civilization with the new." In Jersey City in 1896, the library's mission was to instill "higher standards of intelligence and morality which tend to make better citizens." In Milwaukee in 1913, the library was dubbed "an agency for amalgamating the citizenship and enlightening the new citizen." In Buffalo in 1912, librarians were convinced that there existed "no easier or more direct method of promoting better citizenship than by the distribution of good books."[13] As late as 1923, Pittsburgh librarians characterized the public library as "pro-everything and anti-nothing which promises to contribute to the welfare of the district" and by extension viewed the public library as "a common meeting ground for all races, creeds, and sects."[14]

Library Cooperation in the Americanization Movement

Americanization as a concept, even before it had attached itself to a movement, was a term that connoted many meanings to many people, but for librarians it meant simply a two-part process: instruction in the English language and preparation for citizenship. Librarians viewed the former as leading quite naturally to the latter, believing that newly Americanized immigrants, who could now read and write in the language of their adopted country, would show their gratitude by becoming naturalized citizens.[15]

As the drive for immigration restriction ebbed and flowed during the period from 1876 to 1924 and eventually crested during World War I, librarians viewed Americanization as either a service to the immigrant community, in periods of relative calm, or as their patriotic duty, in periods of heated debate and agitation. Regardless of the intensity with which they approached Americanization, however, librarians never questioned or debated in print whether Americanization was an appropriate mission for the American public library: it was *the* goal of library work with immigrants.

Librarians throughout the country were sensitive as well to what other or-ganizations—social, educational, cultural, religious, philanthropic, patriotic, and political—were doing to promote Americanization and sought means for their respective libraries to cooperate with these agencies. As early as 1897, the Los

Angeles Public Library began a tradition of cooperation by supplying books for the Los Angeles Settlements Association.

This tradition of cooperative service continued in 1910 with the Young Men's Christian Association. The Los Angeles Public Library agreed to place two to three thousand books for use of immigrant laborers employed by the various camps constructing the Los Angeles aqueduct. Later, in 1919, the library cooperated with settlement workers to provide Japanese books and magazines for the clubhouse at the East San Pedro fishing village.

By 1901, the New Orleans Public Library had an agreement with the Young Men's Hebrew Association to extend library service to the immigrant Jewish community. The New York Public Library in 1908 cooperated with the Industrial Department of the Young Men's Christian Association to place books in factories and the Presbyterian Board of Home Missions to place books in foreign churches. Four years later, in 1912, the New York Public Library participated in cooperative programs with municipal departments of health and child welfare to provide instruction in hygiene and sanitation to the immigrant community.

Library cooperation with settlements, a clear manifestation of librarians' affinity for social work, was reported in Detroit in 1907. The public library there provided French books to a settlement maintained by a patriotic society. Similarly, in Cleveland, in 1915, the library contributed regularly to the newsletter published by a local settlement house.[16]

Library cooperation with governmental agencies, both federal and municipal, was manifested in remarkably similar ways across the country. The Buffalo Public Library in 1917 cooperated closely with both the Naturalization Bureau and the Polish Citizens Protective Association to sponsor classes in Polish and English, and the classes emphasized library resources and opportunities for Americanization.

In 1917, the Detroit Public Library reported that every member of the library staff had visited a hearing at the local Naturalization Bureau and had witnessed the examination of an immigrant for either first or second papers. The Cleveland Public Library in 1923 cooperated with the Citizen's Bureau, which taught an intensive twelve-week course to prepare immigrants for the oral examination for citizenship. Librarians and assistants were assigned regularly to these classes both to observe the Americanization process and to inform themselves as to how they could offer assistance in preparing immigrants for it.[17]

Library cooperation with patriotic societies reached its peak during the years surrounding World War I, but was most apparent throughout the period from 1876 to 1924, when libraries provided auditorium and classroom space for the use of a vast array of organizations that promoted the citizenship component of Americanization. The Carnegie Library of Pittsburgh in 1914 provided the space for meetings of a club of Polish boys, which was organized under the auspices of the Daughters of the American Revolution (DAR) and met regularly in the library with a leader provided by the DAR.[18]

Curiously, in the midst of this flurry of harmonious activity with the immigrant community, a single discordant voice was heard. No doubt this lone voice was representative of the inchoate ambivalence of many less articulate, as to whether or not American libraries should continue to use public funds to supply books in the native languages of the immigrant communities they served. Many reasoned that the provision of such materials would hinder the teaching of English and the promotion of citizenship.

An unsigned editorial, which appeared in the October 1894 issue of *Library Journal*, was the first publication to put the question to a national audience and call for comment and debate.[19] The editorial took the stand that American libraries should not provide foreign language materials because this practice encouraged the maintenance of barriers between English-speaking citizens and foreign language-speaking, unnaturalized immigrants.

Surprisingly, the writer of this provocative editorial found no support from fellow librarians, at least none that appeared in print. However, it was soon apparent that the debate was still unresolved in many communities. As much as twenty years later, in 1914, the Queens Borough Public Library reported that "it is a debated question, whether the aliens should be forced to read English books or none, or whether they might not quickly be made more valuable citizens by supplying them with books, including books of information about America, in their own tongues."[20]

The majority response from librarians from New York to Minneapolis, based on extensive personal experience with their immigrant patrons, consistently affirmed that the provision of foreign language materials enhanced, rather than hindered, Americanization.[21] Boston librarians as early as 1907 had pointed out the commercial advantage alone to immigrants who maintained speaking and reading ability in their native languages along with learning English.[22]

On the whole, librarians as a profession viewed immigrants as Americans in the making and themselves as active agents in their Americanization. Librarians demonstrated a progressive laissez-faire attitude toward immigrants, including not only a tolerance for but also an appreciation of cultural differences.

Foreign Language Materials

Throughout the last three decades of the nineteenth century and into the early twentieth century, public libraries throughout the country amassed foreign language collections that reflected the particular needs of the ethnic and national groups represented in their respective communities. These public libraries compiled and published extensive statistics on acquisitions, cataloging, circulation, and other aspects of foreign language collection use and maintenance.

German and French books, the first foreign language collections in most public libraries, were tangible evidence of the influence of the earlier western European immigrants on the early development of American public libraries. These foreign language books, which were made available presumably for scholars, were used more often by American citizens with immigrant heritages, who maintained ties with ancestral homelands through reading literature in the native tongues of their forebears.

Acquisition of Foreign Language Materials. Foreign language books were imported directly from Europe, but more often they were acquired through vendors and dealers in the major centers of domestic and international trade, principally New York. This was the reported practice of librarians in San Francisco in 1904 in the West as well as in Queens Borough in 1909 in the Northeast.

Acquisitions librarians in Brooklyn in 1904 and Cleveland in 1910 and 1924 went on buying trips abroad with a dual purpose: (1) to purchase books not only for their own respective libraries, but also in cooperation with other public libraries collecting in the same languages, and (2) to familiarize themselves with the cultural and educational opportunities as well as the book trades of the homelands of their immigrant patrons. Even before the United States became involved in World War I, the public libraries in Los Angeles on the West Coast in 1917 and Baltimore on the East Coast in 1916 both reported difficulty in getting foreign language books from abroad. They complained that they had to rely solely on the badly depleted stocks of American vendors and dealers.[23]

Public libraries in both Brooklyn and Queens in 1910 were among the first to appropriate specific amounts for the purchase of foreign language books, a practice that eventually led to the use of formulas to allocate purchases. In Los Angeles in 1923, librarians began to purchase foreign language books "in accordance with a rule that the ratio of expenditure shall correspond with the ratio of circulation in each language." The not surprising result was that Spanish received 30 percent of the acquisitions budget for foreign language materials that year.[24]

Circulation of Foreign Language Materials. The Milwaukee Public Library reported that the circulation of books in German literature represented 10 percent of total circulation during the second year of its existence in 1879. The Providence Public Library in 1883 reported that there were sufficient numbers of residents who spoke French and German to warrant purchases in those languages.

The Louisville Free Public Library, which had included foreign language book statistics in its first annual report in 1905, reported only two years later, in 1907, an increasing demand for foreign books, particularly in German. The Queens Borough Public Library reported an increase in foreign language-book circulation from 7,793 in 1909 to 29,985 only four years later, in 1913.[25]

Cataloging of Foreign Language Materials. Books in foreign languages were selected, acquired, and cataloged, and locations for their maintenance and distribution were found with the assistance of religious leaders, scholars, and other prominent citizens from particular ethnic or national groups. Expert advice and assistance was received as well from professors in foreign languages and social work from local universities and colleges and from social workers from the settlements located throughout the foreign sections of the major cities. The Newark Public Library acknowledged the assistance of local Polish societies in 1898, and the Brooklyn Public Library, the assistance of a priest in 1906. The Cleveland Public Library welcomed the assistance of loans from the private collection of a Bohemian newspaper editor in 1908, and the Enoch Pratt Free Library of Baltimore, the assistance of a Bohemian literary club in 1912. Libraries in Philadelphia, Pittsburgh, and St. Louis throughout the period from 1911 through

1922 welcomed assistance from immigrants in the development and administration of foreign language collections.[26]

Distribution of Foreign Language Materials. As public libraries grew they began to offer their services and resources not only at the central library, but also from distribution points in various locations throughout the city. They experimented with ingenious patterns of distribution, including home libraries, which were small, personalized collections for individuals, clubs, and societies with limited geographical access to libraries, as reported by public libraries in Cleveland in 1909, Milwaukee in 1911, and New York in 1914.

Delivery stations or deposits in factories, department stores, and other business establishments that served the needs of remote immigrant neighborhoods were reported by the public libraries in Jersey City during its first year in 1891, Brooklyn in 1903, and Chicago in 1910. Traveling libraries, modeled after the well-developed systems operated by state library commissions in the scarcely populated areas of the Midwest as early as 1902, were adapted to serve the needs of fluid urban immigrant communities by public libraries in Cleveland in 1903, Queens Borough in 1906, and Chicago in 1911.[27]

Branch Libraries. The most effective distribution point by far for the immigrant communities scattered throughout the large urban centers was the branch library, which achieved the status of community center in many immigrant communities. Since many immigrants tended to settle along ethnic or national lines in well-defined neighborhoods, usually near places of employment, the branch libraries serving such areas at their very inceptions took on the distinctive characteristics of their immigrant clienteles. When, for example, a branch library located on the edge of the Vieux Carre in New Orleans was opened in 1908, the main address was given in French.[28]

Representative branches serving the Polish community included the William Ives Branch in Buffalo, from 1906 onward, and the Richmond Branch in Philadelphia, beginning in 1907. The Bohemian (Czech) community received exemplary service from the Soulard Branch in St. Louis, where the Bohemian residents printed souvenir programs in Bohemian of the opening festivities in 1910, and from the internationally famous Webster Branch in New York as early as 1913. In Denver, in 1913, the Charles Dickinson Branch was already noted for its services to Jewish immigrants.[29]

Centralization of Foreign Language Materials. By 1910 in St. Louis and 1911 in Cleveland, another library distribution pattern emerged. Books in certain foreign languages, for which the need was either widespread or ephemeral, were maintained at the main library building as a central reserve collection for redistribution throughout the city based on librarians' requests. Books in other foreign languages, used primarily by specific ethnic or national groups who settled in close proximity to a branch library, were treated as permanent repository collections and maintained at designated branches. This basic distribution pattern was adopted by the public libraries in Pittsburgh in 1912, New York in 1913, Queens Borough in 1916, and Milwaukee in 1924.[30]

Foreign Language Departments. The natural outgrowth of the large central reserve collections was the establishment of foreign language departments in the main library buildings. The foreign language materials, which had often been integrated into the main stacks, were now pulled, reshelved, and housed in designated areas of the main library building for the convenience of foreign language readers and scholars. Called variously foreign language departments or divisions, these special collections sprang up in public libraries across the country beginning in 1907 in Providence and followed by Cleveland in 1909, Los Angeles in 1920, and Detroit in 1924.[31]

Foreign Language Services

Community Surveys. Librarians' knowledge of the makeup of the various immigrant communities enhanced the development of foreign language collections and, eventually, their circulation throughout large urban areas. Libraries surveyed their communities to discover, among other characteristics, the population, the city streets encompassed, the ethnic and national groups represented, the religious affiliations, the public and parochial schools, the labor unions, the fraternal and social organizations, and businesses. This process of documenting the resources of the neighborhoods served by local branches was the normal practice for branch librarians and their assistants.

The information obtained in the community survey not only became a source of information for the librarians themselves, but also provided the basis for reference and referral service for their immigrant clienteles. The Brooklyn Public Library, as early as 1908, referred to the benefits to be derived from studying neighborhoods from a "sociological point of view," and the Queens Borough Public Library reported similar activity in 1910.

The Cleveland Public Library reported in 1914 the practice of using library assistants who were proficient in various foreign languages to do the community survey in immigrant neighborhoods, where their fluency could be used to greatest advantage. The primary result was the construction of color-coded maps to show where certain nationalities resided.

The Los Angeles Public Library used a team approach to conduct a major community survey from 1917 to 1918, under the auspices of the California State Commission of Education. The team, which was composed of librarians, evening schoolteachers, and representatives from other educational and social welfare agencies, produced a nationality map similar to that of the Cleveland Public Library.

The community survey conducted by the Carnegie Library of Pittsburgh in 1918 yielded the data for the development of card files, accessible by fraternal and philanthropic organizations, businesses, newspapers, churches and synagogues, schools and playgrounds as well as by names of professionals, including translators, interpreters, and foreign language teachers. The most extensive and well-organized community survey of American activities in immigrant branches was conducted between 1918 and 1919 in St. Louis. Excerpts from this survey were published in 1919 in *Library Journal*.[32]

Reference Services. As foreign language collections grew, librarians became increasingly concerned with providing access to these materials, both through more in-depth cataloging practices and through reference services provided by librarians and assistants proficient in immigrant languages. As early as 1881, catalogers in Milwaukee were classifying German language books by subject to allow for their integration into the collection, while catalogers in Cleveland in 1909 were still classifying foreign language books by a simple letter designation and maintaining only a rudimentary shelf list arranged alphabetically. By 1912, however, catalogers in Cleveland were making entries for books in Russian and other nonroman alphabets, including Yiddish, Greek, Arabic, and Serbian, in transliterated as well as translated forms, with the aid of newly acquired typewriters equipped with special keyboards.[33]

Foreign Language Assistants. The need for library staff fluent in foreign languages was met by the employment of foreign language assistants beginning in the later part of the nineteenth century and continuing as standard practice in the early twentieth century. In 1899, the Buffalo Public Library employed Josepha Kudlicka as Polish assistant to help serve the burgeoning Polish community in Buffalo. Thus a trend was set that was followed by public libraries across the nation. The Cleveland Public Library reported in 1908 and 1912 the employment of foreign language assistants who spoke German, Polish, Bohemian (Czech), Slovak, Slovenian, and Croatian. The Enoch Pratt Free Library of Baltimore in 1923 boasted of the employment of a Polish assistant. The Boston Public Library, in 1923, pointed with pride to assistants who spoke Arabic, Italian, Yiddish, and Greek. The Milwaukee Public Library announced in 1911 the availability of a trained linguist in the reference department, and the Detroit Public Library followed in 1916 with the acknowledgment of staff members familiar with "alien" languages spoken and read by the "foreigners" of Detroit.[34]

In addition to making immigrant patrons more comfortable or "more at home" in the public library, these foreign language assistants facilitated the publication of printed finding aids and bibliographies for foreign language materials. These were provided both free and at a nominal cost, and were often shared with other libraries and published in library periodicals.

The Cleveland Public Library published a German catalog as early as 1876, and the San Francisco Public Library published a catalog of foreign literature in 1898. The Detroit Public Library sold a French catalog for twenty-five cents in 1889, and four years later distributed a Bohemian catalog at no charge. The Louisville Free Public Library provided lists of German books in 1914. An early instance of interlibrary cooperation in the printing of catalogs in foreign languages occurred in 1913 when the Carnegie Library of Pittsburgh received from the New York Public Library linotype slugs in languages for which no matrices were available.[35]

Immigrant Children's Services and the Public and Parochial Schools. Public libraries struggled to maintain a semblance of balance between services for adults and services for children. Public librarians would admit readily that the most effective agency for the Americanization of immigrant children was the public school. They were also aware of the paradox that it was principally through the children that the parents would be reached. Thus children's books in English, which were read by children for entertainment, served an equally important educational function as the first English reader for foreign-born adults.

Immigrant children, who were exposed daily to the Americanizing influences of the public school, learned English quickly and were often the first English teachers of their parents. In 1903, Clara Whitehill Hunt, superintendent of the Children's Department of the Brooklyn Public Library, noting this phenomenon, was convinced that a children's book often "acts as a missionary to father and mother and small sisters, as well as to the lad who takes it home."[36]

In 1900, the Cleveland Public Library reported the rapid assimilation of immigrant children, especially the acquisition of the English language through the public schools. There it was observed that while more than two-thirds of the children who used the Main Library were born of foreign parents, less than .005 percent of the books issued on juvenile cards were in foreign languages.

The New York Public Library boasted in 1907 that one-third of their total circulation was among children. In 1914, the Buffalo Public Library sent to Polish parents, by way of their children, letters written in Polish and English, that explained library services, including story hours in Polish and English. As late as 1920, the Carnegie Library of Pittsburgh affirmed that foreign-born parents were Americanized best through their children, who, in turn, carried home "lessons of courtesy, cleanliness, thrift, care of public property, [and] love of country," all instilled in them at the public library.[37]

Immigrant children were often introduced initially to the public library through the public school. In 1898, the Buffalo Public Library established the innovative practice of supplying public school classrooms with library deposit collections, later known simply as the Buffalo Plan, which was welcomed by public school officials. The Buffalo Public Library reported enthusiastically three years later, in 1901, that library work with the public schools was potentially the most valuable service provided. As a concomitant result, "its direct influence upon the intellectual and ethical improvement of the city can hardly be overestimated." School-library cooperation was a continuing priority in funding and programming in Buffalo in 1921. That year the Buffalo Public Library reported with pride that the number of classroom libraries, many in immigrant neighborhood schools, had risen from 163 deposits in 1898, with a circulation of 27,469, to 1,103 deposits in 1921, with a circulation of 555,445.[38]

Although not on a scale as extensive as the Buffalo Plan, classroom deposit collections, including English primers and other materials selected for immigrant children and, by extension, their parents, were reported by public libraries in St. Louis in 1914 and Chicago in 1923. The Cleveland Public Library in 1912 reported its cooperation with the parochial schools located near immigrant branches.

The Los Angeles Public Library in 1920 instituted a series of Teachers' Teas for teachers of immigrant education, teachers of English in high and intermediate schools, vocational teachers, and Japanese teachers. These popular events

borrowers. Contacts were made also with elderly immigrants too old to learn English well enough to survive outside the confines of the immigrant community.[46]

Advertising Library Service to Immigrants. The distribution throughout the immigrant community of circulars, placards, and flyers that were printed in English and various foreign languages was reported as early as 1887, when the Milwaukee Public Library distributed circulars in English and German to the public schools. In 1908 and 1909, the Providence Public Library reported the printing and widespread distribution of library application blanks and information booklets in foreign languages, which had been translated by immigrant patrons at no charge.

The Cleveland Public Library in 1909 printed similar leaflets in German, Slovenian, and Polish explaining hours of opening and how to obtain borrowers' cards. These were given in quantities to immigrant borrowers to distribute to their friends and neighbors who might not know of the library.

Placards in Polish were distributed to neighborhood stores and factories by the Buffalo Public Library in 1910. Handbills in English, Polish, and Yiddish were inserted into pay envelopes in factories employing immigrant workers by the St. Louis Public Library in 1910. In Pittsburgh in 1917, the ministers in Swedish churches advertised Swedish books in the Carnegie Library of Pittsburgh, and librarians sent postcards in Hungarian to potential borrowers of Hungarian books. The Denver Public Library in 1916 distributed handbills in Yiddish to every house within a radius of eight blocks of the public library branch serving the Jewish immigrant community. In Queens Borough in 1912 and two years later, in Denver in 1914, the public libraries supplied slides that presented basic information on library hours and services to local moving picture shows in immigrant neighborhoods.[47]

Advertising in Foreign Language Newspapers. The most successful method of publicizing the library and its services was through the local foreign language newspapers. Their pro-assimilationist editorials and articles made them immensely effective, although often overlooked, agents for the Americanization of the immigrant community.

The Detroit Public Library in 1900 sent notices to German newspapers on current acquisitions in German. Similar notices and short bibliographies were supplied to Bohemian newspapers by the Cleveland Public Library in 1906 and the Enoch Pratt Free Library of Baltimore in 1913, and to German newspapers by the Louisville Free Public Library in 1914. The Denver Public Library in 1916 was sending weekly notices to the *Denver Jewish News* regarding new acquisitions in Yiddish.[48]

Continuing Education for Librarians Serving Immigrants. Native-born American librarians, as well as their foreign-born assistants, were desirous of expanding their knowledge of foreign languages and literatures. They sought not only to serve their immigrant clienteles better, but also to demonstrate their respect for other cultures.

The children's librarians at the New York Public Library began to meet regularly in 1909 to review and discuss children's books in foreign languages circulated in various immigrant branches throughout the city. In 1911, a

Cleveland librarian and her assistants reported their studies in Russian literature with an educated Russian immigrant patron. Three years later, in 1914, librarians in Boston reported their studying of French, German, and Italian.

In 1914, the branch librarians serving Buffalo's immigrant communities were meeting regularly to share common concerns and plan cooperatively for the improvement of services. By 1924, Cleveland librarians had formed a citywide Branch Committee on Work with the Foreign Born for the purpose of preparing and distributing annotated bibliographies of recommended foreign language titles.

In 1920, the Brooklyn Public Library invited progressive librarians experienced with immigrant clienteles, notably Jane Maud Campbell, director of Work with the Foreign Born with the Massachusetts Free Public Library Commission, to address and inform staff members on Americanization-related topics such as "Citizenship for Foreign Speaking People." On a state level, librarians in Pennsylvania met in Philadelphia in 1921 to discuss library work with children of foreign-born parents.[49]

Special Events to Raise Community Consciousness of Immigrant Concerns. A natural outgrowth of librarians' desires to become more aware of immigrant cultures and to promote a tolerant attitude among the American-born community was the programming of special events and lecture series. These were not only educational for the foreign born, but also consciousness-raising for the native-born Americans.

In 1912, the Carnegie Library of Pittsburgh held special receptions in the library, often referred to as "entertainments," to highlight new acquisitions for the foreign language collections. Also, that same year, the Providence Public Library began what was to become a well-established series of lectures under the direction of the Immigrant Education Bureau. The Cleveland Public Library in 1914 opened a Russian Tea Room in one of the immigrant branches and provided tea with wafers for two cents.[50]

Ironically, it was during the two-year period from 1919 to 1920, when the Red Scare was in full swing, that libraries offered the most ingenious and innovative programming. In 1920, the St. Louis Public Library began a series of Visitors' Nights, which featured various ethnic and national groups represented in its cosmopolitan population. These festive occasions included exhibits of arts, crafts, and books, speeches in foreign languages and in English, folk songs, and slide presentations.

Similar events were held in the public libraries of Pittsburgh in 1919, Los Angeles in 1920, and Brooklyn in 1920, all during this period of heightened tension between the native-born and foreign-born American communities.The Free Library of Philadelphia in 1919 began a series of Parents' Meetings for parents of foreign birth, which featured their children singing the songs, reading the stories, and dancing the dances representative of their native lands.[51]

Library Service to Immigrants during World War I

When World War I began in Europe, the enthusiasm of American librarians for Americanization efforts did not wane. Rather, their zeal was intensified by the realization that one-quarter of the entire male population old enough to vote was born abroad and fewer than half of these men had become citizens. In anticipation of the involvement of the United States, the armed forces personnel responsible for training foreign-born citizens for participation in the American military units discovered an equally sobering truth. Many immigrant citizens could neither speak nor understand English well enough to respond to instructions or orders.[52]

In 1914, well before American involvement in World War I, the Cleveland Public Library reported that the Stamp Club meeting there, which was composed of German, Bohemian, Polish, and English immigrants, had disbanded due to differences of opinion that surfaced when the tumult began in Europe. One year later, in 1915, Stamp Club minutes noted the recall of unnaturalized immigrant reservists to Italy and the Austrian provinces for military service. The Detroit Public Library reported in 1916 that readers often vented their pent-up racial prejudices in terse annotations, which were discovered in books and periodicals returned to library assistants for reshelving.[53]

Once the United States entered World War I, individual public libraries as well as the American Library Association itself pulled all the stops in order to demonstrate their patriotism and support for the war effort. The Chicago Public Library in 1918, for example, became a central collection station for the Middle West region in the massive ALA "Books for Everybody" campaign, which collected and distributed, both home and abroad, books for American soldiers and sailors. The Cleveland Public Library that same year, 1918, reported that leaves of absence had been granted to librarians and assistants for war work.[54]

Censorship and Patriotism

Incongruously, the Queens Borough Public Library in 1918 reported not only a gathering held in honor of Polish reservists about to return to Poland to fight in World War I, but also the withdrawal of all German books by order of the board of trustees. Statistics of German book stock disappeared in published reports for 1919 and 1920 of the Queens Borough Public Library only to reappear in 1921, after hostilities had subsided and tempers had cooled. The New Orleans Public Library, during the period from 1916 to 1919, announced that "in compliance with an act of the Louisiana Legislature, all German books have been withdrawn from every department."[55]

Although relatively few libraries reported such blatant censorship, whether sanctioned by local library boards or state legislatures, it was quite clear that German books in public libraries across the country as well as the patrons who read them were suspect. The St. Louis Public Library in 1918 summed up the situation succinctly in a "casualty list" for nonfiction library books:

DEAD—Pro-German literature.
MISSING SINCE APRIL, 1917—Books on neutrality.
SERIOUSLY WOUNDED IN ACTION—Books on socialism.
DISABLED THROUGH SHELL SHOCK—Books on pacifism.[56]

The Cleveland Public Library reported in 1918 that "not only was the Library no longer neutral, but it had its own contributions to make toward the winning of the war," including censorship of library materials for the public good. The Cleveland Public Library was committed during the duration of World War I to "eliminate all books and magazines which tend to divide public sentiment in its support of the government and favor giving aid and comfort to those nations with which we are at war." In Cleveland, therefore, as in other urban centers, the public library assumed a new mission, that of being "an active instrument of propaganda." This change did not supplant the old mission of Americanization, but rather lent stronger emphasis and urgency to it.[57]

Library Services for Immigrants after World War I

During the years of the Red Scare following World War I, the American populace called for pulling in the reins on immigration and adopting a more isolationist posture in foreign affairs. While nativist-inspired Palmer raids were ferreting out politically radical immigrants for possible deportation, public librarians, who recoiled at their recent wartime exploits as purveyors of propaganda and perpetrators of censorship, rededicated themselves anew to Americanization, but within a framework of tolerance. Avowing that all immigrants, even those of German ancestry, had unique "gifts" or contributions to make to American society, librarians were anxious to make them manifest to the general public through books and special programs.[58]

Librarians began to cry out for the replenishment of their foreign language collections, which had suffered due to wartime interruptions of the international book trade, wear and tear on the few titles available, attrition, and, in some cases, removal of censored titles. Librarians pleaded as well for advice on how to select and acquire the classics in foreign languages. The availability of these classics would lead immigrants by stages not only to English translations of these well-loved titles, but also to lighter fiction in foreign languages.

Increasingly, the demand arose for books in both foreign languages and simplified English about the United States: its history, customs, laws, values, industry, economics, agriculture, and ideals. While the need for such books was great, their availability in all the foreign languages spoken by the American immigrant community was limited.[59]

ALA Committee on Work with the Foreign Born

John Foster Carr, a publisher and propagandist for Americanization, was convinced that the American public library remained the most effective Americanizing force. He joined the American Library Association in 1913, with the hope that American libraries would use his publications in their Americanization work with immigrants. A year later, in 1914, Carr founded the Immigrant Publication Society of New York, which published his guidebooks for immigrants as well as handbooks and pamphlets on Americanization-related topics for librarians and social workers.

In early 1918, Carr convinced the ALA leadership of the growing need for national coordination of library work with immigrants. It came as no surprise, therefore, when that same year Carr was appointed the first chair of the ALA Committee on Work with the Foreign Born. The committee was charged "to collect from libraries and to supply to them information on desirable methods of assisting in the education of the foreign born, in American ideals and customs and the American language."[60] The ALA CWFB under Carr's leadership from 1918 onward espoused not only the cause of Americanization but also a spirit of tolerance for cultural diversity. These goals had formerly been considered diametrically opposed.

Evidence of this amalgamation of Americanization and tolerance for foreign cultures was manifested by librarians in the public libraries they served as well as by the community and national Americanization efforts in which they participated. The New York Public Library, which served the largest concentration of immigrants in the nation, reported in 1919 an increase in the use of Yiddish books as a result of a cooperative effort with labor-related schools to give instruction to children and adults in the Yiddish language and Yiddish literature. The same library reported later, in 1921, that the evening schools, which were located in the immigrant communities and supported by the municipal board of education, were crowded with immigrants eager to learn English. The New York Council of Jewish Women conducted a class at Hamilton Fish Park Branch for illiterate women who would be deported unless they learned English.[61]

Librarians serving immigrant branches, many of whom served on the ALA CWFB, were particularly in the forefront of reconciling the various factions of the native-born and foreign-born communities. This proactive involvement in community-based Americanization programs was exemplified by Eleanor (Edwards) Ledbetter, of the Broadway Branch in Cleveland, and Josephine Gratiaa, of the Soulard Branch in St. Louis.[62]

Carr, as chair of the ALA CWFB, made a keynote address on the public library's part in Americanization during the Americanization Conference held in May 1919 in Washington, DC, under the auspices of the Americanization Division of the U.S. Bureau of Education. At the same conference, Ledbetter, as a representative of the Cleveland Americanization Committee, commented extemporaneously on the success of citywide Americanization efforts to strengthen bonds between the foreign- and native-born communities in Cleveland.[63]

Library publications after World War I evoked both a more tolerant attitude and a national pride in cultural diversity. A bibliography entitled *Heroes of Freedom*, which was prepared in 1919 by Marion Horton, principal of the Los Angeles Library School, for the California State Commission of Immigration, focused on the national heroes of various foreign countries. A bibliography on the foreign born of California was prepared in 1921 by the Los Angeles Library School for the California Federation of Women's Clubs.

In 1918, the Carnegie Library of Pittsburgh compiled for the Americanization Section of the Field Division of the Council of National Defense in Washington, DC, a bibliography of books that were found useful and interesting by the library's foreign-born patrons. The Buffalo Public Library in 1920 compiled a bibliography on the racial components of the city's population.[64]

In addition to the leadership of the ALA CWFB, a few vocal librarians expressed in print both their support for tolerance in Americanization as well as their horror at governmentally sanctioned, coercive tactics, including the deportation of un-Americanized immigrants. The most articulate librarian to emerge was Della R. Prescott of the Newark Public Library, who demanded not only tolerance of diversity but also social justice for immigrant library users.[65]

Through the efforts of individual librarians like Prescott as well as the leadership of the fledgling ALA CWFB, the ALA leadership was made aware also of the need for national financial support for library work with immigrants. The timing was particularly auspicious. The ALA, heady with the successes it had experienced in providing materials and services to the armed forces during World War I, was beginning to plan for an all-embracing program to extend library services to what were then identified as underserved populations, notably the immigrant community.

Service to Immigrants after World War II

In 1920, the ALA Executive Board proposed an ambitious Enlarged Program and launched a campaign to raise the needed revenue of two million dollars, $60,000 of which was to fund, over a three-year period, a program to enhance library citizenship activities. Carr, as chair of the ALA CWFB, was to administer these funds. The justification for this bold move included the significant statistics that more than 800 public libraries throughout the country had expressed an interest in this type of service, and more than 300 were already actively providing it.[66]

Although the ALA Enlarged Program ultimately floundered due to a lack of financial support from a divided membership, the ALA CWFB, to its credit, continued to promote and provide this type of service on a shoestring. Indeed, the ALA CWFB was quite active under the leadership of Carr during the initial years and, later in the early 1920s, under the leadership of Eleanor (Edwards) Ledbetter of the Cleveland Public Library.

Under its auspices and Ledbetter's keen editorial supervision, the ALA CWFB published in *Library Journal*, between 1921 and 1924, a series of articles with bibliographies. They treated the various ethnic and national groups represented in urban centers throughout the country. The bibliographies were written especially for librarians serving immigrant clienteles, but were useful also for personnel in other organizations involved in Americanization activities.[67]

Ironically, the immigrant groups who formed the focal points of the publications of the ALA CWFB were the southern and eastern European immigrants for whom the Congress was even then establishing immigration quotas. The passage of the National Origins Act of 1924 not only restricted the number of future emigrants from the Eastern Hemisphere, especially southern and eastern Europe and Asia, but also rendered these initial efforts of the ALA CWFB of limited value.

Carnegie Corporation Study of Immigrants

Concurrent with librarians' efforts to infuse a tolerance for diversity within existing library Americanization programs following World War I, the Carnegie Corporation, which also embraced a progressive philosophy toward free immigration, sponsored a study to determine the most beneficial means of promoting Americanization. Defining Americanization much more broadly than librarians had, the Carnegie Corporation was interested in the total assimilation process—the ways in which immigrants adapted to the American patterns of life and behavior.

The Carnegie Corporation assembled a team of experts to survey existing programs of Americanization. Each expert was responsible for one of ten areas of life that directly affected the welfare of immigrants. John Daniels of the New York State Department of Education, formerly secretary of the North American Civic League for Immigrants, reported on neighborhood agencies. Frank Victor Thompson, assistant superintendent of schools in Boston, investigated educational opportunities of immigrants. Isaac Thomas and Robert Ezra Park of the University of Chicago and Herbert Adolphus Miller of Oberlin College reflected upon immigrant heritages and their effects on assimilation. Park also reported on the immigrant press. Peter Alexander Speek, chief of the Slavic Section of the Library of Congress, studied immigrants in rural areas. Michael Marks Davis, director of the Boston Dispensary, addressed health standards and health care for immigrants. Sophonisba Preston Breckinridge of the University of Chicago, formerly secretary of the Immigrants' Protective League of Chicago, investigated the home and family life of immigrants. John Palmer Gavit, a director and consulting editor at the publishing house of Harper and Brothers, studied the naturalization process and the political life of immigrants. Kate Holladay Claghorn of the New York School of Philanthropy addressed the area of legal protection and correction for immigrants. William Morris Leiserson of the University of Toledo investigated industrial and economic opportunities for immigrants. Allen T. Burns, formerly director of the Cleveland Foundation, was appointed supervisor of the study, and Charles Clarence Williamson, a librarian, then president of the Special Libraries Association, was appointed statistician.

Monographs based on individual portions of the study were published by Harper and Brothers in the early 1920s.[68] While not dealing with libraries per se, the monographs of Thompson on the public schools; Thomas, Park, and Miller on immigrant heritages; Park on the immigrant press; and Gavit on the naturalization process all evoked the progressive philosophy shared by many librarians involved in Americanization activities.[69]

John Daniels, the expert responsible for studying community-based organizations involved in Americanization, scrutinized the activities of public libraries along with other social agencies, including settlement houses, community councils, and neighborhood associations. Citing specifically the accomplishments of librarian Jane Maud Campbell with the teeming immigrant community of Passaic, New Jersey, Daniels was convinced that the public library was the ideal institution for accomplishing the Americanization of the immigrant community, and also the most effective.[70]

Library Work with Immigrants Recognized Internationally

Reports on the community-based activities of the immigrant branches as well as foreign language departments and entire library systems enlivened not only the pages of state, regional, and national library periodicals and foreign language newspapers, but also major English language newspapers and periodicals of general cultural and educational interest. Library services to the immigrant community attracted the interest of foreign visitors and dignitaries as well.

In 1905, visitors to the Free Library of Philadelphia published accounts of their visits in periodicals and newspapers in England, France, Germany, Italy, Sweden, Norway, and Switzerland. In 1919, visitors to the Central Children's Room in the New York Public Library, who were interested in promoting children's services in their respective countries, carried back glowing reports of their observations to colleagues in England, France, Belgium, South America, Mexico, China, and Japan.

Under the auspices of the ALA, American public libraries participated in international events and achieved international publicity on American public library services to immigrants. The 1914 and 1915 annual reports of the Brooklyn Public Library mentioned the ALA exhibit at the Leipzig Book Fair. This exhibit featured a model of Brooklyn's Carroll Park Branch as a representative immigrant neighborhood branch and charts explaining the traveling library system for foreign language books in Brooklyn.[71]

Attitudes of Librarians Working with Immigrants

By the turn of the twentieth century, librarians had noted and begun to report on differences in immigrant groups. Librarians noted those immigrant groups who came to the library voluntarily very shortly after their arrival in the United States and those who were frequent users. Conversely, librarians noted those immigrant groups who had to be convinced through home visiting and various means of publicity that the library was the friend of the immigrant and native-born American alike. Librarians observed immigrant groups who valued education for its intrinsic worth as well as those who viewed too much emphasis on schooling and learning as an irrelevant postponement of earning a living.[72]

Growing from paternalism in the years up to and through World War I to respect in their relationships with immigrants in the years following the Red Scare, librarians matured as professionals through their careful observation of and day-to-day contact with immigrant patrons. As librarians grew in their knowledge of their respective immigrant clienteles, they became much more aware than the general public of the very essential truth that immigrants were individuals, not one massive block of humanity. Librarians learned also that each immigrant and, in turn, each immigrant group had different priorities and goals, as well as different strategies for attaining them.

Librarians' penchant for pigeonholing immigrants was revealed most clearly in their comments on the library use patterns, social interaction skills, and personality traits of their immigrant clienteles. A candid Cleveland librarian learned through home visits in 1908 that the immigrant neighborhood served by her branch was composed of "thrifty and hard-working" Irish-Americans and German-Americans. These immigrants were "proud of their children and anxious to give them as much education as they will take, which in a good many instances is not a great deal." [73]

A St. Louis librarian surmised in 1914 that Italians were "clannish and a little suspicious of mixing with their American neighbors," since they were "much inclined to keep their old-world traditions." Buffalo librarians in 1913 and 1914 commented that the Jews were the greatest readers, an observation they attributed to the "ardent desire for education among the Jewish people." A Baltimore librarian in 1912 noted the dependency of her patrons on the summer work on the farms outside Baltimore. She reported that "during the fall and winter months, the Branch is well patronized by foreigners, but in the beginning of spring they hand in their cards, saying they are too busy to read."[74]

Librarians, who as a matter of course would veil in patronizing phrases any condescension they may have felt for immigrant patrons, were occasionally quite unsuccessful in hiding their disdain. A case in point involved a particularly critical Cleveland librarian, who in 1922 expressed a wide range of prejudices not only toward eastern European Gypsies, "the least welcome of our kaleidoscopic patronage," and "slow-minded" African Americans, but also the "uneducated from abroad," all of whom "present problems of various sorts."[75]

Notwithstanding their lapses into criticism of immigrants, librarians were equally unstinting, even effulgent, in praise of what they categorized as the admirable traits of immigrants. Librarians praised their appreciativeness, their fluency with languages, and their good taste in reading, notably a preference for nonfiction over fiction.

Referring to the Jewish boys who frequented her branch, a Baltimore librarian in 1913 noted that "they seem more to appreciate the privilege of a free library than do the boys of native parents." Commenting on the innate intelligence of Russian immigrants from the neighborhood surrounding her branch, a St. Louis librarian in 1913 reported that "there is probably no better place to observe the ease and quickness with which the Russian learns our language than in the library." Librarians often extolled the language ability of the immigrants with whom they came in contact. A Buffalo librarian in 1916 observed that "the Jewish people, who make up the largest part of the patrons of this Branch, quickly acquire English and prefer to read books in English to those in their native tongue."[76]

The New York Public Library in 1907 pointed with pride to the statistic that "the largest amount of non-fiction read is, as usual, on the Lower East Side." The Lower East Side represented, both for New Yorkers and the general public at large, a prototypical immigrant community. In 1911, the Cleveland Public Library conducted an experiment to determine the books requested most frequently for school library deposits and "found that the proportion of fiction ordered in American districts was higher than in the foreign districts." Boston librarians in 1913 reported that "we have found that children of foreign parentage read a better class of books than their American brothers and sisters." Based on their subjective analysis of circulation records, Newark librarians discovered in 1921 "that foreigners who read are more eager for really good books than Americans who read." They observed, furthermore, "that men who work at the benches in factories often read better books than do their colleagues in the offices beyond the glass doors."[77]

Attitudes of Immigrants toward Libraries

Paradoxically, immigrants did not shun Americanization, which was the sole goal of librarians in their work with immigrant clienteles. Americanization represented their ticket to economic and social success in American society. For many immigrants, it was the coercive tactics of Americanizers and not the process itself that they feared.

Immigrants who attained the goal of being Americanized, that is, educated in the language and civics of America, felt a sense of pride and empowerment, while those who never attained that goal felt a profound sense of separateness, of being out of touch with American society. For the Americanized immigrant, America offered unlimited opportunities, including occupational and geographical mobility. For the un-Americanized immigrant, America was a land of empty promises, where the ghetto was not a home but a prison.[78]

CONCLUSION

From 1876 to 1924, librarians found Americanization an appropriate mission for the public library, and although they often argued and debated the methods and tactics used to accomplish it, they never lost sight of this mission. When librarians began their work to Americanize the immigrant community during the last three decades of the nineteenth century, they assumed the role of sovereign alchemists. Librarians possessed the magic—the know-how—to impose Americanization on immigrants.

By World War I, librarians were not only promoting Americanization to the foreign-born community but also justifying to the native-born community the needs and rights of immigrants to public library service. During the Red Scare following World War I and later, librarians willingly assumed the roles of advocates for immigrants and propagandists for free immigration.

Throughout this turbulent half century from 1876 to 1924, librarians remained focused on what they were trying to accomplish with their immigrant clienteles. Librarians were literally caught up in the human side of their work. They often confessed that they learned as much from their immigrant patrons as they taught them.[79]

Ironically, then, as immigrants were being transformed into Americans, librarians were also being transformed through their contacts with immigrants. The sovereign alchemists acted as catalysts in the metamorphosis of immigrants into American citizens. In the process they, too, were changed, metamorphosed into more tolerant Americanizers, more progressive citizens, and more responsive professionals.

NOTES

1. European emigrants represented 22,796,950, or 87 percent of the total of 26,188,472 immigrants entering the United States in the forty-eight-year period from 1876 to 1924. Calculated using the table "Immigrants, by Country: 1820 to 1970," in U.S. Department of Commerce, Bureau of the Census, *Historical Statistics of the United States: Colonial Times to 1970*, Part 1, Bicentennial ed. (Washington, DC: GPO, 1975), 105–6.

2. Maldwyn Allen Jones, *American Immigration* (Chicago: University of Chicago Press, 1960), 204–5.

3. Ibid., chap. 6: "Nativism, Sectional Controversy, and Civil War, 1830–65," 147–76 passim.

4. John Bodnar, *The Transplanted: A History of Immigrants in Urban America* (Bloomington: Indiana University Press, 1985), chap. 1: "The Homeland and Capitalism," 1–56; Jones, *American Immigration*, chap. 7: "New Sources of Immigration, 1860–1914," 177–206; and Dino Cinel, *From Italy to San Francisco: The Immigrant Experience* (Stanford, CA: Stanford University Press, 1982), chap. 4: "The Problems of Resettlement in Italy," 71–100.

5. Jones, *American Immigration*, 251–53, 262–63, 266–68; and John Higham, *Send These to Me: Immigrants in Urban America*, rev. ed. (Baltimore: Johns Hopkins University Press, 1984), chap. 3: "The Transformation of the Statue of Liberty," 71–80.

6. Jones, *American Immigration*, 177–83, 259–60, 268–70; and U. S. Immigration Commission, *Report of the Immigration Commission* (61st Congress, 2d and 3d sessions), 41 vols. (Washington, DC: GPO, 1911).

7. "The Public Library and Allied Agencies," in *The Library without the Walls*, Reprints of Papers and Addresses, selected and annotated by Laura M. Janzow (New York: H. W. Wilson, 1927), 323–49.

8. Jones, *American Immigration*, 273–74.

9. Ibid., 276–77, 279–80.

10. Buffalo Public Library, AR 1907, 19–20; and Brooklyn Public Library, AR 1905, 20.

11. New York Public Library, AR 1908, 16, AR 1914, 42; Cleveland Public Library, AR 1899, 21, AR 1914, 82; San Francisco Public Library, AR 1904/5, 17; Providence Public Library, AR 1908, 8; and Denver Public Library, AR 1912, 7. See also "King Oscar's Traveling Library," *Minnesota Public Library Commission Notes* 2 (Jan. 1908): 101–2.

12. Buffalo Public Library, AR 1914, 21; Boston Public Library, AR 1919/20, 50; and Cleveland Public Library, AR 1907, 49, AR 1911, 75. See also James Hulme Canfield, "The Library in Relation to Special Classes of Readers: Books for the Foreign Population—I," *LJ* 31 (Aug. 1906): 65–67; Sarka Hrbek [i.e., Hrbkova], "The Library and the Foreign-Born

Citizen," *Public Libraries* 15 (Mar. 1910): 98–104; Peter Roberts, "The Library and the Foreign-Speaking Man," *LJ* 36 (Oct. 1911): 496–99; and Don D. Lescohier, "The Library in Americanization," *Wisconsin Library Bulletin* 16 (Jan. 1920): 3–6.

13. Brooklyn Public Library, AR 1900/1, 16; Cleveland Public Library, AR 1910, 81; Jersey City Public Library, AR 1895/96, 4; Milwaukee Public Library, AR 1913, 12; and Buffalo Public Library, AR 1912, 8.

14. Carnegie Library of Pittsburgh, AR 1923, 9–10.

15. Carol Aronovici, "Americanization, Its Meaning and Function," *Minnesota Public Library Commission Notes* 5 (Dec. 1918): 181–82; and "Americanization of Foreigners," *Maine Library Bulletin* 8 (Jan. 1919): 75. See also "Developing Americanism," *New York Libraries* 5 (May 1916): 74–75; H. H. Wheaton, "An Americanization Program for Libraries," *ALA Bulletin* 10 (July 1916): 265–69; Wheaton, "Libraries and the 'America First' Campaign," *LJ* 42 (Jan. 1917): 21–22; "Libraries as Americanizers," *Minnesota Public Library Commission Notes* 5 (Sept. 1918): 174; Jasmine Britton, "The Library's Share in Americanization," *LJ* 43 (Oct. 1918): 723–27; "The Library's Part in Americanizing Foreigners," *New York Libraries* 6 (Aug. 1918): 88–89, which also appeared in *LJ* 43 (Nov. 1918): 848; and M. M. Guhin, "Americanization in South Dakota," *South Dakota Library Bulletin* 6 (Sept. 1920): 46–49.

16. Los Angeles Public Library, AR 1896/97, 10, AR 1909/10, 9, AR 1918/19, 31; New Orleans Public Library, AR 1901, 1; New York Public Library, AR 1908, 39, AR 1912, 95; Detroit Public Library, AR 1907, 13; and Cleveland Public Library, AR 1915, 70. See also Margaret Palmer, "The Library and the Immigrant," *Minnesota Public Library Commission Notes* 2 (Dec. 1909): 192–95; North American Civic League for Immigrants, New York-New Jersey Committee, *Education of the Immigrant, Abstracts of Papers Read at a Public Conference under the Auspices of the New York–New Jersey Committee of the North American Civic League for Immigrants, held at New York City, May 16 and 17, 1913* (Washington, DC: GPO, 1913); John J. Arnold, "Americanization and Libraries," *Illinois Libraries* 1 (Apr. 1919): 15–19.

17. Buffalo Public Library, AR 1917, 22–23; Detroit Public Library, AR 1916/17, 13; and Cleveland Public Library, AR 1922/23, 32. See also "Libraries as Social Centers," *American Library Annual* 1915–16: 67–68, which describes naturalization activities in Philadelphia, Cleveland, New York, and Los Angeles; "Work with Foreigners," *American Library Annual* 1916-17: 54-55, which describes naturalization activities in Portland (OR) and Detroit; and "'New Americans' and the Tacoma Public Library," *LJ* 45 (1 Mar. 1920): 218, which describes naturalization activities in Tacoma (WA).

18. Carnegie Library of Pittsburgh, AR 1913/14, 38.

19. *LJ* 19 (Oct. 1894): 328.

20. Queens Borough (NY) Public Library, AR 1914, 7.

21. Aksel G. S. Josephson, "Foreign Books in American Libraries," *LJ* 19 (Nov. 1894): 364; Gratia Countryman, "Shall Public Libraries Buy Foreign Literature for the Benefit of the Foreign Population?" *LJ* 23 (June 1898): 229–31; Edwin White Gaillard, "Why Public Libraries Should Supply Books in Foreign Languages," *LJ* 28 (Feb. 1903): 67; and "Books for Immigrants," *New York Libraries* 1 (July 1908): 98.

22. Boston Public Library, AR 1906/7, 58.

23. San Francisco Public Library, AR 1903/4, 19; Queens Borough Public Library, AR 1909, 23; Brooklyn Public Library, AR 1904, 23; Cleveland Public Library, AR 1910, 30–31, AR 1923/24, 17; Los Angeles Public Library, AR 1916/17, 16; and Enoch Pratt Free Library of Baltimore, AR 1916, 22. See also Arabel Martin, "Buying of Foreign Books for Small Libraries," *Minnesota Public Library Commission Notes* 9 (Dec. 1906): 30–31.

24. Brooklyn Public Library, AR 1910, 31–32; Queens Borough Public Library, AR 1910, 14; and Los Angeles Public Library, AR 1922/23, 10.

25. Milwaukee Public Library, AR 1878/79, 15; Providence Public Library, AR 1883, 7; Louisville Free Public Library, AR 1904/5, 40, AR 1906/7, 40; and Queens Borough Public Library, AR 1909, 10, AR 1913, 45.

26. Newark Public Library, AR 1898, 15; Brooklyn Public Library, AR 1906, 27; Cleveland Public Library, AR 1908, 63; Enoch Pratt Free Library of Baltimore, AR 1912, 18; Free Library of Philadelphia, AR 1911, 18, AR 1912, 29; St. Louis Public Library, AR 1902/3, 15, AR 1913/14, 89, AR 1921/22, 35; and Carnegie Library of Pittsburgh, AR 1917, 45. See also Peter Roberts, "What Can Libraries Do to Aid the Foreign Speaking Peoples in America?" *Pennsylvania Library Notes* 3 (Oct. 1910): 16–23; and "What One Library Is Doing in the Making of Americans," *New York Libraries* 5 (May 1916): 110, which describes activities in St. Louis.

27. Cleveland Public Library, AR 1903, 37, AR 1909, 50; Milwaukee Public Library, AR 1910/11, 19; New York Public Library, AR 1914, 46–47; Jersey City Public Library, AR 1890/91, 7; Brooklyn Public Library, AR 1903, 55; Chicago Public Library, 1915/16, 20; and Queens Borough Public Library, AR 1910, 34. See also *Hand Book of Library Organization*, compiled by the Library Commissions of Minnesota, Iowa and Wisconsin (Minneapolis: Minnesota State Library Commission, 1902), 29–30, 63–64, 67; "Traveling Libraries of Foreign Books," *Wisconsin Library Bulletin* 1 (Sept. 1905): 74–75; Karen M. Jacobson, "What Minnesota Does for Its Foreign Citizens," *Minnesota Public Library Commission Notes* 9 (Dec. 1906): 31–32; Sarah Comstock, "Eight Million Books a Year: How the New York Public Library Distributes Them Through Forty-One Branch Libraries to More than Three Million People—The Service It Performs for the Blind, for Foreigners Who Cannot Read English, and for the Children Who Are Just Learning to Love Books," *World's Work* 26 (May 1913): 100–108; and "Work with Foreigners," *Pennsylvania Library Notes* 8 (Jan. 1916): 6–7.

28. New Orleans Public Library, AR 1908, 18.

29. Buffalo Public Library, AR 1906, 17–18; Free Library of Philadelphia, AR 1907, 25; St. Louis Public Library, AR 1909/10, 68; New York Public Library, AR 1913, 72, AR 1923, 60; Denver Public Library, AR 1913, 12; M. R. H., "Some Work of the Library with Bohemians," *LJ* 35 (June 1910): 265, which treats the Webster Branch of the New York Public Library; C. E. Howard, "The Carnegie Library of Pittsburgh, and the Foreigner," *Pennsylvania Library Notes* 3 (Oct. 1910): 12-16, which treats the Wylie Avenue Branch; and [Ruth Crawford], "The Library and the Immigrant in St. Louis," *LJ* 41 (July 1916): 478–79, which treats the Divoll, Crunden, and Soulard Branches.

30. St. Louis Public Library, AR 1909/10, 42; Cleveland Public Library, AR 1911, 31–32; Carnegie Library of Pittsburgh, AR 1911/12, 24; Queens Borough Public Library, AR 1916, 27; and Milwaukee Public Library, AR 1924, 18.

31. Providence Public Library, AR 1907, 8–10; Cleveland Public Library, AR 1909, 22; Los Angeles Public Library, AR 1919/20, 18–19; and Detroit Public Library, AR 1923/24, 19–20. See also Marguerite Reid, "Our New Americans," *MLCB* 2 (Mar. 1912): 29–36, which describes the Foreign Department of the Providence Public Library.

32. Brooklyn Public Library, AR 1908, 19-20; Queens Borough Public Library, AR 1910, 14–15; Cleveland Public Library, AR 1914, 102–3; Los Angeles Public Library, AR 1917/18, 23; Carnegie Library of Pittsburgh, AR 1918, 13; and St. Louis Public Library, AR 1918/19, 77–130. See also "Books for the Foreigners," *Pennsylvania Library Notes* 8 (Jan. 1916): 7–10; Katherine Evans Blake, "Americanization," *Minnesota Public Library Commission Notes* 5 (June 1918): 150–1; and Josephine Gratiaa, "Making Americans: How the Library Helps," *LJ* 44 (Nov. 1919): 729–30.

33. Milwaukee Public Library, AR 1880/81, 21; and Cleveland Public Library, AR 1909, 32, AR 1912, 44. See also "Selection of Books in Foreign Languages," *American Library Annual* 1915–16: 51.

34. Buffalo Public Library, AR 1899, 34; Cleveland Public Library, AR 1908, 69, AR 1912, 75–76; Enoch Pratt Free Library of Baltimore, 1923, 54; Boston Public Library, AR 1922/23, 54; Milwaukee Public Library, AR 1910/11, 16; and Detroit Public Library, AR 1915/16, 6. See also Josepha Kudlicka, "Library Work among Foreigners," *Public Libraries* 15 (Nov. 1910): 375–76.

35. Cleveland Public Library, AR 1876, 3; San Francisco Public Library, AR 1897/98, 13; Detroit Public Library, AR 1889, 16, AR 1903, 21; Louisville Free Public Library, AR 1913/14, 21; and Carnegie Library of Pittsburgh, AR 1912/13, 39. See also, "Helps in Government and Language for Immigrants," *Public Libraries* 16 (Mar. 1911): 111–12, a bibliography compiled by the Buffalo Public Library; and Marguerite Reid and John G. Moulton, "Aids in Work with Foreigners," *MLCB* 2 (Mar. 1912): 37–56, a bibliography compiled by librarians from the Providence Public Library and Haverhill (MA) Public Library respectively.

36. Brooklyn Public Library, AR 1903, 45.

37. Cleveland Public Library, AR 1900, 23; New York Public Library, AR 1907, 37; Buffalo Public Library, AR 1914, 21; and Carnegie Library of Pittsburgh, AR 1920, 49. See also Leon M. Solis-Cohen, "Library Work in the Brooklyn Ghetto," *LJ* 33 (Dec. 1908): 485–88; and Aniela Poray, "The Foreign Child and the Book," *LJ* 40 (Apr. 1915): 233–39, which describes work with immigrant children in Detroit.

38. Buffalo Public Library, AR 1901, 13, AR 1921, 23. See also "Libraries for Schools," in U.S. Bureau of Education, *Report of the Commissioner of Education for the Year 1887-88* (Washington, DC: GPO, 1889), 115, which describes school library work in Minnesota; [J. D. Wolcott], "Library Service to Immigrants," in U.S. Bureau of Education, *Report of the Commissioner of Education for the Year Ended June 10, 1915*, vol. 1 (Washington, DC: GPO, 1915), 527–31, which includes accounts of library work with immigrants in Massachusetts, Connecticut, Minnesota, Nebraska, Wisconsin, California, Rhode Island, New York, New Jersey, Pennsylvania, Ohio, Illinois, Missouri, and Washington; Albert Shiels, "The Immigrant, the School and the Library," *ALA Bulletin* 10 (July 1916): 257–63; and Marion Horton, "Here in the Land of Promise," *LJ* 44 (Mar. 1919): 139–42.

39. St. Louis Public Library, AR 1913/14, 93; Chicago Public Library, AR 1923, 23; Cleveland Public Library, AR 1912, 77; and Los Angeles Public Library, AR 1919/20, 32.

40. St. Louis Public Library, AR 1910/11, 65–66.

41. Boston Public Library, AR 1904/5, 14–15.

42. Newark Public Library, AR 1903, 25; Jersey City Public Library, AR 1912/13, 8; Buffalo Public Library, AR 1911, 17, AR 1917, 12–13; Los Angeles Public Library, AR 1916/17, 22; and Milwaukee Public Library, AR 1922, 17.

43. Boston Public Library, AR 1921/22, 64.

44. New York Public Library, AR 1909, 59; Carnegie Library of Pittsburgh, AR 1919, 42; St. Louis Public Library, AR 1913/14, 50; Cleveland Public Library, AR 1922/23, 14; and Free Library of Philadelphia, AR 1919, 23–24. See also W. F. Stevens, "Use of the Library by Foreigners as Shown by the Carnegie Library of Homestead, Pa.," *LJ* 35 (Apr. 1910): 161–62; and "Translation Service from the Business Men's League of St. Louis," *LJ* 42 (July 1917): 519.

45. Los Angeles Public Library, AR 1917/18, 23; and St. Louis Public Library, AR 1923/24, 63.

46. Cleveland Public Library, AR 1908, 54–55; New York Public Library, AR 1908, 32–33; Milwaukee Public Library, AR 1910/11, 19; St. Louis Public Library, AR 1912/13, 95; Enoch Pratt Free Library of Baltimore, AR 1913, 59; Queens Borough Public Library, AR 1913, 21; Buffalo Public Library, AR 1917, 17; and Carnegie Library of Pittsburgh, AR 1917, 58. See also Josephine M. McPike, "The Foreign Child at a St. Louis Branch," *LJ* 40 (Dec. 1915): 851–55.

47. Milwaukee Public Library, AR 1886/87, 8; Providence Public Library, AR 1908, 3, AR 1909, 6; Cleveland Public Library, AR 1909, 59; Buffalo Public Library, AR 1910, 17; St. Louis Public Library, AR 1909/10, 66; Carnegie Library of Pittsburgh, AR 1917, 48, 58; Denver Public Library, AR 1914, 8, AR 1916, 8; and Queens Borough Public Library, AR 1912, 26.

48. Detroit Public Library, AR 1900, 18; Cleveland Public Library, AR 1906, 63; Enoch Pratt Free Library of Baltimore, AR 1913, 25; Louisville Free Public Library, AR 1913/14, 21; and Denver Public Library, AR 1916, 8. See also Della R. Prescott, "Americanization thru Foreign Print," *LJ* 43 (Dec. 1918): 884–85; Della R. Prescott, "Work with Foreign Newspapers in Newark Free Public Library," *LJ* 44 (Feb. 1919): 77–78; and Mordecai Soltes, *The Yiddish Press, an Americanizing Agency* (New York: Teachers College, Columbia University, 1925, copr. 1924; reprint, New York: Arno Press and the New York Times, 1969).

49. New York Public Library, AR 1909, 54–55; Cleveland Public Library, AR 1911, 79, AR 1923/24, 51; Boston Public Library, AR 1913/14, 64; Buffalo Public Library, AR 1914, 20; Brooklyn Public Library, AR 1920, 20; and Free Library of Philadelphia, AR 1921, 19.

50. Carnegie Library of Pittsburgh, AR 1911/12, 24; Providence Public Library, AR 1912, 7; and Cleveland Public Library, AR 1914, 112.

51. St. Louis Public Library, AR 1919/20, 28–29; Carnegie Library of Pittsburgh, AR 1919, 68; Los Angeles Public Library, AR 1919/20, 26; Brooklyn Public Library, AR 1920, 18; and Free Library of Philadelphia, AR 1919, 20. See also Adelaide B. Maltby, "Immigrants as Contributors to Library Progress," *ALA Bulletin* 7 (July 1913): 150–54, which describes ethnic festivals at the Tompkins Square Branch of the New York Public Library; "Work with Foreigners," *American Library Annual* 1915–16: 51, which includes a description of an ethnic festival in Chelsea (MA); "Work with Foreigners," *LJ* 40 (Apr. 1915): 292–93, which describes ethnic festivals in Binghamton (NY) and Chelsea (MA); "Holiday Receptions for Foreigners," *LJ* 40 (June 1915): 450, which describes ethnic festivals in St. Paul (MN), Philadelphia, Cleveland, Baltimore, and Los Angeles; "Work with Greeks," *LJ* 40 (Aug. 1915): 621, which describes ethnic festivals in Denver and Syracuse (NY); and "Work with Foreigners," *LJ* 40 (Sept. 1915): 684, which describes ethnic festivals and other activities sponsored by the Massachusetts Free Public Library Commission.

52. "The Library's Part in Making Americans," *New York Libraries* 4 (Aug. 1915): 235–36.

53. Cleveland Public Library, AR 1914, 105, AR 1915, 29; and Detroit Public Library, AR 1915/16, 6.

54. Chicago Public Library, AR 1917/18, 9; and Cleveland Public Library, AR 1917/18, 16. See also "The Public Library and Patriotism," *Minnesota Public Library Commission Notes* 5 (June 1917): 81–83; and Faith L. Allen, "Children and Patriotism," *Wisconsin Library Bulletin* 14 (Feb. 1918): 46–47.

55. Queens Borough Public Library, AR 1918, 13, AR 1919, 28, AR 1920, 33, AR 1921, 24; and New Orleans Public Library, AR 1916/19, 11.

56. St. Louis Public Library, AR 1917/18, 44–45.

57. Cleveland Public Library, AR 1917/18, 14–15. See also, Wayne A. Wiegand, *"An Active Instrument for Propaganda": The American Public Library during World War I*, foreword by Edward G. Holley, Beta Phi Mu Monograph no. 1 (Westport, CT: Greenwood, 1989), chap. 5: "Discarding Disloyal Literature: Public Library Censorship During Wartime," 87–112 passim.

58. Ida Faye Wright, "The Gifts of the Nations," *LJ* 45 (1 Mar. 1920): 215–16; Jessie M. Woodford, "How a Little Booth Helped a Big Movement," *LJ* 45 (1 Mar. 1920): 217; and Ernestine Rose, "How the Public Library Helps the Foreigner Make His American Contribution," in National Education Association of the United States, *Addresses and Proceedings of the Sixtieth Annual Meeting* (Washington, DC: NEA, 1922), 1001–2.

59. New York Public Library, AR 1920, 51, AR 1921, 58. See also Aksel G. S. Josephson, "Books for the Immigrants: I. Swedish," *LJ* 33 (Dec. 1908): 505; Caroline F. Webster, "Library Work with Foreigners," *ALA Bulletin* 9 (July 1915): 192–95; Gratiaa, "Making Americans: How the Library Helps," 729–30; Mary L. Sutliff, "The Spirit of America," *Wisconsin Library Bulletin* 16 (Mar. 1920): 34–36; and "Americanization Work in Seattle Public Library," *Public Libraries* 25 (Oct. 1920): 448–49.

60. *LJ* 43 (Feb. 1918): 120.

61. New York Public Library, AR 1919, 39, AR 1921, 58.

62. Cleveland Public Library, AR 1917/18, 16; and St. Louis Public Library, AR 1919/20, 66–67, AR 1920/21, 65.

63. Americanization Conference, *Proceedings [of the] Americanization Conference, Held under the Auspices of the Americanization Division, Bureau of Education, Department of the Interior, Washington, May 12, 13, 14, 15, 1919* (Washington, DC: GPO, 1919), see especially, Carr's address entitled "The Library, the Friend of the Foreign Born," 376–79, and Ledbetter's comments on the Cleveland Americanization Committee, 240.

64. Los Angeles Public Library, AR 1918/19, 21, 37, AR 1920/21, 40; Carnegie Library of Pittsburgh, AR 1918, 13; and Buffalo Public Library, AR 1920, 11. See also, "Books for and Concerning Foreign-Born People," *Maine Library Bulletin* 8 (Jan. 1919): 75–79; and Marguerite Tafuris, "The Immigrant: A Composite Portrait," *Wilson Library Bulletin* 1 (June 1919): 349.

65. Della R. Prescott, "What Americanization Is Not," *LJ* 45 (1 Mar. 1920): 218; and Frank Crane, "The Ten Points of Americanism," *LJ* 45 (1 Mar. 1920): 214–15.

66. "Work with the Foreign Born and Preparation for Citizenship," *ALA Bulletin* 14 (July 1920): 299–300; and Orpha Maud Peters, "Libraries in Relation to Citizenship and Americanization," *LJ* 44 (Dec. 1919): 759.

67. David Pinski and Jennie Meyrowitz, "Yiddish Literature," *LJ* 46 (1 Dec. 1921): 977–79; Eleanor (Edwards) Ledbetter, "The Polish Immigrant and the Library," *LJ* 47 (15 Jan. 1922): 67–70, *LJ* 47 (1 June 1922): 496–98; Marion Horton, "Library Work with the Japanese," *LJ* 47 (15 Feb. 1922): 157–60; Josephine Gratiaa, "Roumanians in the United States and Their Relations to Public Libraries," *LJ* 47 (1 May 1922): 400–404; Margery Quigley, "The Greek Immigrant and the Library," *LJ* 47 (15 Oct. 1922): 863–65; Ledbetter, "The Czechoslovak Immigrant and the Library," *LJ* 48 (1 Nov. 1923): 911–15; and May M. Sweet, "Italians and the Public Library," *LJ* 49 (15 Nov. 1924): 977–81. See also ALA CWFB Minutes, *ALA Bulletin* 16 (July 1922): 228, *ALA Bulletin* 17 (July 1923): 209, and *ALA Bulletin* 19 (July 1925): 220; Esther Johnston, "Report of the New York Library Association—Committee on Work with the Foreign Born," *ALA Bulletin* 16 (July 1922): 371–74; and ALA CWFB, "Dealers in Foreign Books," *LJ* 47 (Aug. 1922): 647–48.

68. "Carnegie Corporation to Study Americanization," *LJ* 43 (May 1918): 339; and "Personnel of Americanization Survey," *LJ* 43 (July 1918): 505. The ten studies, which were originally published by Harper and Brothers of New York, were republished, along

with critical commentaries, in 1971, by Patterson Smith of Montclair, NJ. See their series entitled Americanization Studies: The Acculturation of Immigrant Groups into American Society, republished under the editorship of William S. Bernard, 10 vols. (Montclair, NJ: Patterson Smith, 1971, copr. 1920).

69. The study of Thompson (1920) on the public schools was entitled *Schooling of the Immigrant*; the study of Thomas, Park, and Miller (1921) on the social and political backgrounds of various immigrant groups was entitled *Old World Traits Transplanted*; the study of Park (1922) on the immigrant press was entitled *The Immigrant Press and Its Control*; and the study of Gavit (1922) on naturalization was entitled *Americans by Choice*.

70. John Daniels, *America via the Neighborhood*, with a new introduction by Florence G. Cassidy. Americanization Studies: The Acculturation of Immigrant Groups into American Society, republished under the editorship of William S. Bernard (New York: Harper and Brothers, 1920; reprint, Montclair, NJ: Patterson Smith, 1971), 273–84. See Daniels's commendation of Campbell's library work with immigrants, 277–79. See also, John Daniels, "Americanization by Indirection," *LJ* 45 (1 Nov. 1920): 871–76; and Herbert Adolphus Miller, "The True Americanization of the Foreign Child," *ALA Bulletin* 13 (July 1919): 130–32.

71. Free Library of Philadelphia, AR 1905, n.p.; New York Public Library, AR 1919, 48; and Brooklyn Public Library, AR 1914, 30, AR 1915, 60. See also Mabel Potter Daggett, "The Library's Part in Making Americans: Free Books Are Helping Our Foreign-Born Citizens to a Bigger and Better Patriotism," *Delineator* 77 (Jan. 1911): 17–18, which treats library work with immigrants in New York, Cleveland, Chicago, Newark, Grand Rapids (MI), Hagerstown (MD), Binghamton (NY), and Pittsburgh.

72. This realization is in agreement with Bodnar's conclusions regarding the diversity of American immigrant groups. See Bodnar, *The Transplanted*, "Introduction," xv–xxi; and chap. 7: "America on Immigrant Terms: Folklife, Education, and Politics," 184–205. See also, Arthur E. Bostwick, "Books for the Foreign Population—II," *LJ* 31 (Aug. 1906): 67–70; Flora B. Roberts, "The Library and the Foreign Citizen," *Public Libraries* 17 (May 1912): 166–69; and Agnes Hansen, "Work with Foreigners," *ALA Bulletin* 9 (July 1915): 196–98.

73. Cleveland Public Library, AR 1908, 54–55.

74. St. Louis Public Library, AR 1913/14, 50–51, 72; Buffalo Public Library, AR 1913, 8–9, AR 1914, 23; and Enoch Pratt Free Library of Baltimore, AR 1912, 44.

75. Cleveland Public Library, AR 1921/22, 23. See also the tone of condescension that pervades Anna G. Hall, "Work with Foreigners in a Small Factory Town," *New York Libraries* 5 (Nov. 1916): 159–61, summarized in *LJ* 42 (May 1917): 410.

76. Enoch Pratt Free Library of Baltimore, AR 1913, 47–48; St. Louis Public Library, AR 1912/13, 80–81; and Buffalo Public Library, AR 1916, 24.

77. New York Public Library, AR 1907, 23; Cleveland Public Library, AR 1911, 56; Boston Public Library, AR 1912/13, 63; and Newark Public Library, AR 1921, 13. See also, Carl W. Ackerman, "The Book-worms of New York: How the Public Libraries Satisfy the Immigrant's Thirst for Knowledge," *Independent* 74 (Jan. 1913): 199–201.

78. Although his conclusions were limited to New York City around the turn of the twentieth century, Thomas Kessner demonstrated the geographical, residential, and occupational mobility of most Jewish and Italian immigrants. See Thomas Kessner, *The Golden Door: Italian and Jewish Immigrant Mobility in New York City, 1880-1915* (New York: Oxford University Press, 1977).

79. Anna J. Fiske, "The Human Interest in Library Work in a Mining District," *Public Libraries* 13 (Mar. 1908): 78–81; F. C. H. Wendel, "The Stranger Within Our Gates: What

Can the Library Do for Him?" *Public Libraries* 19 (Mar. 1911): 89–92; and Mary Antin, "The Immigrant in the Library," *ALA Bulletin* 7 (July 1913): 145–50.

Jane Maud Campbell, circa 1900. Photo courtesy Fay Campbell (Reed) Kaynor, Amherst, MA.

3

The Librarian as Advocate:
Jane Maud Campbell, 1869–1947

During the first decade of the twentieth century, New Jersey, with a foreign population of 26 percent, would become the place of residence for 5 percent of the total immigrants to the United States.[1] There was not only an increase in the total number of immigrants arriving in New Jersey, but also a dramatic shift in the numerical representation of various nationalities.

The increase in immigration from the British Isles, Germany, and Scandinavia, countries of the "old" immigration, had been 8 percent, while the increase in immigration from Italy, Austria-Hungary, and Russia, countries of the "new" immigration, was over 200 percent. Immigrants were leaving their native lands for social and economic betterment in the New World as before, but now an increasing number fled from political and religious persecution, excessive taxation, and compulsory military service.[2]

These trends in immigration, so apparent in New Jersey, did not pass the scrutiny of the 1907 Federal Immigration Commission, whose members had noted similar trends throughout the United States. They weighed the official testimony of experts in immigration, sociology, education, and eugenics, and ultimately placed themselves on record as favoring the restriction of the new immigrants from southern and eastern Europe.[3]

Many New Jersey citizens, like their brethren in other immigrant states, gave lip service to the notion promulgated by the Federal Immigration Commission that the motivation, allegiance, and even the basic intelligence of the new immigrants were questionable at best. At any rate, the new immigrants would be more difficult to Americanize than the old had been.

If ever immigrants needed an advocate, it was surely in the early years of the twentieth century in New Jersey. Such an advocate was to be found in Jane Maud Campbell.

EARLY YEARS IN ENGLAND, SCOTLAND, AND VIRGINIA

An immigrant herself, Campbell was born in England of Scottish parents, George and Jane (Cameron) Campbell, who had met and married in Virginia. Before, during, and immediately after the American Civil War, patriarch George Campbell's shipping business, primarily transporting cotton, tobacco, and other dry goods, had been responsible for making the large Campbell family at home on both sides of the Atlantic, in England and Scotland as well as in Virginia and West Virginia. During the latter decades of the 1800s, after a tobacco blight brought an abrupt end to his shipping enterprise, George Campbell tried to recoup his losses by redirecting his energy and resources to the tanning industry, with family-owned and -operated factories at sites in both Virginia and West Virginia.

After the death of her mother and George Campbell's subsequent marriage to an American, Rosalie Higgenbotham of Richmond, Virginia, the young Maud Campbell was taught until the age of ten by governesses at the Campbells' home in Dulwich, Surrey, England, near London. For the next five years, she was educated at a girls' school near Richmond, Virginia.

In her late teens, Campbell was sent to live with relatives in Scotland. She continued her education at the Ladies' College of the University of Edinburgh, where she received a master's degree in literature. As testimony to the fact that her preparation for life never omitted the practical at the expense of the intellectual, she earned a certificate from the Edinburgh School of Cookery and Domestic Economy.

Shortly after the completion of her studies in Scotland, Campbell immigrated to America permanently to be with her father, then living in New Jersey, where he had expanded his tanning business and where, for a brief time, he had collaborated with his friend, Thomas Alva Edison. George Campbell's children by his first and second wives were now dispersed in England, Virginia, West Virginia, and New Jersey.[4]

Having spent the early years of her adult life as the caregiver and nurturer for her extended but close-knit family and bookkeeper for the family tanning business in West Virginia, Campbell was thirty-two years old before she felt able to exert her independence. In 1901, she applied for and, after a competitive examination, secured a position as assistant in the reference department of the Newark Public Library. Campbell had had no formal library training.

LIBRARY SERVICE TO IMMIGRANTS IN NEW JERSEY

Working under the tutelage of Frank P. Hill, who soon moved on to the Brooklyn Public Library, and, later of his successor, John Cotton Dana, Campbell learned the principles of librarianship. Her duties as reference librarian brought her into contact with various charitable and educational institutions throughout the Newark community. She lectured on the resources and services available through the public library, and as a result of these contacts, she established traveling libraries and deposit stations throughout the city. Undoubtedly, it was during these visits throughout the bustling metropolis of Newark, with a foreign-born population of over 30 percent, that Campbell was made acutely aware of the informational needs of immigrants and the possibilities for meeting those needs through public library service.

After a brief period of eighteen months of "efficient service," to quote Dana, Campbell had distinguished herself to such a degree that she was offered the position of public librarian at both Perth Amboy and Passaic, the New Jersey cities with the largest immigrant populations. Notwithstanding the consistently high praise of Dana, who referred to Campbell as "a very competent woman," the fact that Campbell was an immigrant American undoubtedly swayed the boards of both Perth Amboy and Passaic.[5] In deciding between the two cities, Campbell chose Passaic.

Service in Passaic

Located in the industrial northeast of New Jersey, Passaic was the city where the rags-to-riches Scottish immigrant, Peter Reid, had made his fortune in textile manufacturing. Reid, like his fellow countryman Andrew Carnegie, had chosen the public library, which afforded educational opportunities for rich and poor alike, as the primary beneficiary of his philanthropy.

The new Jane Watson Reid Memorial Library, named in honor of Reid's wife and opened in early 1903, was situated in the heart of the Dundee district of Passaic, where Reid's textile mills flourished. Reid and the library trustees of Passaic took great satisfaction in the knowledge that the Reid Memorial branch as well as the library in the Passaic City Hall were to be administrated by an immigrant and one of Campbell's ability.

Realizing that it was only through experience that she would master and refine, in Passaic, the many facets of librarianship and community service of which she had barely scratched the surface in Newark, Campbell was not afraid or in the least reluctant to seek advice. She learned from other librarians; library trustees; the library's benefactors, notably Peter Reid; community leaders; politicians; editors of the foreign language press; and library patrons themselves, the majority of whom were immigrants. In turn, she never turned down an opportunity to share what she had learned, whether the occasions were state, regional, or national library conventions; church services; or meetings of patriotic societies, charitable institutions, or social welfare organizations.[6]

Her remarks to the American Library Association at its Niagara (NY) annual conference in 1903 not only exuded her unbridled enthusiasm, innate pragmatism, and good sense of humor, but also revealed her vision for public library service in Passaic or any small town in America. Campbell's concept of the public library as a purely democratic institution existing primarily to serve the will of its constituents and her concept of the librarian as advocate for all segments of the library's community were made quite clear.[7]

Campbell's address established her reputation as an excellent speaker and communicator, a talent that would place her before countless audiences throughout her career. The reaction of her friend and former colleague in Newark, Clara

Whitehill Hunt, then superintendent of the Children's Rooms of the Brooklyn Public Library, was a case in point. Hunt wrote William Coggin Kimball, chairman of the Board of Trustees of the Passaic Public Library, to tell him "how beautifully your representative carried off the honors for Passaic last night." Hunt advised Kimball almost prophetically that "you'd better get a tight grip on your librarian, for she made a hit in the ALA."[8]

Campbell recognized the fact that English was not the native language of the majority of Passaic's citizens. She was acutely aware as well of the debate within the American public library community regarding the efficacy of providing extensive collections of books in foreign languages, with the notable exception of the expected collections of literary classics in the original French or German. Librarians, like the citizenry at large, were of two minds: the provision of foreign language books was viewed as either a natural extension of library service to immigrant taxpayers or an unnecessary hindrance to their learning of English.

On this issue, Campbell was unequivocal. Her strategy for helping immigrants to adjust to life in Passaic involved getting to them *before* they could speak English and *before* they were exploited by corrupt politicians, cornered by well-meaning but unwelcome proselytizers, arrested for breaking laws of which they were totally ignorant, or otherwise disenchanted with America and Americans. Campbell was convinced that library work with immigrants involved a dialogue between the librarian and her immigrant patrons. Library service was a give-and-take proposition in which both parties benefited. Librarians had to get to know their immigrant patrons personally and to understand sympathetically their circumstances and needs.[9]

Campbell believed that it was an absolute necessity, not merely an enlightened gesture on the part of librarians, to secure and provide books, newspapers, and periodicals in immigrant languages. Particularly important library materials were those containing information about the customs, history, and government of the United States and the laws, statutes, ordinances, and regulations regarding health, sanitation, employment, and education that were enforced in the city of Passaic and the state of New Jersey.

Immigrants needed technical guides and instructional aids written in their native languages to help them advance in their chosen trades and crafts. Materials to fulfill all these needs as well as to provide a source of relaxation and escape from the long hours in the factories and mills and the constant strain of domestic duties were secured for the Passaic Public Library. Library hours were extended to accommodate the lifestyles of working immigrants.

Campbell, in an address delivered to the Long Island Library Club in Brooklyn, in 1904, within a year of her arrival in Passaic, envisioned the public library not as a frill for the rich and highly educated Americans, but as a bridge to opportunity for the poor and intellectually starved potential American citizens. Campbell further delineated her vision of the public library as both a preserver of humanistic culture and the great leveler of American society.[10]

While other librarians debated the issue of supplying foreign language materials in American public libraries and debated the ramifications of such a policy,

Campbell did not hesitate. She set about to determine the languages spoken by the immigrant majority in Passaic and to convince the Board of Trustees of the Passaic Public Library that in order to serve the needs of its supporters, the library had to provide books, periodicals, and newspapers not only in English but also in the foreign languages spoken by its various constituencies.[11]

Campbell, who spoke only English and perhaps a wee bit of Gaelic, never found the language barrier an insurmountable obstacle. She communicated her humanitarian concern for helping people in need through the universal language of compassion, sympathy, and genuine understanding.

Whenever Campbell needed assistance in selecting, acquiring, and organizing the foreign language books, she turned to the leaders of the immigrant community. The editors of the foreign language press, often scholars in their own right, were generous with newspaper space for advertising the library's foreign language acquisitions and holdings. She consulted regularly with local immigrant booksellers and established foreign language book dealers throughout the country, who advised her on availability, quality, and turnaround time to be expected when importing foreign language materials. Special assistance was received from the immigrant literary and cultural societies, whose members, being thoroughly versed in the literatures of particular ethnic or national groups, were able to help in cataloging the materials acquired.[12]

By the time the collaborative process of petitioning, selecting, acquiring, and organizing had been completed with the various immigrant clienteles of the Passaic Public Library, Campbell found herself administering a collection of books in English as well as eleven foreign languages. Foreign language materials in French, German, Dutch, Italian, Hungarian, Russian, Bohemian, Slovene, Polish, Hebrew, and Yiddish were available to library patrons in Passaic. One year later, in the 1904/5 annual report of the Passaic Public Library, Campbell presented an amazing statistic that proved not only the success of the library-community partnership, but also the fact that the immigrants were appreciative and enthusiastic readers. Campbell reported that "in twelve months the five hundred and fifty books, in the eleven foreign languages we then had, were borrowed 11,114 times."[13]

Five years later, in 1908, Campbell recalled the ambivalence within the library community concerning the provision of books in foreign languages as well as her own ardent support of this practice in an article espousing a philosophy of proactive library service to the immigrant community. Campbell reported the advice or, in many cases, the lack of it, she had received about supplying books in foreign languages from the libraries she had visited shortly after her arrival in Passaic. She also offered words of encouragement to other librarians serving immigrant clienteles.[14]

The librarian from Passaic thus set the trend for other libraries throughout the nation serving immigrant clienteles. The problems encountered in providing books in foreign languages in public libraries, notably the selection of appropriate titles, was suddenly a nationwide concern. The ALA Publishing Board addressed this need by publishing, from 1907 to 1916, in its Foreign Book List series, seven guides for the selection and acquisition of books in German, Hungarian, French, Danish and Norwegian, Swedish, Polish, and Russian.

Under the auspices of the New Jersey Public Library Commission, Campbell compiled for this series a bibliography of recommended titles in the Hungarian language for public libraries, which was later adopted for use by the League of Library Commissions. With characteristic modesty, Campbell, in the introduction to her *Selected List of Hungarian Books*, described the guide as "simply a list of books which Hungarians are proud to recommend and pleased to read themselves." She gave the credit for its publication to a Hungarian immigrant scholar and editor in New York and members of the Hungarian literary society in Passaic.[15]

Despite the impressive nature of the circulation statistics at the Passaic Public Library, Campbell never lost sight of the public library's primary purpose of service—bringing the community together.[16] Campbell was convinced that the library must be not only a place for the distribution of books and other educational materials, but also a community center.

The library was to be a haven for rest and relaxation for adults after long and often dreary days in the textile mills and other factories of Passaic. For children, the public library was to be a quiet place where they could study and complete their school assignments in relatively spacious surroundings, without the constant interruptions associated with the crowded tenement lifestyle.

The public library served as a clubroom for various social groups and debating societies and a recreation area where patrons could play checkers, chess, ping-pong, and other games. Most important, the public library served as the classroom where continuing education opportunities were always available, including Americanization classes, sewing classes, and lectures on a variety of topics.[17]

Although Campbell viewed the library as primarily an educational institution, particularly for adult immigrants, she did not endorse the usurping of the mission of any other social agency. She did believe, however, that the library must remain flexible enough to be able to address other nontraditional, recreational needs when no other community agency was meeting them.[18]

The free lecture series was a tangible example of the cooperation between the library and the immigrant community in Passaic, specifically the foreign societies. For some time, the library had provided the funding and location for lectures in English on various topics of general interest to the immigrant community. The leaders of the foreign societies, notably the Italian, Slovene, Polish, Bohemian, and Hungarian, approached Campbell with the proposition that they would provide capable lecturers in their respective native languages if the library would provide the space for the lectures.

Campbell was most receptive to their proposition, and it became the standard practice to have lectures given in English and then in the languages of the nationalities or ethnic groups sponsoring the events.[19] Such empathy for her patrons revealed that Campbell was, first and foremost, the consummate humanitarian. In all circumstances, local, state, regional, and national, in which social ills were apparent and called for reform, Campbell could always be counted upon to champion the underdog, especially the immigrant. Whether the cause was defending the policy of free immigration, providing books in foreign languages, lobbying for a fair wage for immigrant laborers, or petitioning health and sanitation officials for more frequent inspections of tenements, Campbell never passed up an opportunity to ally herself with her immigrant patrons and to speak for them.[20]

Attitude toward Immigrants

Campbell was an ardent proponent of cultural pluralism. While in firm agreement with other Americanizers that immigrants had to learn English and become citizens to participate fully in the advantages of American life, Campbell espoused the philosophy that there was no one American culture. Rather, American culture was a conglomeration of cultures, each offering a unique gift to the building of American society.[21]

Education of Immigrants

The provision of educational opportunities for immigrants, which served as an avenue of both assimilation and overall progress within American society, was Campbell's constant concern as a librarian and citizen. The compulsory education laws requiring the regular attendance at public schools of children under the age of fourteen assured at least a minimal education for immigrant children, including instruction in the English language and the inculcation of American values.

Immigrant Children. Although Campbell applauded the success of the public school in carrying out its mandate, she also witnessed with deep regret an unforeseen side effect of the Americanization process for immigrant children. Oftentimes this very education of immigrant children led them not only to lose respect for their parents and home authority but also to lose respect for the cultures and native languages of their parents in particular.

Immigrant Adults. Campbell realized that the educational needs of adult immigrants were not as easily or routinely met. In contrast to the public day schools for immigrant children, the evening schools for adult immigrants were not as successful. This unfortunate situation was due primarily to the fact that evening schools were not readily available in all communities throughout New Jersey on a year-round basis and that their establishment, rather than being mandated by state law, remained a local option.

The same philosophy reflected in the argument that the provision of foreign language books in public libraries was a hindrance to learning English also surfaced in the argument that evening school teachers should speak and understand only English. The logic was that adult immigrants would hear only the language that they were expected to master. A further complication of an already difficult situation was the fact that most evening school classes were composed of adult immigrants of more than one nationality.[22]

Once again, Campbell was not reluctant to voice her concerns to those in a position of authority. Campbell discussed her ideas about increasing the educational opportunities for adult immigrants in New Jersey communities with Passaic Public Library trustee William Coggin Kimball. He was serving concurrently as chairman of the New Jersey Public Library Commission along with New Jersey Supreme Court Justice John Franklin Fort, later to be governor of New Jersey. Both Kimball and Fort were impressed with Campbell's ideas and the expertise demonstrated in her work with immigrants in Passaic.

Kimball, in turn, helped Campbell to gain an interview with New Jersey Governor Edward Casper Stokes.[23] Two months later, on 10 April 1906, Governor Stokes, acting upon the authorization of the New Jersey Legislature granted only the previous day, appointed Campbell a member of a commission of three, along with John Dyneley Prince, a professor at Columbia University in New York, and D. F. Merritt, of Montclair, New Jersey. The commission's charge was "to inquire into and report upon the general condition of the immigrants coming into or residents of this State." The 1906 New Jersey Immigration Commission was the first state commission, according to Robert Watchorn, then U.S. Commissioner of Immigration, "to treat the immigration problem in a rational and systematic way."[24]

1906 New Jersey Immigration Commission

Fully aware of being the first woman appointed to a New Jersey commission, Campbell also realized the opportunity her appointment presented to ameliorate the educational as well as social conditions of adult immigrants. She willingly accepted membership on the New Jersey Immigration Commission.[25]

While the New Jersey Immigration Commission progressed toward its goal of assessing the condition of immigrants in New Jersey, Campbell lectured regularly to gain support for its work and for the appointment of other state commissions of immigration. In her address to the Narragansett Pier (RI) annual conference of the ALA, in August 1906, Campbell alluded to her appointment to the New Jersey Immigration Commission and to the potentially far-reaching effect other such state commissions could have on the education of adult immigrants throughout the country. She closed her remarks with a resolution that all ALA members and members of the various state library associations should lobby for the appointment of state commissions. The charge of these state commissions should be "to investigate the general condition of non-English-speaking residents, with the view to their education and enlightenment upon the principles and policy of our government and institutions, and the rights and opportunities of its citizens."[26]

Other than lecturing to civic and educational groups, Campbell's principal strategy as a commissioner was to garner the support of the foreign societies in New Jersey. She visited the president of the National Slavonic Society in New York and explained the mission of the New Jersey Immigration Commission. She solicited his help in convincing the societies in New Jersey to send letters and petitions to Governor Stokes stating their support for the establishment of a permanent governmental agency or bureau to handle immigration affairs in New Jersey. These contacts with the leaders of the immigrant community alone resulted in an avalanche of letters to Governor Stokes.[27]

Jane Maud Campbell (rear, left) with sewing class of immigrant girls at the Passaic (NJ) Public Library, circa 1904/5. Photo courtesy Fay Campbell (Reed) Kaynor, Amherst, MA.

The 1906 New Jersey Immigration Commission completed its mandate in December of that same year. At a banquet in Princeton, New Jersey, the commission, identifying education of the immigrant adult as the key to immigrant assimilation and ultimate progress, recommended the establishment of evening schools on a statewide basis. The commission had established and was maintaining experimental schools for Italians in Passaic and Princeton, and was working with similar schools in conjunction with the educational authorities in Trenton and Burlington. In addition, the commission had published and distributed a primer in Italian and English geared to the needs of the adult immigrant Italian in the process of learning the English language.

Governor Stokes, who referred to Campbell as "a most progressive woman," concurred with her findings and those of the other commissioners and lauded their efforts on behalf of New Jersey. Stokes waxed eloquent regarding the potential for progress that their findings and accomplishments portended.[28]

In 1907, the New Jersey Legislature, having been convinced by the evidence gathered by the 1906 New Jersey Immigration Commission and cognizant of Governor Stokes's approval of its recommendations, passed a law that encouraged communities throughout New Jersey to set up evening schools for adult immigrants. The 1907 adult immigrant education law provided for the boards of education of any New Jersey school district to establish public evening schools for the instruction of foreign-born residents over fourteen years of age in English and civics. Another section of the law, dealing with the funding of these evening schools, included the provision that the state would match any funds raised by a school district for the maintenance of public evening schools for immigrant adults.[29]

Although the commission had accomplished a worthy goal, there was still no mandate that required the establishment of evening schools on a statewide basis. Their establishment remained a local option. Neither was a permanent governmental agency or bureau set up to handle immigration concerns in New Jersey.

Nevertheless, the New Jersey adult immigrant education law set the pattern for the nation. Other states, including New York, California, Massachusetts, Pennsylvania, and Rhode Island, followed the example of New Jersey and appointed commissions to survey the needs of immigrants on a statewide basis.[30] A few years later, in 1913, Campbell recalled with justifiable pride her first meetings with local and state officials in Passaic, which had led eventually to the passage of the 1907 adult immigrant education law. She lauded the efforts of other states by commenting that "the little candle lighted in Passaic in 1906 has cast its beam quite a distance."[31]

NORTH AMERICAN CIVIC LEAGUE FOR IMMIGRANTS

Three years after the passage of the adult immigrant education legislation in New Jersey, in May 1910, Campbell made the decision to leave her position as librarian at Passaic in order to concentrate her efforts in the area of immigrant education. The outpouring of gratitude and appreciation that accompanied her leaving must have deeply touched Campbell, who saw her move as the natural outgrowth of the experiences she had gained in the cosmopolitan industrial center of Passaic.[32]

At their meeting held on 7 May 1910, the trustees of the Passaic Public Library, including her constant supporter, William Coggin Kimball, and Passaic's mayor, Bird W. Spencer, presented Campbell with a beautifully decorated calligraphic citation. The citation extolled her ability, tact, industry, inspiration, and, most important, her advocacy for the poor and foreign born of Passaic.[33]

Mayor Spencer summed up not only his own feelings but also those of the Passaic citizenry at large in a letter to Campbell written on 23 May 1910. Spencer left no doubt that Campbell, as librarian and advocate for the foreign born of Passaic, had had a positive impact not only on all segments of the local community but also throughout the state of New Jersey.[34]

Campbell's response to Spencer was characteristic in its blending of gratitude, humility, and pride of accomplishment. She made it quite clear that Passaic had provided her with the laboratory for trying out her original and experimental ideas for work with the foreign born.[35]

The challenge that had captured Campbell's imagination enough to lure her away from her successful administration of the Passaic Public Library and the many friends she had won over her seven-year tenure was, ironically, outside the field of librarianship per se. The desire to pursue her ideas in the fertile field of adult immigrant education coupled with an employment opportunity offered by Anne Morgan, daughter of philanthropist and businessman John Pierpont Morgan, provided the needed stimulus to accept a new calling. Morgan invited Campbell to assume the position of education secretary for the recently organized New York Committee of the North American Civic League for Immigrants.[36]

The North American Civic League for Immigrants (NACLI), founded in Boston in 1908, was, according to historian Edward George Hartmann, "the first of the active Americanization groups." The outgrowth of a conference of social workers and reform-minded citizens sponsored a year earlier, in February 1907, by the International Committee of the Young Men's Christian Association in New York City, the league chose as its mission "to accomplish the civic betterment of the immigrant."[37]

The NACLI's membership, like the attendees of the YMCA conference, was, in the main, Anglo-conformist in philosophy and represented conservative economic interests.[38] The NACLI was not concerned with the highly political issue of admission or exclusion of immigrants, but rather with the more humanitarian issues of "the protection, education, distribution, and assimilation of immigrants" once they had arrived in the United States.

The NACLI had initially confined its activities, on an experimental basis, to Boston, the second largest port of entry next to New York City. Later, branches were established as well in the large immigrant cities of New York and Philadelphia. The NACLI sponsored extensive programs of lectures in English and foreign languages to evening school classes for immigrants. It published and distributed these lectures in pamphlet form as *Messages for Newcomers to the*

United States to public libraries throughout the United States, "as far west as Seattle and as far south as Houston, Texas." Through the sponsorship of these lectures and publications, the NACLI became a well-known and respected authority on adult immigrant education.[39]

Concurrently with the founding of the NACLI, the New York State Immigration Commission had been appointed, in 1908, by Governor Charles Evans Hughes. The mandate of the New York State Immigration Commission, like its predecessor, the 1906 New Jersey Immigration Commission on which Campbell had served, was to investigate the condition of immigrants throughout the state of New York.

In March 1909, the commission made its final report, which, again like its New Jersey predecessor, emphasized the education of the adult immigrant as the key to immigrant assimilation and progress. Having no organization in existence to take over its work and to see that the legislation it had recommended was enacted, the commission's former members approached the leadership of the NACLI, which by then had established its reputation nationally.[40]

NACLI New York Committee

In December 1909, nine months after the termination of the 1908 New York State Immigration Commission and the beginning of its former members' negotiations with the NACLI, the administrative district under the auspices of the NACLI New York City branch was expanded to incorporate the entire state of New York. The committee was renamed the NACLI New York Committee to reflect the expansion of its jurisdiction from municipal to statewide. Thus, in early 1910, the furtherance of the recommendations of the New York Immigration Commission was assumed as the mission of the fledgling NACLI New York Committee.[41]

The expertise of Campbell, both in the educational and legislative arenas, had not escaped the notice of Anne Morgan and other members of the NACLI New York Committee, who wanted Campbell to accomplish in New York State what she had done so successfully in New Jersey. Despite the NACLI's conservative stance on the political and economic aspects of the immigration issue, Campbell had no qualms in accepting Morgan's invitation to serve the NACLI New York Committee as its education secretary since in this capacity she would be responsible for all its educational activities.[42]

Campbell began her duties with the NACLI New York Committee in the summer of 1910. By September 1910, the committee had been successful in getting the New York State Legislature to pass the immigration bills recommended by the 1908 New York State Immigration Commission. The major bill provided for the establishment of the New York Bureau of Industries and Immigration to oversee immigrant affairs, from banking and employment to legal aid and education.[43] The New York bureau was thus empowered to provide educational opportunities for adult immigrants similar to those already available in New Jersey as a result of the 1907 adult immigrant education legislation sponsored by the 1906 New Jersey Immigration Commission of which Campbell was a member.[44]

With her headquarters in New York City, Campbell, as education secretary of the NACLI New York Committee, was responsible for coordinating the establishment of classes in English and citizenship for newly arrived immigrants in New York City. Her responsibilities also included the on-site development, implementation, and supervision of programs to facilitate the Americanization of the immigrant laborers and their families in temporary labor camps falling outside the jurisdiction of local school districts in upstate New York.

Addressing initially the needs of immigrant children covered by the compulsory education laws, the NACLI New York Committee, using ships' manifests at Ellis Island, compiled lists of the names of school-age children entering the port of New York. These lists were then transferred to the proper school authorities in permanent as well as temporary educational facilities throughout the state of New York. By March 1911, the NACLI New York Committee, in turn, would be successful in convincing the federal authorities to assume the responsibility for providing such lists to school authorities not only in New York but also in New Jersey, Massachusetts, and Illinois, other states where the majority of immigrants was destined to establish residence.[45]

Most of Campbell's time and energy with the NACLI New York Committee, from 1910 to 1913, would be consumed by her work with adult immigrant workers and their families, largely Italians, Poles, Russians, and Austrians. These immigrants were employed in the labor camps in upstate New York, where a vast network of aqueducts to serve the needs of New York City was under construction. The fact that these construction camps did not fall within the boundaries of local school districts, coupled with the fact that their existence was only temporary, necessitated the provision of special accommodations for the camp residents.

In December 1910, the NACLI New York Committee established an experimental camp school in Valhalla, New York, the site of one of the construction camps building the Catskill Aqueduct. The committee used as their models the construction camp schools in Pennsylvania and New York that were established as early as 1905 by the Society of Italian Immigrants under the direction of Sarah Wool Moore.[46]

NACLI New York–New Jersey Committee

In January 1911, the NACLI New York Committee expanded its jurisdiction to include the state of New Jersey and, in recognition of this major administrative change, was renamed the NACLI New York–New Jersey Committee. Shortly thereafter, the NACLI New York–New Jersey Committee convinced New Jersey Governor Woodrow Wilson to appoint the 1911 New Jersey Immigration Commission. The 1911 commission, like its predecessors, the 1906 New Jersey Immigration Commission and the 1908 New York State Immigration Commission, was charged "to make full inquiry, examination and investigation into the conditions, welfare, distribution and industrial opportunities of aliens."[47]

Crippled from the outset by a lack of state funding, this second New Jersey Immigration Commission had to rely solely on the financial support of civic-minded individuals and on the NACLI New York–New Jersey Committee. Still, even with this funding, the 1911 New Jersey Immigration Commission was unable to get legislation passed to establish a permanent state agency to handle immigrant affairs, as had been done in New York State. Indeed, the 1911 commission accomplished nothing of significance other than a most informative report of its findings, which painted a vivid portrait of New Jersey as an immigrant state at the end of the first decade of the twentieth century.[48]

Concurrently with its sponsorship of the 1911 New Jersey Immigration Commission, the NACLI New York–New Jersey Committee, under the leadership of Campbell, continued to advance its work in the construction camp school at Valhalla, New York. By April 1911, a special assembly hall was opened in Valhalla to take care of the educational needs of immigrant children, women, and men. A day school was operated in the hall for the children, while later, in the afternoon, classes in home economics and sewing were held for the women and girls. Completing the daily cycle of the educational program, an evening school for the immigrant men provided instruction in English and preparation for naturalization.

During the summer of 1911, Campbell experimented with the provision of a new recreational program—moving picture shows. These moving picture shows, with musical accompaniment provided by phonograph recordings, were provided to a circuit of fourteen temporary labor camps situated all along the construction route of the Catskill Aqueduct. Recreational activities eventually included a moving picture show every Saturday night and a dance once a month.[49] Campbell thus demonstrated her concern for the provision of leisure activities for immigrants as well as structured educational experiences, since the only other diversions for the construction workers after eight hours of manual labor were gambling and drinking.

A horse and covered wagon were engaged for the summer of 1911, and beginning in June, the experiment was started and continued for eighty-seven days. During these three months, Campbell personally conducted a total of fifty "entertainments" throughout the circuit of construction camps, with a total attendance of almost seven thousand. The moving picture shows were not only recreational but also instructional and informative. They presented in a novel format essential advice on such topics as health regulations, personal hygiene, the laws of the land, and the naturalization process, and technical instruction on various aspects of aqueduct construction. The experiment was so successful that several construction contractors agreed to purchase the moving pictures and projection equipment in order to inaugurate recreational programs for the immigrant laborers in other temporary labor camps.[50]

The ameliorative effect of these educational and recreational experiences, which were provided under Campbell's supervision in the construction camps in the Catskills, was duly noted in an article written by a contractor at Valhalla and published in the September 1911 issue of the *Catskill Water System News*. The contractor described the work of the construction camp school operated by the New York–New Jersey Committee of the league as "successful beyond expectation." He assessed the overall effect of its activities and educational experiences on the construction workers as "a better class of men, a better camp, and a higher standard of living than is generally found, which all makes for efficiency."[51]

Throughout her tenure as education secretary of the NACLI New York State Committee and, later, the NACLI New York–New Jersey Committee, Campbell maintained a rigorous schedule of lecturing that she had begun earlier in Passaic. Campbell's address on the social and educational needs of immigrant women was delivered to an audience of social workers at a meeting of the New Jersey Conference of Charities and Correction held at Princeton, New Jersey, in April 1911. She revealed her depth of understanding of the immigrant situation as well as her advocacy for the suffrage of women, both native-born and foreign-born.[52]

In her address, Campbell acknowledged the prejudice against all immigrants as manifested in the continuing call for immigration restriction. She drew special attention to the ungrounded discrimination against immigrant women and pointed out the often negative side effects of the assimilation process on the immigrant family. The most far-reaching side effect, the widening of the generation gap between immigrant parents and their children, was, ironically, exacerbated by the exposure of immigrant children to the Americanizing influence of the public schools.

For the immigrant woman as well as the immigrant man and immigrant child, Campbell argued, the problems of assimilation and education were synonymous. She was convinced that "the most difficult problem with the immigrant woman is to make her appreciate the advantages of education, which to her is something only for the men and children."[53]

Campbell continually searched for ways to lure immigrant women to take part in educational opportunities offered by the NACLI New York–New Jersey Committee. Sewing, cooking, and child care classes were often the "bait" to get immigrant women out of the confines of their homes and the congested immigrant community. Campbell wanted to bring them into settings where they would be exposed to the Americanizing influences of hearing spoken English and have the opportunity to share everyday experiences with other Americans in the making.[54]

In 1911, the voluminous reports of the 1907 Federal Immigration Commission were made available to the general public. Campbell and her staff read with particular interest sections of the reports dealing with immigrant labor camps. Referring specifically to the mining operations in Pennsylvania, which employed mainly immigrant laborers, the federal commission reports drew attention to the alarming statistic that "the great majority of the injuries and fatalities in the mines occur because the foreigner does not understand words of command."[55] The NACLI New York–New Jersey Committee was not only convinced that the same statistic could be applied to the temporary labor camps, but also convinced that the problem lay in the lack of appropriate materials for teaching English to adult immigrant laborers.[56]

To remedy this lack of pertinent adult-oriented lessons in English, the NACLI New York–New Jersey Committee wrote and printed a series of elementary

English lessons based on words used in the construction work at the temporary labor camps. These instructional materials were arranged appropriately in parallel English-Italian and English-Polish, since the majority of the laborers were Italian and Polish immigrants. Pamphlets and leaflets explaining the naturalization requirements for first and second papers and the basic laws of the United States, including child labor and compulsory education laws and sanitary regulations, were also prepared and printed in English and the foreign languages spoken by the construction workers and their families.[57]

In early 1913, the New York–New Jersey Committee's parent, the NACLI itself, was urging the appointment of yet another state immigration commission. Already having been instrumental in the appointment and support of the 1908 New York State Immigration Commission and the 1911 New Jersey Immigration Commission, the NACLI turned its attention to Massachusetts, another of the five largest immigrant states.[58]

Meanwhile, Campbell and her associates on the NACLI New York–New Jersey Committee were winding up their experimental education work with the immigrant laborers in New York State. The experimental camp school at Valhalla, initiated on an experimental, localized basis under Campbell's direction, was now the model emulated throughout New York State. The influence of the NACLI New York– New Jersey Committee was manifested by the statewide enforcement of a law introduced in the New York State Legislature by the New York State Department of Education. This new legislation provided that public schools established for laborers in temporary construction camps engaged in public work projects should be maintained out of the funds designated for these public work projects.[59] Access to education by immigrant laborers was now legally sanctioned in New York State.

MASSACHUSETTS FREE PUBLIC LIBRARY COMMISSION

By May 1913, the lobbying efforts of the NACLI were successful in getting the Massachusetts Legislature to appoint the 1913 Massachusetts Immigration Commission. The commission was charged to "make a full investigation of the status and general condition of immigrants" within the boundaries of the Commonwealth.[60] Once again, as in previous state commissions, the educational opportunities of immigrants were to be assessed, but this time the commission would examine specifically the existing public library resources, services, and facilities available to immigrants.

The Massachusetts Free Public Library Commission (MFPLC), under the direction of Charles Francis Dorr Belden, was already one step ahead of the Massachusetts Immigration Commission. Approximately two months earlier, on 25 March 1913, Belden had submitted to Governor Eugene Noble Foss, a recommendation relating to the provision of library service to the immigrant population scattered throughout Massachusetts. The recommendation stated that since the fall of 1912 the MFPLC had been investigating the possibility of providing statewide service to cities and towns serving immigrant clienteles, especially those communities whose tax valuation was under $600,000. Belden reported that response to their initial efforts had been most enthusiastic.

To put the statewide plan into effect, Belden recommended that the Massachusetts Legislature should appropriate funds for "the employment of a special field agent or secretary who can study the problems involved." The field agent would "select the books, cooperate with existing associations, and visit the local foreign societies in different towns, and interest the librarians, trustees, teachers, and others in the furtherance of their activities with the foreign population."[61]

Belden reassured Governor Foss that such an appointment would be in the best interests of all Massachusetts citizens and that public libraries were uniquely equipped to reach the foreign-born population. Belden pointed out to Foss that "libraries are recognized as wholly non-political and non-sectarian, and therefore have a special opportunity to welcome newcomers to this country and interest them in all that pertains to good citizenship."[62]

Foss saw in the recommendation from the MFPLC a politically expedient way to ward off the potential problems often associated with a large, un-Americanized immigrant population scattered throughout the state. Two days later, on 27 March 1913, Foss forwarded the MFPLC's request to the Massachusetts Legislature. Governor Foss admitted readily that the fulfillment of the modest request would not solve all the problems associated with immigration, but stated that to do nothing was to court disaster.[63]

Governor Foss's recommendation, in turn, reached a most receptive audience in the Massachusetts Legislature. On 16 May 1913, less than two months after Belden's initial proposal, the Massachusetts Legislature passed a law authorizing the MFPLC to "appoint an agent or secretary to direct educational work for the benefit of the alien population of the commonwealth at a salary . . . not exceeding two thousand dollars."[64]

Belden began the search for an individual to fill this newly approved position. Campbell, having accomplished her goal with the NACLI New York–New Jersey Committee of improving the access of immigrants to educational opportunities in New York and New Jersey, was concurrently looking for another challenge, particularly one that would take her back to librarianship. In the meantime, Campbell had relocated to Massachusetts and secured a temporary position as social agent of the Boston Dwelling House Association while she searched for permanent employment.[65] The timing could not have been more auspicious for either Belden or Campbell.

In late May 1913, approximately one week after the Massachusetts Legislature approved the bill authorizing the appointment of an agent for coordinating library work with foreigners on a statewide basis, the Massachusetts Library Club held its annual meeting at Williams College in Williamstown, Massachusetts. Belden listened with particular interest to the two speakers for this event, both having been engaged to speak on the topic of library work with foreigners. They were John Foster Carr of the Immigrant Publication Society of New York City and Jane Maud Campbell, formerly of the Passaic Public Library.[66]

Campbell's address, entitled "What the Foreigner Has Done for One Library," recounted her experiences working with the immigrant population in New Jersey at the municipal level in Passaic and also on the state level with the 1906 New Jersey Immigration Commission. One can almost imagine Belden's delight when he heard Campbell's address outlining her experiences in providing library services to the immigrant community of Passaic.

Campbell recounted her experiences in selecting, acquiring, and organizing books in eleven foreign languages, her work with foreign societies and foreign language newspapers, and her advocacy for the rights of immigrant taxpayers to information on housing, medical care, and nutrition in foreign languages as well as in English. Campbell emphasized her philosophy that the library's influence should spread beyond the library's walls into the community at large. Her conviction that librarians could be transformed through their contacts with immigrants shone through as well.[67]

Belden, convinced that Campbell was the woman to fill the position, later offered her the position of director of Library Work with Foreigners. On 30 June 1913, barely one month after the Massachusetts Library Club meeting, Belden wrote Edward F. Hamlin, executive secretary, in the State House in Boston, and asked that he submit to Governor Foss and the Massachusetts Legislature the name of Miss J. Maud Campbell. Campbell thus became the first person "appointed by any State to give her entire time and thought to immigration problems in their relation to the social problems of library work."[68]

The 1913 Massachusetts Immigration Commission

Campbell began her duties with the MFPLC in September 1913 and was immediately called upon to share her experience and expertise with the 1913 Massachusetts Immigration Commission. In May of that same year, the commission had just begun its investigation of the condition of immigrants throughout Massachusetts. In cooperation with the Massachusetts Immigration Commission, Campbell conducted a statewide survey of library resources and services available to immigrants. This survey necessitated numerous visits and conversations with the library officials and immigrant leaders in cities and towns with significant immigrant populations throughout the state.

As a result of her efforts, Campbell was able to provide the Massachusetts Immigration Commission with an accurate but bleak description of the situation in Massachusetts with regard to library work with immigrants. Campbell reported that "of 99 libraries reporting a foreign-speaking population in their territory, only 61 have any foreign books."[69]

In accordance with the mandate given the MFPLC, Campbell's efforts on behalf of the immigrant communities in Massachusetts were to be limited primarily to the small towns with a tax base of less than $600,000, a figure soon upgraded to $1,000,000. Campbell determined that the best way to serve the needs of the scattered as well as shifting population of immigrants throughout the state was to establish traveling libraries of books, both in a particular foreign language and in

English for beginners. These traveling libraries could be circulated on a rotation basis upon the request of libraries in towns with immigrant populations.

Traveling Libraries

By early 1914, when the Massachusetts Immigration Commission's report was issued, nineteen traveling libraries in three languages, French, Italian, and Polish, had already begun their circuit throughout the state. In their final report, the commission had recommended that the MFPLC "receive an increased appropriation, so that it may greatly extend the traveling foreign language feature of its work."[70]

Working on a shoestring budget for library materials, Campbell was nevertheless able to increase the number of traveling libraries. This accomplishment in so short a time was due largely to the additional financial support of foreign societies, notably the Dante Alighieri Society and the Circolo Italiano; American patriotic societies, including the National Society of the Colonial Dames of America and the Daughters of the American Revolution; and the Boston-based women's organization, the Woman's Education Association. Always included in the traveling libraries, in addition to primers in English and aids for immigrants preparing for naturalization, were foreign language and elementary English titles about American laws, history, government, and customs.

Conspicuous among the latter category of materials in simple English were the immigrant's guides in Italian, Polish, Yiddish, and English published by John Foster Carr's Immigrant Publication Society, pamphlets on child care and home economics issued by the Metropolitan Life Insurance Company, and textbooks on first aid and other health-related topics supplied by the American National Red Cross in Italian, Polish, Lithuanian, and Slovene. The donations of books by foreign governments also provided welcome additions to the traveling libraries, notably the King Oscar's Traveling Libraries of books in Swedish for Swedish-speaking immigrants.[71]

The traveling library service of the MFPLC administered by Campbell was immensely popular and useful as demonstrated by its phenomenal growth from 19 libraries in three foreign languages, in 1913, to 60 libraries in eight foreign languages one year later. In less than ten years, there would be 280 traveling libraries, including books in twenty foreign languages, circulating throughout the state of Massachusetts.[72]

A little over a year after beginning her regular tour of public libraries across the state of Massachusetts, Campbell was buoyed by the enthusiasm she met from librarians interested in providing library service to immigrants in their communities. She reported in the MFPLC 1913/14 annual report that "a start has thus been made in breaking down the prejudice that has existed against foreigners using the libraries."[73]

Selection and Acquisition of Foreign Language Materials

Routinely, Campbell provided advice on the selection and acquisition of books, pamphlets, and periodicals in foreign languages through correspondence with individual librarians and through articles and bibliographies published regularly in the *Massachusetts Library Club Bulletin*, the official organ of the state library association of which Campbell was a life member and active participant. The bibliographies were compiled for the small to medium-sized libraries scattered across Massachusetts.[74]

An example of a particularly practical bibliography was her selective list of foreign language periodicals, compiled shortly after she arrived at the MFPLC and designed for the library that could afford to subscribe to but one periodical in a particular foreign language. Campbell made recommendations for the best periodical, in terms of style, content, price, and availability, in twenty languages, including Arabic, Armenian, Bohemian, Croatian, Danish, Finnish, French, German, Greek, Italian, Norwegian, Polish, Portuguese, Romanian, Russian, Slovene, Spanish, Swedish, Syrian, and Yiddish.[75]

The ALA Publishing Board in its Foreign Book List series later published another bibliographic guide, the *Selected List of Russian Books*, compiled by Campbell under the auspices of the MFPLC in 1916. The introduction to the bibliography indicated the uniqueness of Campbell's contribution, particularly its usefulness for librarians who did not speak or read Russian but who were responsible for acquiring books and other library materials in Russian for immigrant patrons. Campbell, in her typically modest fashion, gave full credit to two Russian scholars who, because of their familiarity with Russia and the Russian book trade, were "in a position to judge just what sort of books would be most appreciated by the Russian people who use our public libraries."[76]

Library Consultant for Work with Immigrants

As an integral part of her responsibility as director of Library Work with Foreigners, Campbell traveled by train routinely and systematically throughout Massachusetts. She spoke on the efficacy of public libraries in order to raise the collective consciousness of the Massachusetts citizenry to the needs of immigrants for library resources and services. Campbell delivered her message at local library clubs and town meetings, state and national conferences of librarians and social workers, and special library programs given in honor of immigrants. She worked with library trustees, librarians, and schoolteachers as well as the leaders of numerous immigrant societies and organizations.[77]

Education and Publications for Library Work with Immigrants

Beginning in 1916, the MFPLC, in cooperation with Simmons College in Boston, offered annual summer institutes for Massachusetts librarians. These institutes featured classes in and discussion groups on various aspects of librarianship. Campbell's round tables on Americanization and library work with immigrants were regular events at these gatherings.[78]

The dearth of materials in beginners' English about everyday topics, including American history and government, health and hygiene, childcare and nutrition, and agriculture, hindered unnecessarily the Americanization of the immigrant community. In her publications and lectures, Campbell voiced her concerns regarding this scarcity of materials and other educational opportunities for immigrants. She pointed out, for example, the inconsistency that existed between what was preached to immigrants on their arrival in the United States, specifically to leave the industrial cities for farming opportunities in the more healthful rural areas, and the lack of agricultural leaflets written in languages the immigrants could understand.[79]

Through her contacts with immigrant leaders and scholars, particularly the foreign language newspaper editors, and with the financial support of the civic-minded membership of the Old South Association, Campbell was able to address this lack of suitable foreign language materials on topics she defined as "the practical concerns of life in this country." Campbell contacted reputable authors and lecturers in Massachusetts and surrounding states. She convinced them to produce books and pamphlets that could be used by libraries throughout the country. She encouraged them to deliver lectures in foreign languages, including Greek, Italian, Lithuanian, Polish, Portuguese, and Swedish, to immigrant audiences in town halls and public libraries throughout Massachusetts.[80]

Two of Campbell's contacts with immigrant writers and lecturers were particularly fruitful. In 1915, the MFPLC, in cooperation with the Old South Association, engaged Alberto Pecorini, editor of an Italian newspaper in New York, *Il Cittadino*, to lecture in Italian on the opportunities for Italians in America. Pecorini's lectures to Italian audiences throughout Massachusetts covered the need for Italians to learn English, attend evening schools, use public libraries, and keep their children in schools. Campbell's professional relationship with Pecorini was eventually responsible for the publication, in 1920, of his history of the United States. Written in a bilingual format, English-Italian, Pecorini's *The Story of America* became a popular textbook for the adult Italian immigrant learning English.[81]

Another contact with a Greek immigrant writer proved beneficial to the Greek immigrant communities in Massachusetts and throughout the United States. Campbell's acquaintance with Corinna S. Canoutas, the wife of Seraphim George Canoutas, a Boston lawyer and writer, resulted in the publication in 1916 of a cookbook and handbook on childcare written in Greek. This helpful publication called for ingredients available in American grocery stores and was adapted to the lifestyles of Greek immigrant mothers.[82]

During the early years of her service with the MFPLC, Campbell lived in Brookline, Massachusetts, a suburban community within a short commuting distance of her office at the Massachusetts State House in Boston. In 1914, Campbell's father, George, now a widower for the second time and penniless from business losses, came from New Jersey to live with her. In Brookline, Campbell and her father renewed their close relationship. Campbell also welcomed into her home her niece and nephew, Georgia and Thomas Tileston Waterman, the children of her sister, Anne (Campbell) Waterman. The time at home in Brookline was happy for the family-oriented Campbell, who kept the public and private sides of her life very separate.

When George Campbell died in December 1917, almost a year before the conclusion of World War I, Maud Campbell moved from Brookline to a residence on the north side of Boston's Beacon Hill district, two blocks from her office at the Massachusetts State House. In Boston, Campbell had the double advantage not only of being nearer her office but also of living in closer proximity to Boston's North End, the neighborhood with the greatest concentration of immigrants, primarily Italian.[83]

Library Work with Immigrants during World War I

During World War I, Campbell, under the auspices of the MFPLC, was given the additional responsibility for the administration of new services and programs for non-English-speaking soldiers who were temporarily stationed in Massachusetts. Confronted with troops who did not speak or understand commands or instructions in English, the armed forces personnel at Camp Devens in Massachusetts intensified their efforts to provide courses in English for non-English-speaking recruits. Camp educators turned to the MFPLC for assistance in obtaining English textbooks written in the foreign languages understood by the immigrant soldiers.

The virtual standstill of the book trade with European countries together with the scarcity of domestic publications in foreign languages, thwarted the efforts of the MFPLC to provide foreign language library service during wartime. Although the MFPLC was unable to obtain books in some of the foreign languages needed, it was able to supply small quantities of English textbooks in twelve of the foreign languages spoken by the servicemen stationed at Camp Devens. The MFPLC was also able through its traveling library service to supply additional recreational and educational books. As a special service, the MFPLC provided lecturers in foreign languages for hospitalized soldiers, who often understood neither their physicians nor their officers and fellow soldiers.[84]

Captain Ernest J. Hall, an army officer in charge of morale at Camp Devens, wrote Campbell on 20 December 1918, approximately a month after the armistice was signed. Hall thanked her and the MFPLC on behalf of the foreign-born soldiers, who deeply appreciated "the possibility of reading good literature in their native tongue." Hall remarked that the availability of books in Arabic, Armenian, Finnish, French, Greek, Italian, Lithuanian, Polish, Portuguese, Russian, Swedish, and Yiddish had been of "great assistance to the military authorities in maintaining a good spirit among the men, and in developing them mentally while in Camp Devens."[85]

Between 1919 and 1921, the last three years of Campbell's tenure with the MFPLC, the attention of the national library community was drawn to her accomplishments as a leader in the fields of adult immigrant education and library work with immigrants. Due primarily to the exposure given by her numerous publications and speaking engagements, Campbell's reputation and her sphere of influence had grown from statewide and regional to national.

National Service and Recognition

Campbell's services as a consultant were in great demand not only by small to medium-sized libraries in the Northeast, but also by individual library systems in cities serving large immigrant communities in the Midwest, notably Detroit and Cleveland. Indeed, her reputation as a consultant was undoubtedly a deciding factor in her appointment, in 1920, to the ALA Committee on Work with the Foreign Born. This committee had been established only two years earlier in an attempt to raise the national consciousness on the rights and needs of immigrants for library service. Campbell was to serve on the committee for only two years.[86]

The most outstanding recognition of Campbell's talents came in 1920 with the publication of John Daniels's *America via the Neighborhood*. Daniels, a member of the Carnegie Corporation of New York's task force on Americanization, was responsible for identifying the most successful social agencies and organizations, including public libraries, in the campaign to Americanize the immigrant.

Not surprisingly, Daniels discovered that the most successful libraries were those extending their influence beyond the walls of the library into the community. The most successful librarians were those who "conceive the library as an organic part of the community, which may be not only a place of books, but a general center with a broadly educational motive." Daniels singled out for special recognition Campbell's approach to immigrant library service in Passaic. He applauded her service there as "a convincing demonstration" of how libraries could cooperate with the immigrant community to affect its Americanization.[87] By the time Daniels's study was published, Campbell had already applied the same methods at the state level in Massachusetts with equal distinction.

Ironically, in 1921, along with the national recognition she was receiving, Campbell, at the age of fifty-two, was in the throes of a midlife crisis. Her grueling schedule demanded constant travel and numerous speaking engagements. Coupled with the incredible fact that her salary with the MFPLC had not been increased throughout her seven-year tenure, this presented an impossible situation for Campbell. She shared her concerns with family members in Virginia and West Virginia, who were anxious to find an employment opportunity in the South attractive enough to lure her away from Massachusetts.[88]

Resignation and Move to Virginia

In September 1921, that special employment opportunity surfaced: the Jones Memorial Library in Lynchburg, Virginia, was searching for a director. Upon notification of the opening, Campbell immediately forwarded to the search committee her credentials for consideration, and explained why the position was attractive to her.

She made it quite clear why she would desire to leave the security of the now well-developed library situation in Massachusetts for the uncertainty of the underdeveloped library situation of rural Virginia. Although Campbell emphasized the professional challenge offered by the position in Lynchburg, it was apparent from her letter that she was also anxious to return to Virginia, where she had been raised and where most of her relatives lived.[89]

Campbell had made up her mind, but still she had to resign formally. Belden, apparently taken off guard, was rather incredulous that Campbell could consider such a move. Campbell made it clear to Belden and the other commissioners that she was resolute in her decision to leave Boston, effective 31 December 1921, for the challenge awaiting her in Lynchburg. Even the possibility of an increase in salary was not sufficient to dissuade her.[90]

The official and personal responses from her colleagues on the MFPLC as well as librarians, trustees, leaders of the immigrant communities, and "new Americans" across the state all expressed their concern that Campbell would be impossible to replace.[91] Of all Campbell's colleagues and associates, it was perhaps Belden who came closest to fathoming the magnitude of their collective loss. In the official announcement of Campbell's resignation, which appeared in the MFPLC 1921/22 annual report, Belden assessed the dramatic impact of Campbell's contribution to library work with immigrants throughout Massachusetts and, indeed, the nation. He recognized that "under her able leadership the educational work in libraries for aliens attained a high standard."[92]

THE LEGACY OF CAMPBELL TO LIBRARIANSHIP

By the time Belden's paean appeared in print, no replacement for Campbell had been found. She had completed her first year of a twenty-five-year tenure as director of the Jones Memorial Library in Lynchburg, Virginia. Although the setting had changed, Campbell seized yet another opportunity for advocacy of the rights of the downtrodden among the library patrons she served.[93]

The librarian who, to paraphrase Belden, had set the standard for library work with immigrants, transferred her advocacy to the improvement and extension of library services to working-class southerners. Campbell soon discovered that many of them, because of the color of their skin, had suffered the same prejudices and discrimination as northerners who did not speak English. In Lynchburg, as in Passaic, Valhalla, and Boston, Campbell set about once again to demonstrate "the ability of the library to keep our community happy and good-natured, even if we cannot hope to reform the universe."[94]

NOTES

1. Statistical calculations and descriptive data derived from sections entitled "The Alien in New Jersey" and "General Social Condition of Aliens" in NJ Commission of Immigra-

tion, *Report of the Commission of Immigration of the State of New Jersey Appointed Pursuant to the Provisions of Chapter 362 of the Laws of 1911* (Trenton, NJ: MacCrellish and Quigley, State Printers, 1914), 12–21.

2. NJ Commission of Immigration, *Report of the [1911] Commission of Immigration of the State of New Jersey*, 13–14, 17–18.

3. The 1907 Federal Immigration Commission, also known as the Dillingham Commission, published its final report in 1911, the same year the 1911 NJ Immigration Commission began its investigation. Consequently, the latter quoted extensively from the former. See, for example, NJ Commission of Immigration, *Report of the [1911] Immigration Commission of New Jersey*, 11–12, 16–17.

4. Early information on the Campbell family was obtained from two interviews by the author with Fay Campbell (Reed) Kaynor, great-niece of Jane Maud Campbell, in Amherst, MA, on 11 August 1987, and with Kaynor and her mother, Georgia (Waterman) Reed, niece of Jane Maud Campbell, in East Longmeadow, MA, on 12 August 1987. Kaynor, the family historian, shared a typescript of her biography of her great-aunt, which was later published as "'A Most Progressive Woman': Lynchburg's Librarian, Jane Maud Campbell (1869-1947)," *Randolph-Macon Woman's College Alumnae Bulletin* 80 (Dec. 1986): 16–19, 50–51. The Jane Maud Campbell Papers, the gift of Kaynor, are available at the Arthur and Elizabeth Schlesinger Library on the History of Women in America at Radcliffe College, Cambridge, MA. See also "A Cost of Progress," *Newsletter [of] The Arthur and Elizabeth Schlesinger Library on the History of Women in America, Radcliffe College* (Fall 1987): 4; and Anne Engelhart, "Jane Maud Campbell, 1869–1947," [Accession List, Schlesinger Library, Radcliffe College], Oct. 1987, [1].

5. Newark Public Library AR 1901, 3, 18, AR 1902, 15, 21; Passaic Public Library AR 1907/8/9, 8; "Will Have Charge of Passaic Library; Miss J. Maud Campbell, Assistant Head of Local Institution, Accepts Another Position," *Newark News*, 21 Oct. 1902, Campbell Papers; "Miss Campbell's New Charge in Passaic," *Daily Advertiser (Newark)*, 22 Oct. 1902, Campbell Papers; "Private Gifts for Library Endowment," unidentified newspaper, 15 Nov. 1902, Campbell Papers.

6. Passaic Public Library AR 1903, 5–6, 9, 11, AR 1904/5, 9–14, and AR 1905/6, 3, 8–10; Campbell, "The Small City Library," *LJ* 28 (July 1903): 50–52; Campbell, "Supplying Books in Foreign Languages in Public Libraries," *LJ* 29 (Feb. 1904): 65–67, remarks made at the Long Island Library Club, Brooklyn, NY, 3 Dec. 1903; typescript of an address before the Norwalk (CT) Chapter of the Daughters of the American Revolution, 18 Nov. 1904, Campbell Papers; "Influence of the Library; Foreigners Express Appreciation to Trustees and Officers," *Passaic News*, 2 Feb. 1905, photocopy of clipping included in letter, Kaynor to author, 18 Oct. 1986; Campbell, "An Educational Opportunity and the Library," *LJ* 32 (Apr. 1907): 157–58, part of an address before the Bi-State Library Meeting, Atlantic City, NJ, 15 Mar. 1907; Campbell, "The Public Library and the Immigrant [Part I]," *New York Libraries* 1 (July 1908): 100–105, and "The Library and the Immigrant [Part II]," *New York Libraries* 1 (Oct. 1908): 132–36; *New York Libraries* 1 (Oct. 1908): 129; and Campbell, "What the Foreigner Has Done for One Library," *MLCB* 3 (July 1913): 100–106, reprinted in *LJ* 38 (Nov. 1913): 610–15.

7. Campbell, "The Small City Library," 50–51.

8. Clara Whitehill Hunt to William Coggin Kimball, 25 June 1903, Campbell Papers.

9. Typescript of an address before the Norwalk (CT) Chapter of the DAR, 18 Nov. 1904, Campbell Papers.

10. Campbell, "Supplying Books in Foreign Languages in Public Libraries," 65–66.

11. Campbell, "What the Foreigner Has Done for One Library," 101.

12. Ibid., 102.

13. Passaic Public Library AR 1904/5, 10.

14. Campbell, "The Library and the Immigrant," 135–36.

15. Campbell, *Selected List of Hungarian Books*, compiled for the New Jersey Library Commission, Adapted for use by the League of Library Commissions, Foreign Book List no. 2 (Boston: ALA Publishing Board, 1907), 1; and Campbell, "What the Foreigner Has Done for One Library," 102.

16. Typescript of an address before the Norwalk (CT) Chapter of the DAR, 18 Nov. 1904, Campbell Papers.

17. Ibid.

18. Passaic Public Library AR 1904/5, 11.

19. Campbell, "What the Foreigner Has Done for One Library," 103. See also Passaic Public Library AR 1907/8/9, 8.

20. Typescript of an address before the First Presbyterian Church, Jersey City, NJ, 26 May 1907, Campbell Papers.

21. Campbell, "The Public Library and the Immigrant," 101–2.

22. Ibid., 102–3.

23. William Coggin Kimball, Chairman, New Jersey Public Library Commission, to Governor Edward Casper Stokes, Trenton, NJ, 2 Feb. 1906, Governor Edward Casper Stokes Papers, NJ State Archives.

24. Edward Casper Stokes, Governor of New Jersey, to J. Maude [i.e., Maud] Campbell, 11 Apr. 1906, Stokes Papers; Certificate of appointment to the NJ Immigration Commission, inscribed to J. Maude [i.e., Maud] Campbell, witnessed by Edward C. Stokes, 11 Apr. 1906, Campbell Papers; "Help for the Foreign Born: Governor's Commission at Princeton Discusses Problem of Educating Immigrants; Night Schools for Adults . . . ," unidentified newspaper, 15 Dec. 1906, Campbell Papers; and Robert Watchorn, quoted in Campbell, "What the Foreigner Has Done for One Library," 104.

25. Campbell to Edward Casper Stokes, 14 Apr. 1906, Stokes Papers.

26. Campbell, "Books for the Foreign Population—III," *LJ* 31 (Aug. 1906): 72.

27. Campbell, "What the Foreigner Has Done for One Library," 104.

28. "Help for the Foreign Born," Campbell Papers. See also typescript extract from an address of former Governor Edward Casper Stokes, *Passaic Daily News*, 29 Oct. 1912, Campbell Papers.

29. Excerpts from the 1907 NJ adult immigrant education law, quoted in NJ Commission of Immigration, *Report of the [1911] Commission of Immigration of the State of New Jersey*, 121.

30. Edward George Hartmann, *The Movement to Americanize the Immigrant* (New York: Columbia University Press, 1948), 55, 71–76, 83, 86–87. The 1906 NJ Immigration Commission did not publish a report of its findings and recommendations.

31. Campbell, "What the Foreigner Has Done for One Library," 104.

32. Passaic Public Library AR 1909/10, 2.

33. Citation to Campbell, signed by the Trustees of the Passaic Public Library, 7 May 1910, photocopy of original in possession of Kaynor.

34. Bird W. Spencer, Mayor, Passaic, NJ, to J. Maude [i.e. Maud] Campbell, 23 May 1910, Campbell Papers.

35. Campbell to Bird W. Spencer, 27 May 1910, Campbell Papers.

36. North American Civic League for Immigrants, New York-New Jersey Committee, [*Report*], *December 1909–March 1911* (New York: The Committee, 1911), 3–4; and *MLCB* 3 (Oct. 1913): 141. See also letter of recommendation for Campbell signed by Anne Morgan, 1 May 1912, Campbell Papers.

37. Hartmann, *The Movement to Americanize the Immigrant*, 38, and chap. 2: "The North American Civic League for Immigrants and Affiliated Organizations," 38-63 passim.

38. NACLI AR 1910/11, 9.

39. Ibid., 10–11.

40. NACLI, NY-NJ Committee, [*Report*], *December 1909–March 1911*, 5–6; and Hartmann, *The Movement to Americanize the Immigrant*, 53–56.

41. Hartmann, *The Movement to Americanize the Immigrant*, 56.

42. NACLI, NY-NJ Committee, [*Report*], *December 1909–March 1911*, 3–4.

43. Ibid., 35.

44. Ibid., 36.

45. Ibid., 26–28.

46. Ibid., 32–33; and Hartmann, *The Movement to Americanize the Immigrant*, 27–28. See also Jane E. Robbins, "Schools in Temporary Construction Camps," *Immigrants in America Review* 1 (June 1915): 28–30.

47. NACLI, NY-NJ Committee, [*Report*], *December 1909–March 1911*, 38–39; Hartmann, *The Movement to Americanize the Immigrant*, 60, 71–73. Although Hartmann refers to the 1907 NJ adult immigrant education law, he does not mention the 1906 NJ Immigration Commission, which was responsible for its passage. Hartmann, for this reason, refers to the 1908 NY State Immigration Commission as the first state commission rather than the second, as was the case.

48. Hartmann, *The Movement to Americanize the Immigrant*, 71–73.

49. NACLI, NY-NJ Committee, [*Report*], *December 1909–March 1911*, 32–33; and North American Civic League for Immigrants, New York-New Jersey Committee, [*Report*], *December 1, 1909-February 1, 1913* (New York: The Committee, 1913), 14.

50. NACLI, NY-NJ Committee, [*Report*], *December 1, 1909–February 1, 1913*, 14–15.

51. Ibid., 14.

52. Campbell, *Immigrant Women*; *Paper read at the New Jersey Conference of Charities and Correction, Princeton, NJ, April 3, 1911* (New York: New York-New Jersey Committee, North American Civic League for Immigrants, 1911?).

53. Campbell, *Immigrant Women*, 4, 14 (quote).

54. Ibid., 14.

55. NACLI, NJ-NJ Committee, [*Report*], *December 1909–March 1911*, 29–31.

56. Ibid., 29–30.

57. Ibid., 30.

58. Hartmann, *The Movement to Americanize the Immigrant*, 73.

59. NACLI, NY-NJ Committee, [*Report*], *December 1, 1909–February 1, 1913*, 15.

60. Hartmann, *The Movement to Americanize the Immigrant*, 73–76.

61. MFPLC AR 1912/13, 16.

62. Ibid., 17.

63. Ibid.

64. Ibid., 17–18.

65. Ibid., 18.

66. *MLCB* 3 (May 1913): 53–54; and *MLCB* 3 (July 1913): 86.

67. Campbell, "What the Foreigner Has Done for One Library," 100, 106.

68. Charles F. D. Belden, Chairman, MFPLC, to Edward F. Hamlin, Executive Secretary, State House, 30 June 1913, Campbell Papers; "Libraries for the Immigrant; Plans to Reach Foreign Part of Population; Miss J. M. Campbell Made Agent by Commission for This Work," *Boston Globe*, 25 Sept 1913, Campbell Papers; and Charles F. D. Belden, "Library Commission Work in Massachusetts," *LJ* 42 (Jan. 1917): 5–10, an address before the New York Library Club, 26 Oct. 1916.

69. *MLCB* 3 (Oct. 1913): 136–37, 141–42; "Libraries for the Immigrant," Campbell Papers; and MFPLC AR 1912/13, 18-20. See also MA Commission on Immigration, *Report of the [1913] Commission on Immigration on the Problem of Immigration in Massachusetts* (Boston: Wright and Potter, State Printers, 1914), 5, 17, 151–52.

70. MA Commission on Immigration, *Report of the [1913] Commission on Immigration . . . in Massachusetts*, 17, 152; and MFPLC AR 1912/13, 18–20, 24, and AR 1916/17, 18.

71. MFPLC AR 1912/13, 19-25, AR 1913/14, 19, and AR 1915/16, 25–26; *MLCB* 4 (July–Oct. 1914): 98; and Campbell, "Americanizing Books and Periodicals for Immigrants," *ALA Bulletin* 10 (July 1916): 271.

72. MFPLC AR 1912/13, 20, AR 1913/14, 14–15, AR 1914/15, 22–23, AR 1915/16, 22–23, AR 1916/17, 18–20, AR 1917/18, 22–23, AR 1918/19, 20–21, AR 1919/20, 14, AR 1920/21, 15–16, and AR 1921/22, 12–13.

73. MFPLC AR 1913/14, 16.

74. *MLCB* 3 (Oct. 1913): 136; MFPLC AR 1912/13, 25, AR 1913/14, 17, AR 1914/15, 22; and Belden, "Library Commission Work in Massachusetts," 9.

75. Campbell, "Foreign Periodicals," *MLCB* 4 (Mar.–May 1914): 67–69. See also MFPLC AR 1913/14, 18.

76. Campbell, *Selected List of Russian Books,* compiled for the Free Public Library Commission of Massachusetts, Foreign Book List no. 7 (Chicago: ALA, 1916), 3–4. See also MFPLC AR 1915/16, 25.

77. *MLCB* 3 (Oct. 1913): 137, *MLCB* 4 (Jan. 1914): 38, 41–42, *MLCB* 5 (Mar. 1915): 35–36, *MLCB* 6 (Mar.–May 1916): 21–23, (July–Oct. 1916): 68, *MLCB* 9 (Mar. 1919): 14, (Oct. 1919): 13; MFPLC AR 1914/15, 25, AR 1915/16, 24–25, AR 1916/17, 21, AR 1917/18, 24-25, 27, AR 1918/19, 21, and AR 1919/20, 15; Campbell, "Americanizing Books and Periodicals for Immigrants," 269-72, and Georgia (Waterman) Reed, interview by author, 12 Aug. 1987. Reed remembered her aunt, Jane Maud Campbell, joking that she carried her toothbrush in her bustle during these regular jaunts across Massachusetts.

78. *MLCB* 6 (Mar.–May 1916): 20, (July–Oct. 1916): 67, *MLCB* 9 (June 1919): 3, *MLCB* 11 (Oct. 1921): 8; and Belden, "Library Commission Work in Massachusetts," 10.

79. Campbell, "Americanizing Books and Periodicals for Immigrants," 271. See also "The Public Library and the Immigrant, Discussed by Mr. Charles F. D. Belden, Chairman, Free Public Library Commission, Miss J. M. Campbell, Educational Director for Work with Aliens, [and] Mr. William F. Kenney, Trustee, Boston Public Library," *Boston Globe*, 29 Mar. 1914, Campbell Papers.

80. Quote from Campbell, "Americanizing Books and Periodicals for Immigrants," 271. See also *MLCB* 5 (May 1915): 82–83; MFPLC AR 1915/16, 23–24, 27; Belden, "Library Commission Work in Massachusetts," 9; and "Boston Woman Makes Citizens of Immigrants: Miss J. Maud Campbell of Massachusetts Free Library Commission Enlists Help of Foreigners Themselves in Library Experiments; Did Fine Work in New Jersey," *Woman's Journal*, 31 Mar. 1917, Campbell Papers.

81. Alberto Pecorini, *The Story of America*, prepared for the Massachusetts Society of the Colonial Dames (Boston: Marshall Jones, 1920). See also *MLCB* 5 (May 1915): 82–83; *MLCB* 11 (Oct. 1920–Jan. 1921): 6; and MFPLC AR 1914/15, 23–24.

82. *MLCB* 5 (July–Oct. 1915): 115-16; and "Boston Woman Makes Citizens of Immigrants," 31 Mar. 1917, Campbell Papers.

83. Georgia (Waterman) Reed and Fay Campbell (Reed) Kaynor, interview by author, 12 Aug. 1987.

84. MFPLC AR 1917/18, 25–27.

85. Ibid., 26–27.

86. MFPLC AR 1918/19, 17–19, 22; CPL/BB Broadway Branch Publicity Scrapbook [1], clipping, *News Notes Broadway Branch*, 17 Dec. 1919, Ledbetter Papers; *ALA Bulletin* 14 (Oct. 1920): 380; and *ALA Bulletin* 15 (Sept. 1921): 281.

87. John Daniels, *America via the Neighborhood*, with a new introduction by Florence G. Cassidy, Americanization Studies: The Acculturation of Immigrant Groups into American Society, republished under the editorship of William S. Bernard (New York: Harper Brothers, 1920; reprint, Montclair, NJ: Patterson Smith, 1971), vii, 273-84 passim. In her introduction to the republished edition, Florence G. Cassidy points out that Daniels's study "exemplified sanity and objectivity in the midst of the strident voices and confused utterances of the period" (quote, vii).

88. Georgia (Waterman) Reed and Fay Campbell (Reed) Kaynor, interview by author, 12 Aug. 1987.

89. Campbell to Executive Committee of the Jones Memorial Library, Lynchburg, VA, 18 Sept. 1921, Campbell Papers.

90. Campbell to Willie Campbell, Charles Town, WV, 22 Nov. 1921, photocopy of letter in possession of Kaynor.

91. *MLCB* 12 (Jan. 1922): 3; typescript initialed E. K. J. [Edith Kathleen Jones], 27 Dec. 1921?, Campbell Papers.

92. MFPLC AR 1921/22, 4–5. See also, Charles F. D. Belden to Armistead R. Long, Lynchburg, VA, 30 Dec. 1921, Campbell Papers.

93. Kaynor, "A Most Progressive Woman," 50–51.

94. Campbell, "The Small City Library," 52.

John Foster Carr addressing crowd at The New York Public Library during the "Books for Everybody Campaign," circa 1918. He is directly in front of the banner reading "Books Wanted for Our Men in Camp and 'Over There.'" Photo courtesy American Library Association Archives, University of Illinois at Urbana-Champaign.

4

The Publisher as Propagandist: John Foster Carr, 1869–1939

During the half century between the American Civil War and World War I, New York was transformed from a distant outpost of Europe with approximately 1,500,000 inhabitants in 1870 to a thriving metropolis, an economic and cultural hub in its own right, of 5,000,000 in 1915. New York, with its unsurpassed natural harbor, reigned as the major port of entry for immigrants to the United States as well as the terminus for the routing of immigrants westward across the three thousand miles of the American continent. The city personified, according to historian Moses Rischin, "the gateway, toll station, and hostelry through which immigrants passed in their abandonment of the Old World for a better life in the New."

Although many immigrants, particularly those interested in agricultural pursuits, stopped in New York only long enough to get directions to the nearest plot of fertile land, many were attracted by the allure of the city. These urban immigrants, many of whom were unaccustomed to the rural lifestyle, weighed heavily the advantages of access to cultural, religious, and educational institutions and the opportunity to ply here in America the skills learned and crafts mastered in Europe. For these immigrants especially, New York was unquestionably the destination of choice, for it was there that they hoped to join and renew ties with relatives, friends, and acquaintances from their homelands who had settled and established roots earlier.[1]

For the sake of convenience, public library branches were established in the midst of the teeming immigrant neighborhoods. Initially these branches were located in lower Manhattan not far from disembarkation centers at Castle Garden and, later, Ellis Island. As upwardly mobile immigrants left the congested tenements of Manhattan, branches were erected in more affluent neighborhoods in the boroughs of Brooklyn, the Bronx, Queens, and Richmond.[2] The holdings of these branch libraries, reflecting the needs of their immigrant clienteles, included books, pamphlets, and magazines in foreign languages as well as simple English. These materials were designed to give immigrant readers a better understanding of the history, government, literature, and customs of their adopted country and biographies of America's heroes and heroines.

Although librarians were eager to provide Americanization materials in foreign languages, they could not always locate publishers and dealers in the United States. One of the few publishers was John Foster Carr.

EARLY YEARS IN NEW YORK, ENGLAND, AND ITALY

A native New Yorker, Carr was educated at Yale University and Brasenose College of Oxford University. During his seven-year tenure as a devoted Oxonian, Carr's worldview was shaped by his travels in Italy, where Carr came under the seductive spell of Italian culture.[3]

Career in Journalism

On his return to New York, Carr, a man of independent but modest means, launched his career as a journalist and special correspondent in 1903. He wrote numerous feature articles for the widely read and respected periodicals *World's Work*, *Outlook*, and *Suburban Life*, all published in New York. His concern for political and social reform, both domestic and international, found expression in articles on diverse topics ranging from critiques of American international relations with England, Germany, and Russia to the phenomenon of immigration to the United States.[4]

Carr's articles dealing with immigration and the immigrant experience revealed his unique perspective regarding American immigrants gained from firsthand observations in the immigrant colonies in New York and conversations with immigrants themselves. Carr noted in his writings that American immigrants were not a single, united mass of humanity. They could not be discussed or analyzed as a block.

He observed also that the majority of first-generation immigrants in New York tended to live in almost totally self-contained and self-sufficient neighborhoods located near their places of employment. From the immigrant's perspective, this housing and occupational pattern allowed them not only to maintain Old World customs but also to achieve a group consensus regarding accommodation to New World realities. From Carr's perspective, on the other hand, this pattern hindered their rapid Americanization.[5]

Attitude toward Immigrants and Their Americanization

Carr never wavered in his conviction that all immigrants, regardless of their origins, desired to be Americanized. "American civilization has not suffered any change in any of its essentials from the swarming millions of newcomers. But on the contrary, the United States has shown a marvelous power to Americanize the

Carr as an "Anglo-conformist"

desirable immigrant."[6] Speaking for Italian immigrants specifically, Carr espoused similar views on the motivational factors for other new immigrant groups. "Italians come to America, not from a migratory instinct, but either to make a better living or to keep from starving, and they bring nothing with them but a strong body and the will to work."[7]

Imbued with a passionate sense of patriotism and dedication to maintaining the glory of American traditions and accomplishments, Carr was the archetypal Anglo-conformist. He often referred to the "melting pot" assimilation theory, as when he wrote that "Americans are not men of one blood, but a society of men who think alike."[8] Nevertheless, Carr wanted the melting pot to instill American traits while obliterating or melting away foreign traits.[9]

Carr and the Connecticut Daughters of the American Revolution

As early as 1908, it was evident in Carr's correspondence with other like-minded reformers that he had identified the education of the immigrant as the key to hastening the Americanization process. He wrote Clara Lee Bowman, a member of the Bristol chapter of the Connecticut Daughters of the American Revolution, that "we ought to consider the immigrant a greatly desired addition to the nation [and] we should try to help him to become an American in the shortest possible time."

educ. as key

Carr shared with Bowman his mission to educate the immigrant and the means for fulfilling it. His intent was not to preach American ideals to the immigrant but to impress upon him the fact that if he became an American citizen, he could make, in turn, a significant contribution to the betterment of the nation. "He should learn of the advantages of citizenship and the steps to take in order that he may become a citizen. Some such information could with great advantage be conveyed to him in an attractive pamphlet, illustrated, a small and practical guide to the new life among us."

Carr realized that to fulfill his mission, he needed the full cooperation of individuals and organizations that shared the Americanization of the immigrant as a common goal. He would need the support of the public schools, public libraries, and, case in point, patriotic institutions like the Daughters of the American Revolution. "Win him once by real helpfulness and he will then become more accessible to other efforts made to reach him through our public schools . . . as well as through our libraries, for both of these seem to offer the most serviceable and proper means of welcoming these newcomers and informing them with the American spirit."[10]

Shortly after writing this passage in a letter to Bowman, Carr left New York and his responsibilities as a journalist to accept a temporary position as headmaster of the Interlaken School, a private boys' school in LaPorte, Indiana, where he served a brief tenure between 1909 and 1911. Concurrently he maintained his contacts with the officers of the various Connecticut chapters of the DAR. They recognized in Carr's idea of a guidebook for newly arrived immigrants the perfect vehicle for the furtherance of their own organization's goal of patriotic education.

Moral encouragement for the idea of the guidebook was also received, ironically, from the Royal Italian Emigration Commission.[11]

With the financial backing of the Connecticut DAR chapters assured, Carr proceeded to solicit educators and reform-minded individuals for their suggestions as to the content of the proposed guidebook for immigrants. He began to contact potential publishers for suggestions regarding the layout of the information and design of the guidebook. In response to his queries, Carr received helpful suggestions and enthusiastic support from Jane Elizabeth Robbins, executive secretary of the Public Education Association in New York, who served with Carr on the managing board of the Italian-American Civic League. He also received help and advice from Jane Maud Campbell, then librarian of the Passaic Public Library. Campbell had formerly helped to produce an English-Italian primer for immigrants during her tenure with the 1906 New Jersey Immigration Commission.[12]

Immigrant Guide

After negotiations first with Putnam and then with Doubleday, Page and Company, Carr chose the latter as the publisher of the guidebook. Perhaps his former association with Doubleday, Page and Company, the publisher of *World's Work*, was a deciding factor.

During the summer of 1910, Doubleday, Page and Company published Carr's *Guida degli Stati Uniti per l'Immigrante Italiano*, under the auspices of the Connecticut DAR. Carr immediately organized a lecture tour to promote the *Guida*, the convenient appellation used by Carr and DAR members in their correspondence and speaking engagements. The lectures in the main were presented to Connecticut chapters of the DAR in cities where Italian immigrant colonies flourished, notably Hartford, New London, New Haven, Danbury, Torrington, Meriden, New Britain, Bridgeport, Bristol, and Norwalk.[13]

Taking into account Carr's affinity for the Italians and his concern regarding their initial lack of commitment to remaining in America, it was totally consistent with his educational mission that his guidebook would be in the Italian language. The *Guida* was conceived by Carr as "an immigrant Baedeker," a handy compendium of information to answer the known and inchoate questions of the adult Italian immigrant.

Each section of the *Guida* was prepared to fulfill a particular informational need as determined by Carr in personal interviews with Italian immigrants. Each section was later read to groups of immigrants for their candid comments on the appropriateness of the information presented, and their suggestions for its improvement were solicited. To ensure the relevancy and accuracy of the text, Carr presented drafts of pertinent sections of the *Guida* to experts in the fields of law, naturalization, housing, and health for them to augment and revise.[14]

The *Guida*, designed to be portable and durable, was bound in green paper covers and measured approximately seven by five inches. The meagerly illustrated text was arranged in twenty-six topical sections, from "Societies Helpful to the

New Arrival" to "How to Become a Citizen of the United States." The subliminal message that ran through each section was that the good American speaks English, makes education a priority, becomes a citizen, and votes. With regard to education specifically, Carr gave enthusiastic endorsement of educational services offered at no charge to the immigrant, including public schools, evening schools, and free lectures. He urged immigrants to take advantage of the resources for learning English and preparing for citizenship available in the many branches of the New York Public Library, where materials were available in Italian and other foreign languages.

Carr devoted a considerable amount of text in the *Guida* to promote his vision for the distribution of immigrants throughout the nation rather than their concentration in a few congested urban centers. He urged Italian immigrants to leave the congestion of the cities and return to the soil. In addition to his lectures as secretary of the National Liberal Immigration League of New York, Carr frequently made special trips to encourage communities sponsoring immigrant farming enterprises in locations as diverse as Wilmington, North Carolina, and Binghamton, New York. The *Guida* concluded with Carr's "Special Advice to the Immigrant." Italian immigrants were warned not to speak loudly, not to gesticulate, and not to resort to violence. They were urged to dress well, eat better, and pay careful attention to their personal hygiene.[15]

These and other admonitions given by Carr throughout the *Guida* cannot help but raise the hackles of individuals sensitive to prejudicial and discriminatory treatment of minority groups. In comparison to nativist propaganda of the period, however, Carr's Anglo-conformist propaganda was condescending, but not cruel. Nevertheless, the subliminal message underlying the *Guida* was that all immigrants must conform to American ways.

Despite its overtly patronizing and potentially offensive language, the *Guida* was well received. From California to Massachusetts, Carr received congratulatory greetings on The Little Green Book, a popular appellation applied to the *Guida* from educators, lawyers, and businessmen.

Libraries in cities with large immigrant populations, including the New York Public Library, purchased multiple copies of the *Guida*. The Massachusetts Free Public Library Commission endorsed it and recommended its purchase to immigrants and Americans alike. Leaders of the Italian immigrant community, notably Andrea Sbarboro, founder of the Italian-Swiss Agricultural Colony in Asti, California, and officials of the Royal Italian Emigration Commission, praised Carr and his associates in the Connecticut chapters of the DAR for their efforts on behalf of Italian immigrants.[16]

Carr received not only suggestions for the improvement of subsequent editions of the *Guida* but also numerous requests for different versions of the *Guida* to be published in other immigrant languages as well as in English. A very productive working relationship began in April 1911 with Charles Shapiro, a lawyer from Bridgeport, Connecticut, who volunteered to help Carr put together a version of the *Guida* in Yiddish. Carr was enthusiastic about his offer, but was quick to point out that "each new version in a different tongue will also need to be specially adapted to the particular nationality for which it is intended."[17]

Requests for a Polish version of the *Guida* were forthcoming as well, but before either the Yiddish or Polish versions were a reality, however, an English translation of the *Guida* was published in 1911. The English version was issued, according to Carr, "with the double purpose of letting those of our friends, who do not read Italian, know what we are really trying to do, as well as to satisfy a growing demand for the book for teaching foreigners English, as it has been found that it serves this purpose very admirably."[18] Again, the response was positive. The evening schools of Providence, Rhode Island, approved both the Italian and English versions of the *Guida* for use as textbooks in classes with Italian immigrants. The evening schools of Boston and New York were similarly interested.[19]

The Polish and Yiddish versions met enthusiastic response as well, the latter receiving singular praise from the leaders of the American Jewish community. Mary Antin, the noted Russian Jewish immigrant author, wrote that "the book anticipates every question the bewildered immigrant is sure to ask and calls his attention to a multitude of facts that are of the first importance to him at the beginning of his career in a new country. It will prevent millions of blunders, hundreds of failures and tragedies." In a similar vein, Rabbi Henry Pereira Mendes, then President of the Union of Orthodox Jewish Congregations of the United States and Canada, remarked that "the publication of a fifteen-cent book has done more to solve the question [of] how to Americanize the immigrant than one hundred societies."[20]

The responses from businessmen working in close contact with immigrants were particularly valuable to Carr, a case in point being the testimonial of Paul Kreuzpointner, a representative of the Committee on Industrial Education of the American Foundrymen's Association in Altoona, Pennsylvania. Kreuzpointner related that "divers portions of the guide, according to local needs and individual fancy, have formed popular topics for discussions in the boarding houses."[21]

Senator William P. Dillingham praised the *Guida* as a "book which, in my judgment, contains more information necessary to the newly arrived alien than any other which I have ever seen." Dillingham further proclaimed that "its distribution is a service of the highest importance, having in it the promise of untold good to all prospective citizens and to society."[22] The chilling irony of Dillingham's comment was that the commission bearing his name, also known as the 1907 Federal Immigration Commission, was responsible for gaining the Congressional and public support that would lead to the nation's first major legislation to place limitations and tighter controls on immigration to the United States.

Carr also maintained a good working relationship with Terrence V. Powderly, who headed the Division of Information of the Bureau of Immigration and Naturalization, then under the auspices of the U.S. Department of Commerce and Labor. Powderly, who helped with the writing and editing of the section of the *Guida* on naturalization laws and procedures, was impressed with the work of Carr *free immigration*

and the Connecticut chapters of the DAR. At Carr's urging, Powderly agreed to speak at the Annual State Congress of the Connecticut DAR in 1911.[23]

Along with Dillingham and Powderly, other interested parties urged Carr to publish versions of the *Guida* in several immigrant languages. Although requests were received for versions in twenty-four different languages, only versions in Italian, English, Yiddish, and Polish appeared, due solely to a lack of adequate financial backing.

The *Guida*, in all its various manifestations, filled a definite need that few publishers, including the federal government, had addressed effectively. The information was accurate and up-to-date, and its moderate price of fifteen cents rendered it affordable to even the poorest immigrant. Within three years of the appearance of the *Guida* and its subsequent editions, versions, and translations, 22,000 copies were sold or otherwise distributed throughout the country. This impressive statistic was a testament to the *Guida*'s potential for influencing public opinion regarding the immigration question.

The verdict of Mary Alice Willcox, professor emerita at Wellesley College and member of the board of Carr's Immigration Publication Society, was a reasonable gauge of public opinion. The *Guida* was, according to Willcox, "not only a guide to America for the immigrant but a guide to the immigrant for the American." She later elaborated on this essential point that "the greatest value of the 'Guide' is not in the information it gives, useful as that is. Its greatest value is in creating a common knowledge, a common meeting ground for native Americans and foreign-born." She continued that the *Guida* was infused with a "spirit that recognizes not only what the foreigner receives from America, but also what he can give to the country."[24]

The *Guida* firmly established Carr's reputation as an advocate for free immigration. Indeed, he was frequently called upon as representative of either the National Liberal Immigration League or the Italian-American Civic League to lecture and debate in favor of immigration-related issues at public forums.[25] When the People's Institute of Jersey City needed a pro-immigration respondent for a public debate on the subject of the restriction of immigration, it was quite natural to call upon Carr. On 9 April 1911, Carr faced the Reverend Dr. Madison Clinton Peters, a noted New York clergyman, who spoke in favor of restricted immigration. Over one thousand attended this debate alone.[26]

Dante Alighieri Society

Concurrently with his speaking engagements and marketing of The Little Green Book, Carr worked in cooperation with the Connecticut DAR chapters in the second phase of their patriotic education endeavors. As a member and representative of the Societa Nationale Dante Alighieri, an Italian cultural society promoting the welfare and education of Italian immigrants in the United States, Carr served as a liaison between these two dissimilar organizations that, for the moment, shared a common goal.

The Dante Alighieri Society would provide, free of charge, standard libraries of fifty Italian books to American public libraries and DAR reading rooms in communities with Italian immigrant populations. The strategy was simple: to lure the Italians into libraries using the bait of books in their native tongue. Once the immigrants were exposed to the friendly atmosphere of the library and the help of sympathetic librarians, Italian immigrants would be introduced to materials to hasten the process of their Americanization.

Carr, who was well-read and conversant in Italian literature, helped to select the books to be included in the Dante Alighieri Society libraries. He also coordinated the effort to gather the requests from DAR chapter regents as well as mayors and librarians in the major cities of Connecticut. Carr received requests for Dante Alighieri libraries from interested parties in Hartford, New Haven, New London, Stamford, Meriden, Danbury, Derby, and Ansonia. These he forwarded, along with his own personal justifications, to the Dante Alighieri Society headquarters in Rome.[27]

The officers of the Elizabeth Clarke Hull Chapter of the DAR in Ansonia, Connecticut, wrote in their letter of application that their chapter "contributes each year to support evening classes for teaching English in the YMCA, but the Italian residents do not come to these classes as the other foreigners do, and need to be reached in some way. So a library in their own tongue may fill a great need."[28] Charles E. Rowell, Mayor of Stamford, Connecticut, included in his application the fact that "our city has a large Italian population who from their frugal and industrious habits; their honesty in dealing with their fellow men; the accumulation of large amount[s] of real estate, and their willingness to help bear the burden of taxation make them a valuable addition to our population."[29] Carr's recommendation on behalf of the Connecticut DAR chapters as a whole reflected not only his gratitude for their support of the *Guida* but also his recognition of the contribution that women's groups in general had made to public libraries.[30]

The Dante Alighieri Society graciously granted the collections of fifty Italian books, and a year later, in 1912, awarded Carr a diploma in appreciation of his educational work with Italian immigrants in the United States. That same year the King of Italy bestowed upon Carr the Cross of Chevalier of the Order of the Crown. Carr was justifiably proud of this recognition of his efforts but, at the same time, realized the delicate balancing act he must maintain as not only a friend of Italy but also an advocate of Italian immigration.[31]

Carr's professional and personal association with the Connecticut DAR chapters and public libraries yielded, overall, positive results toward the realization of his ever-present goal, the education and Americanization of the immigrant. This excerpt from a letter written to Carr by the public librarian in Derby, Connecticut, was representative: "Our readers seem very glad to get some new Italian books as they had read all that we previously owned. I intend soon to have lists made of all our Italian books and shall try to get one of these lists in every Italian home in Derby, hoping to make more of the Italians familiar with the resources of the library."[32]

the PL as a site of action

American Library Association Service

Positive responses such as this one served to convince Carr that the most appropriate and practical agency for the promulgation of his propaganda for the education of the immigrant was the public library. Carr joined the American Library Association and, beginning in 1913, was a regular speaker at national and state library association meetings.

Addressing the annual meeting of the Massachusetts Library Club at Williamstown, Massachusetts, in 1913, Carr welcomed the challenge of immigration and urged librarians to assume positions of advocacy for immigrants. The same message came forth at the Washington (DC) conference of the ALA in 1914, but with even greater emphasis on the primacy of the public library, not the public school, as a driving force in the education of the immigrant.[33]

In all of his speeches to library associations and organizations, Carr was overt in his flattery of librarians. He once commented that "[t]he librarian . . . publicly urges no offensive theory of the immigrant's need for civilization and moral uplift [and] the librarian's power of help is boundless." Carr alluded in his speeches to examples of creative work already being accomplished by librarians in cities with significant immigrant clienteles. He pointed out specifically the groundbreaking work of Jane Maud Campbell, agent for work with foreigners of the Massachusetts Free Public Library Commission. Carr urged other librarians to follow in her footsteps.[34]

Immigrant Publication Society

Although not a librarian himself, Carr envisioned his role in this vast educational endeavor as that of the publisher and supplier of the materials needed to assist librarians in their work with immigrant clienteles. In 1914, he founded a nonprofit organization whose purposes were the education of immigrants and their distribution throughout the United States.

The Immigrant Publication Society, sometimes referred to during its early years as the Immigration Education Society, was conceived as a membership organization "open to all who are interested in promoting the welfare of the immigrant and through his education, the welfare of the Country." The expenses of the society were paid out of the income derived from the dues of approximately 165 members and the sale of publications to individuals and institutions, primarily libraries, that purchased the society's publications in bulk.

A distinguished board, or "council of direction," was appointed by Carr to oversee the operations of the society. The council included librarians Edwin H. Anderson of the New York Public Library, Charles F. D. Belden of the Boston Public Library, and Frances E. Earhart of the Duluth (MN) Public Library. Educators on the council were Stephen Pierce Duggan of the Institute of International Education, Richard Gottheil of Columbia University and the Educational Alliance of New York, and Mary Alice Willcox, professor emerita of Wellesley College. Prominent social worker Kate Holladay Claghorn, New York School of Social Work, served alongside religious leaders Rabbi Henry Cohen of Galveston,

Texas; Ralph E. Diffendorfer of the Interchurch World Movement; and the Right Reverend Peter J. Muldoon of the National Catholic Welfare Council. Rounding out the council's membership were the Honorable Irving Lehman, justice of the United States Supreme Court, and immigrant leaders and community activists Andrea Sbarboro of the Italian-Swiss Agricultural Colony in Asti (CA), Thomas Siemiradzki of the Polish National Alliance in Cleveland, and Antonio Stella of the Society of Italian Immigrants in New York.[35]

The collective credentials and expertise of this stellar group of advisers notwithstanding, the support of the council of direction was at best moral and nominal. The Immigrant Publication Society remained essentially a one-man operation. Carr nevertheless corresponded extensively with members of the council of direction and valued their suggestions, particularly with regard to the society's publications.

Carr's Immigrant Publication Society sought to publish works that would project to his readership, primarily librarians and occasionally social workers, "a sympathetic approach" to library work with immigrants. Membership in the society included the opportunity to write Carr with questions and suggestions, which he, in turn, answered and shared with the membership at large. Through such correspondence as well as visits to libraries and conversations at state and national library conventions with librarians serving immigrant clienteles, Carr made the critical decisions regarding the publications most needed to advance the Americanization process. In addition to the *Guida* and its various versions and translations, the society also published and marketed other works for the immigrant. The first publication of the Society was *Immigrant and Library: Italian Helps, with Lists of Selected Books*. Written and compiled by Carr and issued in cooperation with the ALA Publishing Board, this publication was essentially a handbook or manual for librarians working with Italian immigrants.[36]

The bibliographies in the handbook were based largely on the titles included in the Italian libraries provided by the Dante Alighieri Society. These were supplemented by titles gleaned from Italian bibliographies and publishers' announcements; bibliographies compiled by the public libraries of New York, Providence, and Springfield (MA); and a bibliography compiled by Marguerite Reid and John G. Moulton for the Massachusetts Library Club, which was later published by the ALA.[37]

Carr's statement of purpose was straightforward, albeit unabashedly censorial. "It has been the purpose to include no expensive books, no difficult books of science or of research, of narrow or purely scholarly interest, no unwholesome or trivial books, no books representing the aesthetic or decadent schools, no English books—for though the number of these is restricted, many useful lists already exist."[38]

The second publication of the society, appearing one year later, in 1915, was "intended as a book of patriotism for the intelligent adult immigrant who has made a little progress in our language." Written by Emma Lilian Dana of the Model School of Hunter College, *Makers of America* was a collective biography of Benjamin Franklin, George Washington, Thomas Jefferson, and Abraham Lincoln.

Carr, a bachelor in his late forties, married Dana within the year on 21 June 1916. Their brief marriage ended with her untimely death in 1921.[39]

The third publication of the society was *Foreigners' Guide to English* by Azniv Beshgeturian, a Boston school teacher of Armenian ancestry. His grammar book was favored by Carr for its "proper emphasis to the neglected matter of practice in pronunciation" and the fact that it was geared to the needs of the adult immigrant.[40]

When it became increasingly evident that the United States would enter World War I, Carr's message assumed an even greater urgency. Acutely aware that publicity was the crucial ingredient to successful library programs for immigrants, Carr hammered away in his speaking engagements that "to the immigrant the library represents the open door of American life and opportunity."[41]

Carr was impressed with the efforts of enthusiastic librarians in major centers of immigrant population. In his address at the Asbury Park (NJ) conference of the ALA, in 1916, he singled out for special commendation the libraries in New York, Chicago, St. Louis, Providence, Detroit, Pittsburgh, Louisville, Jersey City, Buffalo, Boston, Passaic, Altoona (PA), and Springfield (MA). "As I talk to these good librarian folk, I find myself always in an atmosphere of enthusiasm when we speak of work with our immigrants. They tell me—and I have collected hundreds of astounding instances—of miracles wrought, of affecting gratitude, of beautiful friendships formed."[42] Carr predicted that together, the Immigrant Publication Society, supplying the materials needed as well as selection aids, and librarians, supplying their expertise as selectors, teachers, and administrators, could accomplish much more than separately. The Americanization of the immigrant was a mutual goal.

He convinced three enthusiastic librarians to share their strategies employed to publicize the library to the immigrant community. The three pamphlets resulting from Carr's negotiations were essentially case studies of three individual librarians working with immigrants in different but similarly successful situations. These pamphlets were edited and published by the Immigrant Publication Society between 1917 and 1919 under the Library Work with the Foreign Born series.

In the foreword to the first of the three pamphlets, *Bridging the Gulf; Work with the Russian Jews and Other Newcomers*, by Ernestine Rose, Carr identified the audience for these publications. "Librarians, who have long been busied befriending these strangers of queer tongue and queer apparel . . . are anxious to exchange their experiences with others." Carr explained that these pamphlets had been written in response to questions about library work with immigrants. "To answer the most pressing of these questions that come not only from librarians, but from many others; to give help where it is needed, this little booklet has been printed, the first of a series prepared chiefly by librarians, who are expert and successful in this new field."[43]

Rose wrote of her experiences as librarian of the Seward Park Branch of the New York Public Library. The second pamphlet in the series, *Winning Friends and Citizens for America; Work with Poles, Bohemians and Others*, by Eleanor (Edwards) Ledbetter, retold her experiences as librarian of the Broadway Branch of the Cleveland Public Library. The third and last pamphlet in the series, *Exploring a*

Neighborhood; Our Jewish People from Eastern Europe and the Orient, by Mary Frank, then superintendent of the Extension Division of the New York Public Library, recalled her experiences as librarian of the Rivington Street Branch.[44]

Concurrently during the war years for the United States and this productive period for the Immigration Publication Society, Carr himself wrote and published two pamphlets for the Library Work with the Foreign Born series. The first, issued in 1916, *Some of the People We Work For*, was actually a reprint of his address to the Asbury Park (NJ) conference of the ALA. The second, issued in 1918, was *War's End: The Italian Immigrant Speaks of the Future*. This pamphlet focused, as did those of Rose, Ledbetter, and Frank, on the loyalty of immigrants to their adopted country. All of these pamphlets, published during and just after World War I, emphasized the fact that immigrants, despite the involvement of their homelands in the great European conflict, had demonstrated a renewed dedication to American democratic ideals.[45]

ALA SERVICE DURING AND AFTER WORLD WAR I

During the last months of World War I, Carr was employed by the ALA to aid in the campaign to provide library books to men in the armed services. Working without an appropriation for advertising, Carr was able to collect almost single-handedly over 700,000 books in New York alone during the course of fifteen months. Armed with only a megaphone, he positioned himself on the steps of the magnificent central building of the New York Public Library, and there proved himself to be not only a good salesman and publicist, but also a master of what publicity expert Harry Varley termed "crowd psychology." Varley, writing just after the successful completion of the ALA campaign for books, recalled, in a feature article for *Printers' Ink*, Carr's knack for using anecdotes and catchy slogans such as "strip your bookshelves for the boys" to impart his message to the crowds that gathered around him daily.[46] This ALA publicity work proved to be the veritable two-edged sword for Carr. He was able not only to assist the ALA in its unprecedentedly expansive war work, but also to win the respect and, most important, the ear of the ALA Executive Board members and other influential librarians on matters relating to library work with immigrants. Thus, toward the end of World War I, in 1917, the ALA Executive Board appointed Carr as chairman of the newly formed Committee on Work with the Foreign Born, which officially began its thirty-year tenure at the close of the war, in 1918.

ALA Committee on Work with the Foreign Born

Along with Carr, and undoubtedly at his recommendation, the following librarians were appointed members of the committee: A. L. Bailey of the Wilmington (DE) Institute Free Library, Anna A. MacDonald of the Pennsylvania State Library in Harrisburg, Adelaide B. Maltby of the New York Public Library, Annie P. Dingman and Eleanor (Edwards) Ledbetter of the Cleveland Public Library, and Frances E. Earhart of the Duluth (MN) Public Library. Earnhart was also a board member of Carr's Immigrant Publication Society. The ALA Committee on Work with the Foreign Born was charged with the mission "to collect from libraries and supply to them information on the desirable methods of assisting in the education of the foreign-born in American ideals and customs and the English language."[47]

Obviously the missions of the ALA CWFB and the Immigrant Publication Society were mutually compatible, since Carr directed both. Indeed, during the fiscal years 1919 and 1920, when Carr chaired the committee, publication activity of the Society was temporarily suspended. The work of the committee and the society merged.

Carr's articles written for library periodicals during this period reflected his dual commitment. He constantly urged librarians, particularly those not conversant in the foreign languages spoken by their patrons, to exercise extreme care in the selection of foreign language books for immigrants. "If the librarian depends upon the chance and irresponsible advisor," Carr warned, "she will soon find her shelves crowded with books of radical socialism, anarchism, bartenders' guides, books of religious propaganda, trash."

Along with care in the selection of materials for immigrants, librarians were admonished that the use of "rigorous and 'Prussian' methods of Americanization accomplished nothing but bitterness, stirring incredible resentment and antagonism among our foreign born. They directly nourish the Bolshevism that we fear."[48] This brooding postwar paranoia with regard to Communism would haunt Carr throughout the remainder of his life.

During his tenure as chair of the ALA CWFB, Carr worked closely with the leaders of the American library profession to determine the direction for the ALA during peacetime. The Library War Service of the ALA, directed by Herbert Putnam and later Carl H. Milam, had been highly successful and highly visible, thanks in no small measure to the efforts of dedicated ALA employees like Carr.

ALA Enlarged Program

During the war, approximately $6,000,000 had been pledged to carry out varied programs of the ALA, over 4,000,000 books had been donated for the use of the armed services personnel, and over 700 librarians had served in war-related activities. The ALA and its membership were not only pleased with their success but also anxious to continue and extend the programs and activities spawned by the war.

The year 1919 was full of possibilities for a professional organization with a yearning to expand its mission. Dennis Thomison, historian of the ALA, summed up the ambivalence, anxiety, and enthusiasm exhibited by the ALA and its membership during this heady time. "Although the members had always seemed to have a missionary spirit about their organization, the war work was the first proof that ALA was capable of being welfare oriented, rather than being strictly a professional organization."[49]

In May 1919, after months of preliminary discussions among ALA members and the ALA Executive Board, George B. Utley, secretary of the ALA, announced plans for an open meeting of the ALA Council during the Asbury Park (NJ) conference of the ALA to be held in June 1919. At that meeting several areas of potential peacetime initiatives for the ALA would be discussed.[50]

As a result of the debates and discussions among ALA members at the open meeting as well as the deliberations of the ALA Executive Board at the Asbury Park conference, a Committee on an Enlarged Program for American Library Service was appointed. The chairs of all ALA standing committees were asked to attend at least one session with the Enlarged Program committee to present ways in which the proposed Enlarged Program could effect beneficial changes in their committees' areas of responsibility. Carr, as chair of the ALA CWFB, spoke of the accomplishments of libraries and librarians in their work with immigrants and pleaded for funds to establish new programs and to sustain and expand existing citizenship programs.

In October 1919, the Enlarged Program committee presented its preliminary report and recommendations regarding the areas of library service to be addressed.[51] Between October and December 1919, librarians throughout the country, including then ALA President Chalmers Hadley and Milam, voiced their support for the Enlarged Program. Orpha Maud Peters of the Gary (IN) Public Library spoke in favor of funding for the citizenship component of the Enlarged Program, concluding that "there is no doubt that libraries have a most important role to play in Americanizing the foreign people in our midst and in making better citizens not only of people of other nations but of American people as well."[52]

In December 1919, Milam established headquarters for the Enlarged Program in New York. Carr, who had worked previously under Milam in the ALA Library War Service, was now assigned to the Enlarged Program headquarters. Carr's duties were in the areas of publicity as well as finance. Preparation of the budget for the Enlarged Program was largely his responsibility.

The ALA Executive Board, the Enlarged Program committee, and library leaders, including Carr, presented a united front in favor of the Enlarged Program. ALA President Chalmers Hadley reported the association's plans to the membership in an article in the December 1919 issue of *Library Journal*.[53]

A special meeting of the ALA membership at large was called by the executive board for January 1920 to discuss and debate openly the details of the Enlarged Program. Although discussions were heated and lengthy, the Enlarged Program was approved by a majority of those in attendance.

Books for Everybody Campaign

In February 1920, Frank P. Hill, chairman of the Enlarged Program committee, set into motion the wheels of the campaign to raise $2,000,000. To facilitate the massive fund-raising effort for the Enlarged Program, which was officially dubbed the "Books for Everybody" campaign, the country was divided into ten regions with a regional director appointed for each region. In March 1920, a proposed budget for the "Books for Everybody" campaign, as prepared by Carr, was presented to the ALA membership. Of the $2,000,000 budget, $75,000 was budgeted for citizenship and other library programs for immigrants.[54]

Despite official approval of the Enlarged Program, many ALA members did not hesitate to express in print their continued misgivings, particularly with regard to the expansive nature of the Enlarged Program and the expense involved in its implementation. Mary Eileen Ahern, as editor of *Public Libraries*, the rival of the more establishment-oriented *Library Journal*, was a self-appointed leader of the opposition to the Enlarged Program. She and other ALA members suggested that, as an amendment to the Enlarged Program, part of the proposed $2,000,000 to be raised should be set aside as an endowment fund.[55]

Still other members became more willing to express their criticisms as a direct result of a circular letter dated 31 March 1920 and signed by thirteen influential librarians from across the nation. This letter had been mailed to the ALA membership, and was later published in the 15 April 1920 issue of *Library Journal*. The thirteen librarians memorialized by this circular were not opposed to the Enlarged Program per se, but strongly asserted that more stringent guidelines of accountability be imposed.[56]

To reassess the support of the ALA membership at large and to discuss the Enlarged Program further, a second special meeting of the membership was scheduled to be held in Atlantic City (NJ) in late April and early May of 1920, in conjunction with the bistate meeting of the New Jersey and Pennsylvania Library Associations. At this meeting, Frank P. Hill, sensing the lack of unity among the ALA membership regarding the Enlarged Program, as manifested so clearly by the circular letter, resigned as chair. He was replaced by William N. C. Carlton.

A compromise was struck at this second special ALA membership meeting. The "Books for Everybody" campaign for the Enlarged Program would proceed as planned with the provision that half of the money raised would be set aside for an endowment fund. As a result of this compromise, Carr developed a new budget for the Enlarged Program that allowed for the $1,000,000 endowment. He presented a revised budget to the executive board in which the funds earmarked for the "citizenship" area were reduced from $75,000 to $60,000 over a period of three years.[57]

Just before and shortly after that eventful special membership meeting, Carr and Milam began negotiations for a joint appeal for funds in the Greater New York area on behalf of the Immigrant Publication Society and the ALA respectively. Carr would remain on the ALA payroll throughout the campaign, and, as director of the Immigrant Publication Society, would assume personal responsibility for raising the $60,000 budgeted in the Enlarged Program for the citizenship component.

Carr, in a letter to Milam dated 14 April 1920, had also made it quite clear that, if the appeal was successful, the Immigrant Publication Society would assume the bulk of the responsibilities now vested in the ALA CWFB. By 19 May 1920, within a month of the beginning of their negotiations, a formal agreement was made among Milam as ALA Secretary, Carlton as chair of the Enlarged Program committee, Raymond B. Fosdick as chair of the Greater New York "Books for Everybody" campaign, and Carr as director of the Immigrant Publication Society.

To provide further incentives for fund-raising, the ALA Executive Board and the Enlarged Program committee had set a precedent that they would be inclined toward a "willingness to make a joint campaign in other cities with other organizations, where the objects of the appeal are naturally allied, but do not overlap."[58] One week later, on 26 May 1920, Fosdick released a statement on the "Books for Everybody" campaign, clarifying the fact that "[a]ssociated with the American Library Association in New York in this effort is the Immigrant Publication Society, an organization that is producing books breathing the American spirit in many languages and is cooperating closely with public libraries throughout the country."[59]

In early June 1920, in the midst of all the debate over the Enlarged Program, Carr received notification that he had been proclaimed an Officer of the Order of the Crown of Italy in recognition of "his profound and helpful friendship toward Italy." His exuberance was necessarily curtailed pending the need to prepare for the Colorado Springs (CO) annual conference of the ALA, which was to be held a few days later, on 7 June 1920.

At that lackluster conference, the Enlarged Program, including the endowment provision and a revised budget, was surprisingly approved once again. It was widely known that many members known to disagree with the Enlarged Program had refused to participate in the discussions, and others left the meeting before the final vote was taken.[60]

The date for the conclusion of the financial campaign was set for 30 June 1920, but was later extended. By September 1920, the prospects for a disappointingly unsuccessful conclusion to the campaign were foreshadowed in an editorial in the 1 September 1920 issue of *Library Journal*. The editorial stated simply that "the appeal for funds for the Enlarged Program has suffered both from the heat of discussion and the heat of summer, and so has progressed but slowly up to date."[61]

A couple of weeks later, on 16 September 1920, Carr wrote to Charles F. D. Belden of the Boston Public Library, who served as regional director for New England of the "Books for Everybody" campaign. Carr confided to Belden that "things are going badly with the Enlarged Program here, and, as I gather, the condition is not local." Carr, who was scheduled to speak to the Lake Placid meeting of the New York Library Association, urged Belden to come if he possibly could to provide input and moral support for the failing Enlarged Program. Carr added prophetically that "it seems almost the last chance. I hope for discussion and I hope for action."[62]

Belden passed on Carr's letter to Edith Kathleen Jones, of the ALA Library War Service's Merchant Marine Department. Belden requested that she send Carr information on the importance of the ALA Enlarged Program to citizens in Massachusetts, which he could use in his Lake Placid address.

Jones wrote Carr on 20 September 1920. Her comments, which were most sympathetic to the aims of the Enlarged Program but critical of the ALA's attitude and handling of the "Books for Everybody" campaign, must have been reassuring to Carr as he planned the message he would present at Lake Placid two days later. She confided in Carr that "I believe that if we could have held the 'vision splendid' through the difficult months just passed and have worked together as we did during the war . . . that we could have made of the rather narrow, very conservative ALA of pre-war days a really big association which would stand for a power in the country."[63]

On 22 September 1920, Carr delivered an address, "A Greater American Library Association," at the Lake Placid conference of the New York Library Association. Speaking to an obviously divided profession, Carr warned that the campaign was "on the verge of a spectacular failure and the disruption of the Association."[64] Only the hard work, dedication, and united effort of all ALA members could salvage the Enlarged Program.

Carr intended his Lake Placid address as a rally cry for the failing Enlarged Program. Instead, response to his speech was as divided as the ALA membership was over the looming issue of the Enlarged Program that nobody seemed to want anymore. The 1 October 1920 issue of *Library Journal* responded editorially that although Carr gave "a rousing shake-up" at the Lake Placid meeting of the New York Library Association, "he rather over-stated the difficulties within the ALA." In the same issue of *Library Journal* was the report of the regional directors of the "Books for Everybody" campaign that only about $68,000 of the $2,000,000 had been collected or pledged.[65]

Alice S. Tyler, Chalmers Hadley's successor as ALA President, called for more "tolerance and cooperation." Mary Eileen Ahern, while expressing her displeasure with Carr's remarks, unwittingly gave support to Carr's scenario of a divided ALA membership: "First and foremost, Mr. Carr is an employee of the ALA which he assails so bitterly, because the larger part of its membership does not see the subject of the Enlarged Program as he and his group see it."[66]

The responses to Carr's remarks from individual ALA members were not all adverse, however. In her congratulatory letter to Carr, Mary L. Titcomb, regional director for the Middle Atlantic states of the "Books for Everybody" appeal, referred specifically to the negative reaction of Ahern. She confided that she disagreed entirely with Ahern, and added with an ironic twist: "I think it quite time that someone should speak out as you did, and tell us at least a part of the disagreeable truth about ourselves."[67]

Anna A. MacDonald, consulting librarian with the Pennsylvania State Library and Museum and member of the ALA CWFB, told Carr that she was in substantial agreement with him with regard to his view of the ALA's internal administrative and managerial problems. "Every word you said was true, and the sooner the librarians wake up to the fact the better it will be. The ALA has been in the control of a certain group of people and has not grown with the library needs. As loyal as I have always been to it, I cannot help but recognize these facts."[68]

Carr confided in Arthur E. Bostwick, then librarian of the St. Louis Public Library. "May I not say to you confidentially that, in my view, perhaps the crux of our present distressing difficulties is the wretched mismanagement of the Executive Board?" Carr criticized the board for providing "nothing whatever in the way of active leadership."[69] Both Carr and Bostwick knew that without immediate action on the part of the executive board, disaster would befall the ill-fated Enlarged Program.

And it did. The Enlarged Program campaign was terminated as of 30 November 1920. The final tally, after receipts and expenditures were reconciled, was a balance of approximately $80,000, barely 4 percent of the funds needed to carry out the Enlarged Program as planned. The share of proceeds of the campaign raised in conjunction with the joint appeal of the ALA and the Immigrant Publication Society was $2,000, out of $60,000 budgeted for the citizenship component of the Enlarged Program.[70]

The handwriting was on the wall for the ALA CWFB. Their only options were to exist on a shoestring budget or disband. Although the committee chose the former option, Carr stepped down from his position as chair and terminated his membership on the committee.

LATTER YEARS

Carr's only hope of salvaging the Immigrant Publication Society was through his own ingenuity now. He could no longer rely on the assistance of the ALA. The "spectacular failure" of the Enlarged Program had thwarted Carr's dream of the Immigrant Publication Society working in tandem with the ALA CWFB. He resumed with renewed vigor his letter-writing campaigns to solicit succor from new and continuing members of the Immigrant Publication Society and to try to attain grants from foundations. His enthusiasm reached almost pathetic proportions in his attempts to raise funds for a matching grant from the Carnegie Corporation of New York, a dream that was never realized.

In 1923, he wrote a supporter in New Haven (CT), of the need for funds to continue his work: "Our subscriptions, with my utmost help personally, became ever more inadequate to meet the widening call of service, for urgently needed new books, new editions—books for practical education, interpreting America appealingly, helping make our immigrants patriotic citizens, instead of discontented misfits or revolutionists. Books ready for publishing, but no money to pay for their printing!"[71] Carr reaffirmed his unswerving commitment to his calling and the unchanging need for the society's publications. "Our books are teaching the reality of American brotherhood, obedience to law, the winning facts of American life and ideals. . . . The schools need them; the libraries need them; every kind of organization doing this so-called Americanization work needs them. There is nothing they can use in their place."[72]

If Carr was not defeatist in attitude, he was most assuredly deluded. His paranoia regarding the threat of revolutionary elements taking over the United States was increasingly pervasive in his fund-raising letters in the postwar years. Carr often commented on the need for libraries to exercise constant vigilance and extreme care in the selection of books in English as well as in foreign languages. He was convinced that Communist propaganda was not only highly persuasive but also more readily accessible to the common man than American patriotic literature.[73]

Final Years of the Immigrant Publication Society

Carr's goal of educating the immigrant population was now expanded to include the revitalization of the patriotism of old-stock Americans as well. Although the Immigrant Publication Society would never recover the popularity of its golden years from 1914 to 1919, Carr was able to hold things together financially long enough to publish the final publication to appear under the society's imprint. *The Declaration of Independence and the Colonies, with a Literal Reprint of the Declaration of Independence* was published in 1924 and reprinted in 1926. The introduction to this pamphlet, containing rhetoric reminiscent of the fervor evinced first in the *Guida*, a mere fourteen years earlier, proclaimed the "double need" for Carr's patriotic propaganda: to affect the true Americanization of "old" and "new" Americans.[74]

In the latter years of his life, from 1927 until his death in 1939, Carr was plagued by ill health compounded by the constant worry over finances. Whether one agreed with Carr or not, his selflessness and his total dedication to his mission were touching. He confided in his close friend, the artist Sarah J. Eddy, the depth of his concern for the society and its membership. "[I]t is work that is so urgently needed nationally; it is now serving so widely; the results are always so very heartening; so many have helped it and believed in it; it is besides so entirely my life, that I felt that [I] must carry on, come what might." Carr revealed to his friend the depth of his passion for his cause. "[E]ven when things were blackest, I did not lose faith that the work must grow in power and win in the end—if only I did not fail it!"[75]

Eddy's reply was equally poignant. Her observations and advice revealed a glimpse of how Carr was perceived by his close friends and associates, specifically the dedication and humanitarianism he exemplified. "I can only say that the tears came to my eyes as I realized the devotion of your life to your ideal of serving humanity. The beauty of it and the lack of self consciousness appeal to me more deeply than I can tell you." She showed her concern foremost for his health and well being. "I do hope that now you will realize the work depends as much on you that your first care should be to keep yourself well and rested."[76]

Never on a sound financial basis to begin with, the Immigrant Publication Society was steadily losing the financial support it needed to survive, much less to thrive. Carr's failing health, to which he referred in his correspondence during 1927, had rendered it impossible for him to continue his lecturing schedule. This source of income had often been the critical hedge against total financial insolvency.[77]

That same year of 1927, Walter F. Willcox, a professor of economics at Cornell University and brother to Mary Alice Willcox, who served on the Council of Direction of the Immigrant Publication Society, called upon Carr to express his opinions on the National Origins Act of 1924. This relatively new law, which set quotas on immigration from various countries, favored immigration from the Western Hemisphere at the expense of immigration from Europe and Asia. Ironically, the National Origins Act would not become fully operational until 1929, two years after the correspondence between Willcox and Carr.

It was revealing and impressive that Walter F. Willcox, a statistician and member of a national advisory committee studying this issue, would turn to Carr for his opinion. As usual, Carr was well informed on the subject and had definite opinions, which he was happy to share with Willcox. Carr was not only sympathetic to the feelings and pride of immigrants, but also believed strongly that the proposed legislation was alien to American ideals. He stated that a serious drawback of the quota system was made painfully apparent in immigrants' as well as Europeans' attitudes toward America and Americans. "In several of the nations I believe it to be one of the important contributing causes to the now almost rooted dislike of us." Carr was insistent that the arbitrary limitation on immigration belied "our national need of labor, that varies with the years," and also that it failed to take into account the infusion of vitality and richness accompanying the immigration of peoples of diverse cultures.

Carr revealed to Willcox that he was not opposed to tighter, more rigidly enforced immigration regulations, but he was opposed to setting arbitrary limits according to nationality. "My experience leads me to one conclusion: That this tangled problem of immigration legislation will never approach satisfactory solution until the law makes the test exclusively that of the worth to our country, of the country's need, of the individual man or woman. The tests should be physical, mental and moral."

While seeing no need to discriminate according to nationality, Carr was not as resolute with regard to discrimination by race. Carr's matter-of-factness regarding the desirability of excluding Japanese immigrants was not consistent with his typically liberal views, and revealed an insensitivity that rarely surfaced in his writings. "There are necessary restrictions as to race that would require careful definition, considerate definition,—perhaps with Japan reverting in some form to the 'gentleman's agreement.'"

Carr's concluding comments to Willcox reaffirmed his faith in the immigration process and in the individual immigrant who was willing to conform to Anglo-Saxon ideas and ideals. "I think that . . . any fine, aspiring individual who can measure up to the tests, and who has the dream of America in his heart, should find entrance here and a home. That would still be in line with our honored tradition. The best of all! One of many!"[78]

The last decade of Carr's life must have been the occasion for reflection. There were no more society publications forthcoming. Restrictive immigration legislation coupled with rigidly enforced immigration quotas had reduced the demand for them.

THE LEGACY OF CARR TO LIBRARIANSHIP

Carr's lapse into relative obscurity in the annals of American public library history is tied undoubtedly to his association with what Carr himself referred to as the "spectacular failure" of the ALA Enlarged Program. What, then, was Carr's legacy to library work with the immigrant community?

The publications of his Immigrant Publication Society and his leadership in those initial, formative years of the ALA CWFB together set the tone of library opinion toward immigrants and immigration—a progressive tone, which was not in accord with the nativist reverberations emanating from the Congress. Nevertheless, librarians relied on Carr's publications and the advice they contained for the selection and acquisition of library materials for immigrant clienteles.

Librarians, both individually and as a profession, deferred to Carr as a candid and objective "outsider" for his judgment on immigration-related issues. Most important, librarians valued Carr's persuasive propaganda for the public library as the ideal agency for the Americanization of the immigrant.

NOTES

1. Moses Rischin, *The Promised City: New York's Jews, 1870–1914* (Cambridge, MA: Harvard University Press, 1977, copr. 1962) 3, 5–10; and Deborah Dash Moore, *At Home in America: Second Generation New York Jews* (New York: Columbia University Press, 1981), chap. 1: "New York Jews," 2-17.

2. Phyllis Dain, *The New York Public Library: A History of Its Founding and Early Years* (New York: New York Public Library, Astor, Lenox and Tilden Foundations 1972), 288–89, 291–93; and Moore, *At Home in America*, chap. 2: "Jewish Geography," 18–58.

3. *Who Was Who in America: A Companion Volume to Who's Who in America*, vol. 1 (1897–1942) (Chicago: Marquis Who's Who, 1962, copr. 1943), s.v. "Carr, John Foster," 196; "The Immigrant Publication Society," *LJ* 45 (1 Mar. 1920): 213–14; and "Real American Is John Foster Carr Who Speaks Here: Has Made a Study of the People Who Come to Our Shores from Europe," *Elmira (NY) Star Gazette*, 21 Feb. 1917, in John Foster Carr, "The Immigrant Problem in the United States; Pertinent Clippings with Speeches by John Foster Carr, 1910–1917" [scrapbook of newspaper clippings, mounted and bound at the New York Public Library, 1941], 55.

4. See, for example, Carr, "Anglo-American Unity Fast Coming," *World's Work* 6 (Oct. 1903): 4016–17; "The Italian in the United States," *World's Work* 8 (Oct. 1904): 5393–404; "The Plight of Russia," *World's Work* 9 (Nov. 1904): 5531–34; "The Coming of the Italian," *Outlook* 82 (24 Feb. 1906): 418–31; and "A Fire in the Country," *Suburban Life* 6 (Apr. 1908): 206–7.

5. Carr, "The Italian in the United States," 5393–404; and "The Coming of the Italian," 418-31. For example, compare Carr's observations and opinions of Italians in New York with those of scholars of the 1970s and 1980s writing on Italian immigrants and immigration of the late nineteenth and early twentieth centuries, who reached similar conclusions: Virginia Yans-McLaughlin, *Family and Community: Italian Immigrants in Buffalo, 1880–1930* (Urbana: University of Illinois Press, 1982, copr. 1977); Thomas Kessner, *The Golden Door: Italian and Jewish Immigrant Mobility in New York City, 1880–1915* (New York: Oxford University Press, 1977); John W. Briggs, *An Italian Passage: Immigrants to Three American Cities, 1890–1930* (New Haven, CT: Yale University Press, 1978); and Dino Cinel, *From Italy to San Francisco: The Immigrant Experience* (Stanford, CA: Stanford University Press, 1982).

6. Carr, "Anglo-American Unity Fast Coming," 4017.

7. Carr, "The Italian in the United States," 5402.

8. "Is Immigration Desirable? The Rev. Dr. M. C. Peters and John F. Carr Debate the Question," *New York Sun*, 10 Apr. 1911 (quote); and "John Foster Carr Speaks in East Hartford: Celebrated Writer Tells How Italians Are Americanized . . .," *Hartford (CT) Times*, 23 Feb. 1912, both in Carr, "The Immigrant Problem in the United States," 16, 29.

9. Carr, "The Library and the Immigrant," *ALA Bulletin* 8 (July 1914): 144, 147; and Carr, "The Nation's Need and the Library's Opportunity," *New York Libraries* 5 (Feb. 1917): 192–94. Both Elaine Fain and Wayne A. Wiegand cast Carr as an advocate of the melting pot philosophy of assimilation rather than the Anglo-conformity philosophy. See Elaine Fain, "Books for New Citizens: Public Libraries and Americanization Programs, 1905-1925," in *The Quest for Social Justice; The Morris Fromkin Memorial Lectures, 1970–1980*, edited by Ralph M. Aderman (Madison: University of Wisconsin Press, 1983), published for the Golda Meir Library of the University of Wisconsin-Milwaukee, 265–70; and Wayne A. Wiegand, *"An Active Instrument for Propaganda": The American Public Library during World War I*, foreword by Edward G. Holley, Beta Phi Mu monograph no. 1 (Westport, CT: Greenwood, 1989), 103.

10. Carr to Clara Lee Bowman, Bristol, CT, 8 Oct. 1908, Carr Papers.

11. John Foster Carr, "A School with a Clear Aim," *World's Work* 19 (Dec. 1909): 12362–65; Henry Cohen, "The Immigrant Publication Society," *Jewish Charities* 6 (Aug. 1915): 4; *The Story of the Immigrant Publication Society* [brochure] ([New York: The Society, 1920?]), Carr Papers; and Julie Miller, "John Foster Carr, 1869–1939. Papers," [Accession Sheet, Rare Books and Manuscripts Division, New York Public Library], 20 Aug. 1987, Carr Papers.

12. Jane E. Robbins, Executive Secretary, Public Education Association, New York, to Carr, 2 June 1909, Carr Papers; Robbins, Wethersfield, CT, to Carr, 24? July 1909, Carr Papers; Angeline Scott Donley, Circulation Department, NYPL, to Carr, 14 July 1909, Carr Papers; Jane Maud Campbell, Passaic, NJ, to Carr, 9 Sept. 1909, Carr Papers; Carr to Fred W. Carpenter, The White House, Washington, DC, 18 Apr. 1910, 20 Apr. 1910, Carr Papers; Arthur W. Page, Doubleday, Page and Company, New York, to Carr, 3 May 1910, Carr Papers; Francesco Tocci, Treasurer, Italian-American Civic League, New York, to Carr, 20 April 1911, Carr Papers; and *The Italian-American Civic League: An Organization to Promote Civic and Social Welfare Among Italians* [brochure] (New York: The League, 1911?), Carr Papers.

13. Carr, *Guida degli Stati Uniti per l'Immigrante Italiano*, pubblicata a cura della Societa delle Figlie della Rivoluzione Americana, Sezione di Connecticut (New York: Doubleday, Page and Company, 1910); Arthur W. Page, Doubleday, Page and Company, New York, to Carr, 22 June 1910, Carr Papers; and "List of Speeches Delivered by Mr. Carr in Connection with Immigration," typescript, Carr Papers.

14. Mary Alice Willcox, "The American Baedeker," *Journal of Education* 78 (4 Dec. 1913): 571–72; Willcox, "The Little Green Book: How It Is Used in the Schools," *Journal of Education* 78 (18 Dec. 1913): 631-33; Carr, "An Immigrant's Baedeker," *Outlook* 106 (7 Feb. 1914): 287–88; Cohen, "The Immigrant Publication Society," 4; and *The Story of the Immigrant Publication Society*, Carr Papers.

15. Comments based on the English translation of the Italian version of the *Guida*: Carr, *Guide for the Immigrant Italian in the United States of America*; *A Nearly Literal Translation of the Second Yiddish Edition*, published under the auspices of the Connecticut Daughters of the American Revolution (New York: Doubleday, Page and Company, 1911).

16. Carr, *Guide*, 5–15, 17, 19–21, 23–46, 53–55, 59–61. See also "Immigration in the South: Mr. John Foster Carr Talks Interestingly of Immigration and the Undeveloped South—At Chamber of Commerce," *The Morning Star (Wilmington, NC)*, 28 Jan. 1912; "Public Market Must Reduce Cost of Living, Declares Carr: Will Encourage Better and

Extensive Farming, Asserts Man Interested in Improving Conditions of Aliens, and Result in Raising of More Produce," *Binghamton (NY) Press*, 26 Jan. 1917; "Better Education for Aliens Urged: Is Insult to Teach Grown-Up Foreigners by Primers, Carr Says," *Binghamton (NY) Press*, 27 Jan. 1917; and "Aliens Dull and Unintelligent? Not So, Says Carr; Use of Primer Methods Is an Insult to Them, He Declares: All They Lack Is Opportunity: They Embrace It with Avidity: Expert Addresses Public Library Audience and the Rotary Club," *Binghamton (NY) Republican-Herald*, 27 Jan. 1917, all included in Carr, "The Immigrant Problem in the United States," 29, 52–54.

17. Willcox, "The American Baedeker," 571–72; Willcox, "The Little Green Book: How It Is Used in the Schools," 631–33; Carr, "An Immigrant's Baedeker," 287–88; Cohen, "The Immigrant Publication Society," 3–5; *The Story of the Immigrant Publication Society*, Carr Papers; "The Immigrant Publication Society," 213–14; and Carr to Andrea Sbarboro, Italian-Swiss Agricultural Colony, Asti, CA, 12 July 1910, 31 July 1910, Carr Papers.

18. Carr to Mabel W. Wainwright, Hartford, CT, 15 June 1911 (quote), Carr Papers. A second edition of the *Guida* in Italian was published in 1910 by Doubleday, Page and Company, and a third, in 1913, was published by Carr's Immigrant Education Society. See also Carr to Charles H. Shapiro, Bridgeport, CT, 25 Apr. 1911, 2 June 1911, Carr Papers; Shapiro to Carr, 12 June 1911, Carr Papers; Carr to Shapiro, 14 June 1911, Carr Papers; Shapiro to Carr, 19 June 1911, Carr Papers; and Carr to Shapiro, 20 June 1911, Carr Papers.

19. Carr to Clara Lee Bowman, Bristol, CT, 28 June 1911, Carr Papers; Carr, *Guide*, 1911; Carr to J. Bockmeyer, Garden City, Long Island, NY, 20 May 1911, Carr Papers; Carr to Mabel W. Wainwright, Hartford, CT, 15 June 1911, Carr Papers.

20. Gilbert E. Whittemore, Supervisor of Evening Schools, Providence, RI, to Doubleday, Page and Company, Garden City, Long Island, NY, 11 Sept. 1911, Carr Papers; Carr to Whittemore, 28 Sept. 1911, Carr Papers; Carr to Mrs. George M. Minor, New London, CT, 4 Oct. 1911, Carr Papers; Carr, "An Immigrant's Baedeker," 287–88 (quote, 287); Carr, *Guide to the United States for the Jewish Immigrant; A Nearly Literal Translation of the Second Yiddish Edition*, published under the auspices of the Connecticut Daughters of the American Revolution (New York: John Foster Carr, 1912), as well as editions published in 1913 and 1916; *Wegweiser von die Vereinigte Staaten fur des Yiddishen Imigrant* ([Bristol?, CT]: Connecticut Daughters of the American Revolution, 1912); and *Przewodnik po Stanach Zjednoczonych do Uzytku Polskich Imigrantow*, opracowal John Foster Carr ([Bristol?, CT]: Wydawnictwo Stowarzyszenia Corek Amerykanskiej Rewolucyi Stanu Connecticut, 1912).

21. Paul Kreuzpointner, Chairman, Committee on Industrial Education, American Foundrymen's Association, Altoona, PA, to Carr, 28 June 1911, Carr Papers. See also, Carr to Mrs. S. A. Talbot, Construction Camp, Camp School, Brown's Station, NY, 1 Aug. 1911, Carr Papers.

22. William P. Dillingham, Committee on Privileges and Elections, U.S. Senate, to Charles Nagel, Secretary, Department of Commerce, 5 June 1911 [Dillingham's letter of introduction for Carr to Nagel], Carr Papers; Carr, "An Immigrant's Baedeker," 287; and Terrence V. Powderly to Carr, 10 Aug. 1911, Carr Papers. For information on the Dillingham Commission, see Maldwyn Allen Jones, *American Immigration* (Chicago: University of Chicago Press, 1960), 177–83.

23. Terrence V. Powderly, Division of Information, Bureau of Immigration and Naturalization, U.S. Department of Commerce and Labor, Washington, DC, to Carr, 8 Aug. 1911, Carr Papers; Carr to Powderly, 23 June 1911, Carr Papers; and "Annual Meeting of the DAR: Second Church Filled with Members of the Order," *New London (CT) Daily Globe*, 26 Oct. 1911, in Carr, "The Immigrant Problem in the United States," 23.

24. Willcox, "The American Baedeker," 571–72; Willcox, "The Little Green Book: How It Is Used in the Schools," 631–33 (quote, 633); and Willcox, "The Use of the Immigrant's Guide in the Library," *MLCB* 4 (Mar.–May 1914): 69–73 (quote, 71–72).

25. "Manufacturers in Annual Convention: Immigration and Patent Law Discussed ... J. F. Carr Pleads for Open Door Policy for Immigration ...," *Journal of Commerce*, 16 May 1911, in Carr, "The Immigrant Problem in the United States," 18. See also "List of Speeches Delivered by Mr. Carr in Connection with Immigration," Carr Papers.

26. Winston Paul, Secretary, The People's Institute of Jersey City, NJ, to N. Behar, 13 Mar. 1911, Carr Papers; Bessie Pope, Secretary, Executive Committee, The People's Institute of Jersey City, NJ, to Carr, 20 Mar. 1911, Carr Papers. See also "People's Institute for a County Investigation . . . Interesting Debate About Immigration," *Hudson Observer*, 10 Apr. 1911; "Restricting Emigrants, Pro and Con," *The Jersey Journal*, 10 Apr. 1911; and "Is Immigration Desirable?," all included in Carr, "The Immigrant Problem in the United States," 14-16.

27. Carr to Mrs. Wilbur F. Rogers ("Aunt Mary"), Meriden, CT, 15 Feb. 1911, 25 Feb. 1911, Carr Papers; Carr to Mrs. Gilbert Horner, Danbury, CT, 4 Apr. 1911, Carr Papers; Carr to Mrs. George M. Minor, Waterford, CT, 27 June 1911, Carr Papers; Carr to Clara Lee Bowman, Bristol, CT, 28 June 1911, Carr Papers; Carr to Dr. Attolico, 21 Feb. 1911; and Carr to Helen Kilduff Gay, Public Library of New London, CT, 6 Jan. 1912, Carr Papers.

28. Mary T. Clark, Librarian, and Catherine H. Judson, Regent, Elizabeth Clarke Hull Chapter, DAR, Ansonia, CT, to Carr, 11 Feb. 1911, Carr Papers.

29. Charles E. Rowell, Mayor, Stamford, CT, to Carr, 17 Feb. 1911, Carr Papers.

30. Carr to Dr. Attolico, 21 Feb. 1911, Carr Papers.

31. "John Foster Carr Is Decorated by Italy: King Makes Him Officer of Crown in Recognition of Effort for Emigrants," *Morning Herald (NY)*, 7 June 1920, Carr Papers; and Carr to Mrs. George M. Minor, Waterford, CT, 27 June 1911, Carr Papers.

32. Minnie B. Cotter, Librarian, Public Library, Derby, CT, to Carr, 10 Feb. 1912, Carr Papers.

33. Carr, "What the Library Can Do for Our Foreign-Born," *LJ* 38 (Oct. 1913): 566–68; and Carr, "The Library and the Immigrant," 142. See also, "The Librarian," *Boston Evening Transcript*, 27 May 1914, in Carr, "The Immigrant Problem in the United States," 35.

34. Carr, "The Library and the Immigrant," 142–46.

35. Cohen, "The Immigrant Publication Society," 3-5; *The Story of the Immigrant Publication Society*, Carr Papers; and "The Immigrant Publication Society," 213–14.

36. Carr, *Immigrant and Library: Italian Helps, with Lists of Selected Books* (New York: Immigrant Education Society, 1914), which was issued in cooperation with the ALA Publishing Board. See also "The Librarian," *Boston Evening Transcript*, 10 June 1914, in Carr, "The Immigrant Problem in the United States," 36.

37. Cohen, "The Immigrant Publication Society;" and Carr, *Immigrant and Library: Italian Helps*, 9–10.

38. Carr, *Immigrant and Library: Italian Helps*, 14–15.

39. Emma Lilian Dana, *Makers of America: Franklin, Washington, Jefferson, Lincoln* (New York: Immigrant Publication Society, 1915); Julie Miller, "John Foster Carr, 1869-1939. Papers," [Accession Sheet], Carr Papers; and *Who Was Who in America*, 1:196, s.v. "Carr, John Foster."

40. Azniv Beshgeturian, *Foreigners' Guide to English* (New York: Immigrant Publication Society, 1914); Carr, "'Making Americans': A Preliminary and Tentative List of Books," *LJ* 45 (1 Mar. 1920): 209–12; Cohen, "The Immigrant Publication Society," 5; and *The Story of the Immigrant Publication Society*, Carr Papers.

41. Carr, "Some of the People We Work For," *LJ* 41 (Aug. 1916): 555 (quote); Carr, "The Nation's Need and the Library's Opportunity," 194; and "Aliens Storming All Our Libraries: 'Books for Everybody' Movement Aims to Supply Enormous Demand and Aid Americanization Work," *Sunday Herald*, Magazine Section, 6 June 1920, Carr Papers.

42. Carr, "Some of the People We Work For," 552–57, (quote, 554-55). See also Carr, "The Library, the Friend of the Foreign Born," in *Proceedings [of the] Americanization Conference, Held under the Auspices of the Americanization Division, Bureau of Education, Department of the Interior, Washington, May 12, 13, 14, 15, 1919* (Washington, DC: GPO, 1919), 376–79, speech delivered by Theresa Hitchler; and Carr, Campaign Director, to Carl H. Milam, Library of Congress, Washington, DC, 13 May 1919, Carr Papers.

43. Ernestine Rose, *Bridging the Gulf; Work with the Russian Jews and Other New-comers*, Library Work with the Foreign Born, edited by John Foster Carr (New York: Immigrant Publication Society, 1917), "Foreword," 3.

44. Eleanor (Edwards) Ledbetter, *Winning Friends and Citizens for America; Work with Poles, Bohemians, and Others*, Library Work with the Foreign Born, edited by John Foster Carr (New York: Immigrant Publication Society, 1918); Mary Frank, *Exploring a Neighborhood; Our Jewish People from Eastern Europe and the Orient*, edited and with additional notes on Jewish immigrant life, by John Foster Carr (New York: Immigrant Publication Society, 1919); and *LJ* 44 (Mar. 1919): 138. A slightly different version of Frank's essay, with Carr listed as coauthor, was published later as "Exploring a Neighborhood," *Century* 98 (July 1919): 375–90. Carr's admiration for Ledbetter was evident in his article entitled "The Library in Americanization Work," *Illinois Libraries* 1 (Oct. 1919): 60–61, which summarizes Ledbetter's library work with immigrants in Cleveland.

45. Carr, *Some of the People We Work For; Address Delivered before the American Library Association, Asbury Park, New Jersey* (New York: Immigrant Publication Society, 1916?); and Carr, *War's End: The Italian Immigrant Speaks of the Future* (New York: Immigrant Publication Society, 1918), 1. See also Carr, "Some of the People We Work For," 552–57.

46. Harry Varley, "Gauging the Sentiment Appeal in Selling Charity to the Crowd: The New York Library Book Campaign, a Study in Mob Psychology," *Printers' Ink* 107 (19 June 1919): 65–68; and Carr to Carl H. Milam, 14 Apr. 1920, Carr Papers.

47. *ALA Bulletin* 11 (Jan. 1917): 33 (quote), (July 1917): 336; *ALA Bulletin* 12 (Nov. 1918): 405; and *ALA Bulletin* 13 (Sept. 1919): 451.

48. Carr, "Books in Foreign Languages and Americanization," *LJ* 44 (Apr. 1919): 246.

49. Dennis Thomison, *A History of the American Library Association, 1876–1972* (Chicago: ALA, 1980, copr. 1978), 70–71.

50. George B. Utley, "Shall a Permanent Endowment Be Undertaken for Peace Time Work of the ALA?" *ALA Bulletin* 13 (May 1919): 92–93, also published in *LJ* 44 (June 1919): 382–83.

51. ALA Executive Board Minutes, *ALA Bulletin* 13 (July 1919): 359–61; ALA Council Minutes, *ALA Bulletin* 13 (July 1919): 361–71; LJ 44 (Oct. 1919): 625–26; and "American Library Association Preliminary Report of Committee on Enlarged Program for American Library Service," *LJ* 44 (Oct. 1919): 645–63.

52. Adam Strohm, "Laying Our Course," *LJ* 44 (Nov. 1919): 691–94; *LJ* 44 (Dec. 1919): 751; Chalmers Hadley, "The Proposed Enlarged Program of the ALA: A Statement by the President of the ALA," *LJ* 44 (Dec. 1919): 753–54; Carl H. Milam, "What's Left of Library War Service," *LJ* 44 (Dec. 1919): 755–56; Orpha Maud Peters, "Libraries in Relation to Citizenship and Americanization," *LJ* 44 (Dec. 1919): 759; Carl H. Milam, "A Call for Munitions," *LJ* 44 (Dec. 1919): 765; and Thomison, *History of the ALA*, 75–76.

53. Hadley, "The Proposed Enlarged Program of the ALA," 754.

54. *ALA Bulletin* 14 (Jan. 1920): 1; "The Enlarged Program Proceedings, January 1-3, 1920," *ALA Bulletin* 14 (Jan. 1920): 2–9; J. Randolph Coolidge, "Achievement Thru Conviction," *LJ* 45 (1 Feb. 1920): 103–4 [text of speech delivered to the ALA special membership meeting in Chicago, 2 January 1920]; "The Opportunity and the Outlook," *LJ* 45 (1 Jan. 1920): 11–12; "At Chicago," *LJ* 45 (15 Jan. 1920): 55–56; ALA Council Minutes, *LJ* 45 (15 Jan. 1920): 76–79; Harold L. Wheeler, "That Two Million Dollars," *LJ* 45 (15 Jan. 1920): 82–83; "Look Down the Hill," *LJ* 45 (15 Feb. 1920): 165–66; Frank P. Hill, "Regional Directors of the ALA 'Books for Everybody' Appeal," *LJ* 45 (15 Feb. 1920): 173; "Proposed Budget for the ALA Two Million Dollar Fund," *LJ* 45 (15 Mar. 1920): 271–72; and *LJ* 45 (15 Mar. 1920): 274–75.

55. Scholasticus, "Is the ALA Attempting Too Much?" *LJ* 45 (1 Jan. 1920): 38; "A Plaint!" *Public Libraries* 25 (Feb. 1920): 73; M. E. A[hern], "The Called Meeting of the ALA," *Public Libraries* 25 (Feb. 1920): 80–82; and *LJ* 45 (15 Mar. 1920): 274–75.

56. *LJ* 45 (15 Apr. 1920): 361, (1 May 1920): 408; "Circular Letter on the Enlarged Program," *LJ* 45 (15 Apr. 1920): 363–64, cited in Thomison, *History of the ALA*, 80, 268; "ALA Interests Concerning the Enlarged Program," *Public Libraries* 25 (June 1920): 328; and Thomison, *History of the ALA*, 80.

57. George B. Utley, "American Library Association: Atlantic City Special Conference, Colorado Springs Conference," *LJ* 45 (15 Feb. 1920): 177; *LJ* 45 (1 May 1920): 408; "Proposed Budget Plan Prepared by John Foster Carr, and Submitted as Information to the Joint Committee Appointed by the Executive Board of the American Library Association at Atlantic City on April 30th, 1920 [revised May 4th, 1920]," typescript, Carr Papers; *LJ* 45 (15 May 1920): 453; and ALA Council Minutes, *LJ* 45 (15 May 1920): 455–61.

58. Carr to Carl H. Milam, "Preliminary Draft of the Understanding between the American Library Association's Committee on Enlarged Program and the Immigrant Publication Society," 14 Apr. 1920, Carr Papers; Typescript form signed by F. C. Hicks, Frederick W. Jenkins, Richard R. Bowker, New York, 17 May 1920, Carr Papers; and Carl H. Milam, Secretary, ALA, and W. N. C. Carlton, Chairman, Committee on Enlarged Program, ALA, to Raymond B. Fosdick, New York, 19 May 1920, Carr Papers.

59. "Statement," by Raymond B. Fosdick, Chairman, Executive Committee, American Library Association "Books for Everybody" Movement, in Greater New York, typescript, 26 May 1920, Carr Papers.

60. "John Foster Carr Is Decorated by Italy," Carr Papers; "Report of the Committee on an Enlarged Program for American Library Service," *ALA Bulletin* 14 (July 1920): 297–309; "American Library Association Enlarged Program: Trustees' Meeting Held at Boston Public Library,"*LJ* 45 (1 June 1920): 506–7; and Thomison, *History of the ALA*, 81.

61. *LJ* 45 (1 Sept. 1920): 701; and Thomison, *History of the ALA*, 81.

62. Carr to Charles F. D. Belden, Boston Public Library, 16 Sept. 1920, Carr Papers.

63. Edith Kathleen Jones, ALA Library War Service, Merchant Marine Department, Dispatch Agent, Boston Public Library, to Carr, 20 Sept. 1920, Carr Papers.

64. Carr, "A Greater American Library Association," *LJ* 45 (1 Oct. 1920): 775–8, (quote, 777); and New York Library Association Minutes, "Library Week at Lake Placid," *LJ* 45 (1 Oct. 1920): 808.

65. *LJ* 45 (1 Oct. 1920): 791 (quote); and "The Status of the 'Books for Everybody' Campaign as Reported by the Regional Directors on July 15th," *LJ* 45 (1 Oct. 1920): 798-800.

66. ALA Minutes, *LJ* 45 (1 Oct. 1920): 796–98; Alice S. Tyler, "Tolerance and Co-operation: A Message from the President of the ALA," *LJ* 45 (1 Nov. 1920): 890 (quote), reprinted in *Public Libraries* 25 (Nov. 1920): 518–19; and "A Mistaken Notion," *Public*

Libraries 25 (Nov. 1920): 500–501. See also Carr's reply to Tyler: "A Greater ALA—A Letter to the President," *LJ* 45 (1 Dec. 1920): 979.

67. Mary L. Titcomb, Washington County Free Library, Hagerstown (MD), to Carr, 10 Nov. 1920, Carr Papers; Carr to Titcomb, 11 Nov. 1920, Carr Papers; and Hill, "Regional Directors of the ALA 'Books for Everybody' Appeal," 173.

68. Anna A. MacDonald, Consulting Librarian, Pennsylvania State Library and Museum, Library Extension Division, Harrisburg (PA), to Carr, 30 Nov. 1920, Carr Papers.

69. Carr to Arthur E. Bostwick, St. Louis Public Library, 8 Oct. 1920, Carr Papers.

70. *LJ* 45 (1 Dec. 1920): 981–82; Typescript memorandum, 12 Jan. 1921, Carr Papers; and Thomison, *History of the ALA*, 81–84.

71. Carr to Mary B. Bristol, New Haven, CT, 23 July 1923, Carr Papers.

72. Carr to Bristol, 22 Sept. 1923, Carr Papers.

73. Ibid. See also Carr to Mary F. Lovell, Superintendent, Department of Humane Education, World's Woman's Christian Temperance Union, Jenkintown, PA, 23 June 1927, Carr Papers.

74. Carr, *The Declaration of Independence and the Colonies, with a Literal Reprint of the Declaration of Independence* (New York: Immigrant Publication Society, 1924), 4. Reprinted in 1926.

75. Carr to Sarah J. Eddy, Bristol Ferry, RI, 26 Jan. 1927, Carr Papers.

76. Sarah J. Eddy, Pasadena, CA, to Carr, 5 Feb. 1927, Carr Papers.

77. See, for example, Carr to Sarah J. Eddy, Bristol Ferry, RI, 3 June 1927, Carr Papers; Carr to Dr. Kate Holladay Claghorn, New York School of Social Work, New York, 18 June 1927, Carr Papers; and Carr to Mrs. Eli Whitney, New Haven, CT, 22 June 1927, Carr Papers.

78. Walter F. Willcox, Department of Economics, Cornell University, Ithaca, NY, to Carr, 30 June 1927, Carr Papers; Jones, *American Immigration*, 279; and Carr to Walter F. Willcox, Ithaca, NY, 7 July 1927, Carr Papers.

"Women from Guadaloupe." Photograph courtesy William Williams Papers, Manuscripts and Archives Division, The New York Public Library, Astor, Lenox and Tilden Foundations.

5

Libraries, Immigrants, and Restricted Immigration, 1924–1948

The passage of the National Origins Act of 1924 marked the end of free American immigration. Conferring the weight of federal sanction to both exclusion and discrimination, the National Origins Act, even before it became fully operational in 1929, changed dramatically and irrevocably both the composition and the quantity of American immigration.

While immigration from countries outside the Western Hemisphere was henceforth limited to approximately 150,000 immigrants per year, immigration from the countries of the Americas and the Caribbean remained unrestricted. Among the countries outside the Western Hemisphere directly affected by the quota system, preference was given in the form of larger quotas for immigrants from the countries of northern and western Europe, which were the original homelands of the "old" immigrants.[1]

RESTRICTED IMMIGRATION AND THE NATION

Such blatant, but nevertheless legal, discrimination against the "new" immigrants was the legacy of the Dillingham Commission of 1907. The commission's lengthy 1911 report to Congress, which purported to prove the racial inferiority of southern and eastern Europeans, was yet another in a string of partial victories for nativists, who were bent on reversing the immigrant tide altogether.[2] The even partial success of the nativist crusade for restriction was manifested by a telling statistical comparison. From 1876 through 1924, the number of immigrants entering the United States from all sources had averaged just fewer than 550,000 annually. From 1925 through 1948, the average number of immigrants never reached 150,000 per year.[3]

Ironically, even if the National Origins Act had not been passed, the confluence of demographic, political, and economic factors both in Europe and the United

States would have worked to stem the tide of European emigration to the United States between 1924 and 1948. Demographically, the decrease in European population during this period, directly attributable to a decline in the birthrate, was exacerbated by the monumental loss of lives Europe experienced during World War I. Politically, the rise of totalitarian regimes, which relied on manpower for the pursuit of military expansion, made migration within as well as emigration out of Europe more difficult. Economically, potential European emigrants found little incentive to leave behind the prosperity that accompanied industrialization and social reforms in their homelands for the deprivation of the Great Depression of the 1930s, which followed in the wake of the stock market crash of 1929, in the United States.[4]

National Origins Act of 1924

The decline in European immigration from 1924 onward, the legacy and intent of the National Origins Act, was in stark contrast to the dramatic increase in arrivals from countries of the Western Hemisphere as well as the Philippine Islands. From 1898, when the Philippines became the possession of the United States as a result of the Spanish-American War, until 1934, when they became an independent commonwealth, the Philippine Islands had had the distinction of being the only Far Eastern country whose inhabitants had not been excluded by American immigration policy.

Heavily concentrated on the Pacific Coast where they were employed as seasonal agricultural workers, Filipino immigrants were subjected to the hostility of West Coast labor unionists and other restrictionists. From 1928 onward, these West Coast restrictionists began to demand the exclusion of Filipino immigrants in order to complete the pattern of Oriental exclusion.[5] From 1935, when the Philippine Islands declared their independence from the United States, throughout the World War II era, Filipino immigration to the United States remained minimal, never reaching the one thousand mark until 1948.[6]

The exemption of the countries of the Western Hemisphere from the quota system was in part a concession to southwestern ranchers and farmers. Over the years, they had grown to rely on Mexican migrants as a cheap source of labor. Another important influence, however, was the strength of Pan-Americanism, a diplomatic preference for other countries of the Americas as an expression of mutual revulsion for the Old World.

For decades after 1924, although restrictionists continued to demand the abolition of the Western Hemisphere exemption, their demand that immigration from the Americas should be placed on a quota basis was rejected in the interests of what eventually became known as the Good Neighbor policy. Thus, after 1924, newcomers from the Western Hemisphere formed a larger proportion of the total immigration than before. The majority now came from Mexico, Canada, and the West Indies.[7]

Good Neighbor Policy

Mexican Immigration. Mexicans from 1900 onward had come to the United States on a large-scale basis initially to help with railroad building and agricultural expansion in the Southwest. From 1900 to 1930, more and more Mexicans were lured to the United States by the boom in the fruit and vegetable industries and the movement of the center of cotton cultivation westward.[8] The number of Mexicans officially reported as entering the United States swelled from approximately 50,000 between 1901 and 1910 to just over 459,000 between 1921 and 1930.[9]

Many Mexican laborers were unable to fulfill the literacy test requirements. This fact, coupled with the expense and delay involved in obtaining American visas stipulated by the 1924 immigration legislation, caused great numbers of Mexicans to enter the United States illegally as "wetbacks." American labor contractors, whose desire for cheap, unskilled, migratory labor was insatiable, smuggled them in. Although declining during the depression years of the 1930s, Mexican immigration to the United States recovered from 1942 onward, when the federal government undertook the organized recruitment of Mexicans for seasonal agricultural work and railroad maintenance.

As a direct result of the increasing mechanization of agricultural endeavors in the Southwest, however, Mexicans began to spread out to the mountain states and particularly to the Midwest, where industrial opportunities awaited them in Chicago, Toledo, and Detroit. Mexicans, who came from a homogenous folk culture, had depended on migratory labor for their livelihoods. They were ill prepared for a rapid transition to a complex, highly industrialized, urban society.

Throughout the 1920s and into the 1940s, however, Mexicans began to form their own agricultural labor unions, to join established industrial labor unions, and to strike against exploitation. As their settlements took on permanence, Mexicans began the inexorable move up the occupational ladder along with their immigrant compatriots from other parts of the Western Hemisphere.[10]

Canadian Immigration. During the first three decades of the twentieth century, Canadians of British ancestry had migrated from Ontario to the great industrial centers of the Midwest. French-Canadians moved to join compatriots in the communities that they had established in the mill towns of New England. By the early 1930s, however, Canadian migration had run its course due to the depression. Then, too, the rapid industrialization of Canada during and after World War II removed the incentive for further mass migration of Canadians into the United States.[11]

Caribbean Immigration. The first decade of the twentieth century witnessed as well the beginnings of a movement of immigrants into the United States from the islands of the Caribbean. Falling off during the depression years and increasing dramatically after World War II, Caribbean immigration up to 1945 was composed mainly of blacks from the British West Indies, French West Indies, Cuba, and Haiti. After 1945, it consisted overwhelmingly of Puerto Ricans of Spanish descent.

The racial dynamic between West Indian blacks, who settled largely in urban centers on the Atlantic seaboard, and African Americans as well as among both black groups and Puerto Ricans of Spanish descent was a source of continuing tension. West Indian blacks, who were usually more educated and decidedly British in speech patterns and cultural outlooks, looked down upon African Americans for their alleged ignorance and supineness. African Americans, who suffered from years of educational and economic deprivation, resented the supposed aloofness and aggressiveness of the West Indian blacks. The economic role of Puerto Rican immigrants had been to fill the need for unskilled and semiskilled labor left by the virtual ending of immigration from southern and eastern Europe.[12]

Immigration during the Great Depression

During the early years of the Great Depression, the Hoover administration, in response to the demands of nativists, ordered more stringent adherence to the immigration regulation. A new regulation prohibited the admission of persons likely to become public charges. During the Roosevelt administration until 1937, strict enforcement of this particular regulation effectively excluded all but the most prosperous European immigrants.[13]

From 1931 to 1940, fewer than 350,000 Europeans entered the United States. In fact, the total number of emigrants, no matter what their origins, who chose America as a destination during the depression decade was just under 530,000. The dramatic increase in the return immigration of many immigrants, who left behind the financial woes associated with the depression in the United States in search of better opportunities elsewhere, even in their former homelands, produced a negligible net gain in population.[14]

From 1933 onward, the majority of European immigrants were refugees from Nazi Germany, overwhelmingly Jews, who fled Hitler's anti-Semitic campaign. As early as 1934, Roosevelt had instructed American consuls to give due consideration to all refugees' applications for admission. In 1940, he permitted the State Department to circumvent the established quotas for German immigrants by permitting consuls outside Germany to issue visas to German refugees. Still, only a fraction, approximately 250,000, was able to reach the United States during the period from 1934 to 1941.[15] Ironically, the total of all refugees admitted in any given year was well within the limits of the existing quotas.

Pre–World War II Refugees

The pre–World War II refugees were predominantly middle-class, white-collar workers, professionals and businessmen, artists, musicians, architects, and scientists, including Nobel Prize winners and scholars in every academic discipline. These refugees were sophisticated, well-educated urbanites who adapted readily to big city life. Unlike the unskilled immigrants of the new immigration in the fifty years prior to 1924, they found the language barrier an insurmountable hindrance to attaining the type of employment to which they were suited.

Most had to resort to menial jobs, since many states and professional associations, including those representing the legal, educational, and medical professions, barred aliens. Although they faced more discrimination than did their predecessors of the earlier immigration, prewar refugees were more fortunate. They found a greater number of organized voluntary agencies to which they could turn for assistance in the ordeal of resettlement, including the National Refugee Service and the Hebrew Sheltering and Immigrant Aid Society.[16]

Immigration during World War II

Coincidentally with the end of the Great Depression, the entry of the United States into World War II brought new economic opportunities for European refugees and native-born Americans alike. The increasing demand for manpower in war-related industries and the relaxing of the exclusive attitude of professional associations and public authorities together smoothed the way for refugees to move into positions for which they were qualified. Refugees as a group, even those who never regained the prestige and wealth they were forced to leave behind in their European homelands, were extremely anxious to become naturalized citizens as proof both of their loyalty and their gratitude to the United States.

German-Americans and Italian-Americans. Many immigrants, particularly German-Americans and Italian-Americans, maintained strong sympathies with their homelands. They often disagreed with American foreign policy with regard to Germany and Italy respectively. Their expressed and inchoate antagonisms were quelled, however, by the Japanese attack on Pearl Harbor.

Though there were almost one million enemy aliens in the United States in 1941, in addition to millions of unnaturalized aliens who had been born in enemy territory, all but a handful were unwavering in their American allegiance. Of the 700,000 enemy aliens from Italy and the 300,000 enemy aliens from Germany, only a few hundred were interned. The rest suffered no serious discrimination either in war-related industries or in the armed services.[17]

Internment of Japanese-Americans. Such was not the case with Japanese aliens and Americans of Japanese ancestry. Concentrated on the Pacific Coast, mainly in California, the Japanese, who had remained the object of suspicion and animosity by nativists, now became the victims of a tragedy.

A little more than two months after the Japanese attack on Pearl Harbor, John L. DeWitt, commanding general of the Western Defense Command, called for the immediate evacuation of all Japanese from the Pacific Coast area. DeWitt's action was not unilateral. Rather, it was sanctioned by President Franklin Delano Roosevelt, endorsed by both houses of Congress, and sustained by the Supreme Court. More than 110,000 people of Japanese ancestry, two-thirds of whom were American citizens, were transferred under the supervision of the U.S. Army to ten relocation centers situated in isolated parts of the western and central United States.

There, behind barbed wire and under armed guard, the majority of the evacuees sat out the war, deprived of their occupations and property, not to mention their constitutional and legal rights. Ironically, the great majority of Japanese-Americans remained staunchly loyal to the United States throughout this regrettable ordeal, and more than 12,000 Nisei—people born in America of Japanese immigrant parentage—served with honor and distinction in American combat units during World War II.

Having proven their loyalty by surviving the ordeal of internment or by service in the armed forces, many Japanese-Americans returned to the Pacific Coast after World War II. Others spread throughout the nation and developed permanent communities in Chicago, Minneapolis, Denver, Philadelphia, and Cleveland. Before 1941, most Japanese-Americans had been truck farmers, gardeners, fishermen, and domestic servants. After World War II, they became factory workers, small businessmen, doctors, teachers, and lawyers.[18]

Throughout World War II, European emigration remained at a low level. Not only were most Europeans conscripted for war service in their native lands, but also the disruption of transatlantic communications prevented the free flow of emigrants. Immediately after World War II, all available shipping was used to return American armed services personnel home.

As conditions improved, the United States once again began to attract skilled and semiskilled immigrants from European countries favored by the quota system, notably Great Britain and Germany. These immigrants were especially anxious to escape the devastation of postwar Europe.

Immigration after World War II

The passage of special acts of 1946 relaxed the quota requirements for the benefit of European wives, fiancées, and children of American servicemen. These acts made it possible for some 150,000 wives and fiancées, 25,000 children, and a few hundred husbands to enter the United States from Europe in the five years after the war. A subsequent amendment to the immigration law in 1947, in favor of Oriental war brides, permitted similarly the entry of approximately 5,000 Chinese and 800 Japanese wives.[19]

Displaced Persons and Refugees

After World War II, the dilemma facing the world community was finding homes and employment for displaced persons. These included the survivors of the Nazi concentration camps, forced laborers brought to Germany from the occupied countries, and those who fled from the Baltic states before the Russian advance in 1944 and 1945. The number of post–World War II refugees was further increased by anti-Semitic outbreaks in Poland and Romania and by the flight of Czechs, Yugoslavs, and Poles from Communist domination.

Acknowledging that this was an international rather than an American problem, the Truman administration urged the Congress to have the United States set an example by admitting a generous proportion of the displaced persons and refugees. Congressmen, especially those from the rural regions of the South and Midwest, opposed a liberal program for displaced persons and postwar refugees, as did many veterans' organizations and hereditary patriotic societies. These legislators feared that the admission of refugees and displaced persons not only would deprive returning veterans of jobs and housing, but also would flood the country with subversive elements.

Thwarted by congressional inaction, in December 1945 President Truman issued a presidential directive that gave displaced persons and postwar refugees priority within the existing quotas. However, since most were from countries with low quotas, only 41,000 refugees and displaced persons were allowed to enter the United States during the next two and a half years.[20]

Displaced Persons Act of 1948

Finally, in 1948, Congress passed the Displaced Persons Act, which was amended in 1950 to allow for the admission of some 400,000 people during a four-year period. Neither the displaced persons nor the postwar refugees were allowed to enter as nonquota immigrants. The emergency relief measures in effect from 1948 to 1953 provided that those entering on such terms were to be charged to future quotas of their countries of origin.

In contrast to the prewar refugees who had come to the United States in the heart of the depression, the displaced persons and postwar refugees came during a time of renewed economic expansion, when employment of all kinds was relatively easy to obtain. Also, since the majority of these immigrants were either unskilled or semiskilled laborers, their ignorance of English was usually no bar to immediate employment. Finding suitable employment and enjoying a more tolerant reception than had the prewar refugees of the 1930s, displaced persons and postwar refugees of the late 1940s were generally able to make more rapid social and emotional adjustments.[21]

Effect of Immigrants on American Culture

After 1924, the strict enforcement of the National Origins Act coupled with the Great Depression, World War II, and the postwar boom not only changed the composition and quantity of American immigration, but also worked together to dissolve ethnic and national ties within the immigrant community. The depression and its hardships drew renewed attention to class divisions among Americans in general. These class divisions tended to override cultural differences of workers, which had heretofore kept various ethnic elements apart in the workplace. The advent of Roosevelt's New Deal had the totally unforeseen effect of teaching immigrants to rely on governmental agencies rather than on their own mutual aid societies, which had flourished in the immigrant community during the first three decades of the twentieth century.

Notwithstanding the evacuations of Japanese-Americans, the race riots in Detroit and New York, and the Los Angeles "zoot-suit" riots of 1943 against Mexican-Americans, the latter years of the war witnessed both increasing ethnic unity within individual immigrant groups and increasing identification among divergent immigrant groups as Americans. The close contact and increased personal interaction between people of diverse ethnic and national origins in the armed forces and war-related industries together worked toward the dissolution of class divisions. This carried over into the postwar era. With the gas chambers and ovens of Hitler's death camps serving as grim reminders of the lengths to which racial hatred could and did lead, Americans as a nation became more tolerant of cultural diversity.[22]

Ethnic and Religious Ties

While ethnic ties and loyalties persisted even generations after the passage of the National Origins Act of 1924, it was equally apparent that this legislation had provided the impetus for change in the very foundations of group loyalty within the immigrant community. Particularly for the second generation of the immigrant community, which had never known the old country, the ethnic tie became increasingly meaningless. Occupational and residential mobility, religious affiliation, political clout, and assimilation within American society gained ascendancy in immigrants' priorities.

As religion became increasingly the major focus of social activity for most Americans, religious affiliation, not membership in an ethnic or national group, became the primary method of self-identification and social grouping. In many cases, religious affiliation established the bounds within which intermarriage might occur. By 1948, then, the most meaningful differentiation of the American populace was not by national or ethnic origin but by religious preference—Protestant, Catholic, or Jew. Similarly, with the gradual disintegration of their ethnic ghettos, the new European immigrants, who were now empowered by both occupational and geographical mobility, made their first great strides toward the anonymity of American middle-class life.[23]

Ironically, it was the impact of the new immigrants, the very group targeted for extinction by the National Origins Act, that was most dramatic in the realm of American politics. When the second generation of the immigrant community began to exercise collectively their political power in the voting booths, they almost single-handedly transformed the United States from a country with a normally Republican majority to one with a Democratic majority.[24]

Second-Generation Americans

Estranged from their parents by their American education, many children of immigrants, by the shedding of exotic surnames as well as the adoption of American dress, speech, and interests, made deliberate attempts to repudiate their immigrant heritages and thus improve their status as Americans. As a further consequence of this collective repudiation of Old World traits and allegiances, the great immigrant organizations that had been established by and for the earlier immigrants from southern and eastern Europe lost steadily in membership, vitality, and purpose.

Immigrant Press

The phenomenal growth of mass communications tended to undermine those very institutions that had been most effective in giving expression to ethnicity. Most notably, the immigrant press was unable to withstand competition from picture tabloids, which made their appearance in the 1920s. They simply could not hold the second-generation immigrant readership, even by changing from the traditional foreign language to English. By the close of the 1940s, more than one-third of the total number of foreign language publications in the United States had passed out of existence.

The successive rise of the movies in the 1910s and the radio in the 1920s brought about the demise of the immigrant theater. The spread of television from the 1930s onward accentuated the trend whereby all Americans, regardless of origins, were exposed to a common set of influences.[25]

RESTRICTED IMMIGRATION AND PUBLIC LIBRARIES

From 1924 onward, the Americanization efforts of various educational and social welfare agencies, including public libraries, were no longer exclusively directed toward the European immigrant of the new immigration, but more and more to the Western Hemisphere immigrant. For European immigrants, an unexpected outcome of the drastic curtailment of their immigration was the acceleration of the Americanization of the earlier arrivals. For Western Hemisphere immigrants, their Americanization was increasingly viewed as an integral part of the more all-encompassing adult education movement. The adult education movement was attuned as well to the needs of illiterate American-born adults, including blacks and whites from the rural South. Pittsburgh librarians in 1925 remarked that "the uneducated adults are pathetically anxious for spellers, grammars, American histories, and easy reading books; in fact, a part of the use of the so-called 'English for New Americans' has been with Negro people." Similarly, St. Louis librarians in 1928 noted that "when Americanized groups have left the immediate neighborhood, their places have been filled, in most cases, by illiterate native-born Americans from the Ozark regions of Missouri and Arkansas."[26]

The Library and Internationalism

The once distinctly separate and narrowly focused goals of American public libraries to Americanize immigrants as well as to educate the general populace were merging into a single goal. Libraries worked to build a literate citizenry composed of both foreign- and native-born Americans who were imbued with a spirit of internationalism. Americanization activities in general continued to be centered at the local level. Through the ALA Committee on Work with the Foreign Born, the national coordination of Americanization programs as well as other library programs for immigrants was realized.

In July 1924, the ALA, with funding from the Carnegie Corporation, appointed a Library Commission on the Library and Adult Education. Composed of seven librarians representing public, school, and academic libraries, the commission's charge was "to study the adult education movement, and the work of libraries for adults and for older boys and girls out of school, and to report its findings and recommendations to the ALA Council." Of the seven librarians, five were public librarians serving large, diverse immigrant clienteles, including Judson Toll Jennings of Seattle, Matthew Simpson Dudgeon of Milwaukee, Charles Francis Dorr Belden of Boston, Charles Everett Rush of Indianapolis, and Linda Anne Eastman of Cleveland. The commission's report, which was published in 1926, described the nature and extent of library educational work with adult immigrants. It concluded that "the dividing line between general library work with the foreign born and that which can be considered as distinctly educational cannot be sharply drawn."[27]

The Cleveland Public Library reflected this broadening of the mission of the public library toward the immigrant community in a policy statement in 1926. The policy suggested that libraries should now be concerned with "the larger service of 'internationalization' of all readers, American and foreign-born, to the enrichment of American literature and life, rather than simply seeking to 'Americanize' its foreign-born clientele." Two years later, in 1928, the Cleveland Public Library entertained, as a further refinement of this movement toward internationalism, a change not only in philosophy but also in the terminology used to describe library work with immigrants. The Cleveland Public Library advocated dropping the term "Americanization" altogether. Cleveland librarians preferred the more accurate and all-inclusive term "adult elementary education." This term would include not only immigrant education, but also educational endeavors of an elementary scope directed toward illiterate adults and those who never completed elementary school.[28]

While in no way denigrating the Cleveland Public Library's progressive attitude toward library educational work with immigrants, the Detroit Public Library in 1926 cautioned that Americanization, pure and simple, should not be abandoned as a goal of American public libraries serving immigrant clienteles. "The huge immigration of the first quarter of this century can be looked upon as an emergency, the effects of which still have to be met. Somehow or other the millions of aliens who came here in those years have to be accepted. Their influence is inevitable. For better or worse they modify the culture of America, and it is the part of a wise foresight to see that their presence is an asset rather than a hindrance to the best development of the civilization which is evolving here." Detroit librarians conceded pragmatically that "an adult can never be deprived of his nationality, but he can be made a citizen, and it is the business of the educational agencies of the city to see that the immigrant has the incentive and the opportunity to become an educated and useful one."[29]

In the first years after the National Origins Act of 1924 went into effect, most American public libraries supported philosophies of Americanization that fell somewhere between the more conservative philosophy reflected by the Detroit Public Library and the more progressive philosophy of the Cleveland Public

Library. At neither extreme did Americanization any longer connote the eradication of the immigrant's pride in and devotion to his native country.

Dovetailing with the ALA's *Libraries and Adult Education*, for which research began in 1924 and publication was in 1926, was ALA's *A Survey of Libraries in the United States*, for which research began in 1926 and publication was completed by 1927. These two Carnegie Corporation–sponsored studies represented major achievements in documenting library resources and services as they had developed since 1876. Based on the responses of approximately twelve hundred American public libraries, *A Survey of Libraries in the United States* presented in four volumes a detailed summary of general library resources and services offered in libraries throughout the nation as well as specific resources and services offered for immigrant clienteles.[30]

Regrettably, the section of the survey directly related to public library work with immigrants was based on the responses received from less than forty libraries. The responses were treated in five basic areas: (1) book selection, (2) cooperation with other American social and educational agencies, (3) cooperation with parochial and public schools and foreign social organizations, (4) work with adult education classes, both day and evening programs, and (5) library publicity.

The section on book selection included statistics of the book stock of twenty-eight public libraries in thirty-three foreign languages. The twenty-eight cities represented all of the major census divisions of the country, but primarily cities in the Northeast and Midwest states. The thirty-three languages represented, with the exception of extremely limited Japanese holdings in public libraries in Los Angeles and Portland (OR), could all be classified as Indo-European. Among the most progressive programs in 1927 were those in Cleveland, Detroit, Gary (IN), Grand Rapids (MI), Indianapolis, Minneapolis, New Bedford (MA), New York, and St. Louis.[31]

Four years later, in 1931, William Madison Randall, a professor at the Graduate Library School of the University of Chicago, published a study of the availability of foreign language materials in public libraries and their circulation per capita. He used the data presented on the foreign language holdings of the twenty-eight libraries in the 1927 *Survey of American Libraries* as well as the data on general library holdings from the 1927 *American Library Directory*. Randall discovered significantly that the ratio of foreign language books provided by public libraries to the foreign-born population was consistently lower than the ratio of English language books provided by public libraries to the native-born population.

Randall found that there was no positive relationship between the number of foreign language books per capita and circulation per book, as there was for English books. He concluded that many libraries were failing to provide reading matter in immigrant languages that was as popular and attractive as that provided in the English language. As a direct affirmation of Randall's findings, the Detroit Public Library in 1931 reported that while the city's foreign language–speaking population was 251,689, there was only one foreign language book for every nine people.[32]

ALA Committee on Work with the Foreign Born

Considering Randall's recommendations and Detroit's experience, perhaps the most helpful service offered the American public library community on behalf of immigrant clienteles was the advice, publications, and educational opportunities provided by the ALA CWFB from 1924 through 1948. The leaders of the committee during this period were exceptional, especially Eleanor (Edwards) Ledbetter of the Broadway Branch of the Cleveland Public Library, Edna Phillips of the Massachusetts Board of Library Commissioners in Boston, and Margaret Gabriel Hickman of the Foreign Language Department of the Los Angeles Public Library, who each served lengthy terms.

The ALA CWFB was a clearinghouse for Americanization information. Through correspondence, publications, and their personal examples, committee members demystified the selection and acquisition of foreign language books for librarians throughout the country. They offered expert advice on publicizing the library's resources for the immigrant community, and served as advocates for immigrant clienteles regardless of their origins.

Continuing the tradition begun in the early 1920s under the leadership of John Foster Carr and Eleanor (Edwards) Ledbetter, the ALA CWFB published pamphlets on the reading interests of immigrant groups. These included extensive bibliographies and suggestions for purchases both in the immigrant language treated and in English translation. Pamphlets were published on the Polish immigrant in 1924, the Italian immigrant in 1925, the Greek immigrant in 1926, and the German immigrant in 1929.[33]

The final pamphlet in the series, *Reading Service to the Foreign Born*, appeared in 1929. This handbook offered general advice to librarians working with all immigrant groups on the selection, acquisition, and cataloging of foreign language books and Americanization aids. Lists of the names and addresses of domestic and foreign dealers in foreign language books were included. Suggestions on the transliteration of nonroman alphabets were given. The handbook stressed the need to be aware of and to cooperate with other educational and social agencies involved in the promotion of Americanization and "inter-racial understanding." These included state library commissions and associations, the Foreign Language Information Service, and various foreign societies.[34]

Ironically, these bibliographic pamphlets of the ALA CWFB were limited exclusively to European countries, notably those of eastern and southern Europe, whose immigration quotas were comparatively small as a result of the National Origins Act of 1924. Nevertheless, the pamphlets filled a real need, particularly for librarians in the large urban centers of the Northeast and Midwest, where large concentrations of first-generation eastern and southern European immigrants existed and where Americanization was not an accomplished fact.

Libraries during the Great Depression

The Great Depression was a period of ironic contrasts and inequities for American public libraries. During the late 1920s and early 1930s, library collections throughout the country suffered from the lack of funds to purchase library materials. Later, in the late 1930s and early 1940s, library services in some areas of the country were actually expanded due to the availability of workers funded by the federal manpower programs of President Franklin Delano Roosevelt's New Deal.

In 1927, the Brooklyn Public Library complained that the shortage of money had necessitated a cutback in purchases of foreign language materials. Buffalo in 1932 lamented the fact that branches would be closed on a five-month rotation plan until the financial situation improved. The public libraries in St. Louis and Los Angeles in 1931 as well as Cleveland in 1932, all having the resources to maintain at least minimal service, saw a silver lining in the economic thundercloud hovering over the nation.

The Cleveland Public Library commented that "in times of depression and unemployment, the use of the library increases in inverse ratio to the decrease in business and industry." The Los Angeles Public Library noted that attendance at free lectures and exhibits "flourished in this year of surplus leisure." In the final analysis, the St. Louis Public Library assessed that "the unemployment problem has proved to be an unwitting boon to the adult education movement."[35]

Throughout these destitute years, the ALA CWFB concentrated its efforts on publishing bibliographies to aid in the selection and acquisition of foreign language books. The committee was particularly interested in books that would introduce immigrants to the United States, its politics and government, its economy and geography, and its cultural and educational opportunities. In cooperation with the editorial staff of *Booklist*, the ALA CWFB published at least twenty-three bibliographies in nineteen different foreign languages during the period from 1937 to 1941. Once again, the languages treated were primarily, although not exclusively, Indo-European, including Armenian, Croatian, Czech, Danish, Dutch, Finnish, French, German, Greek, Hungarian, Italian, Norwegian, Polish, Portuguese, Russian, Serbian, Spanish, Swedish, and Yiddish.[36]

Despite the partial success of the *Booklist* bibliographies, librarians in 1940 and again in 1941 had begun to complain to the ALA CWFB that they were having great difficulties acquiring the titles listed in the bibliographies. By 1942, the publication of this series of bibliographies was suspended for the duration of World War II, never to be revived. The librarians at the Queens Borough Public Library in 1944 expressed a related concern. They decried ramifications of the concomitant paper shortage, resulting in the poor grade of paper, print, and binding used in the limited materials available.[37]

By the late 1930s, libraries acknowledged with universal gratitude the help that came to them through the federal manpower programs, notably the Public Works Administration (PWA), the Works Progress Administration (WPA), and the National Youth Administration (NYA). For many libraries, these manpower programs made it possible for them not only to survive but also to initiate creative programs for the immigrant community.

In 1937, the Queens Borough Public Library, in cooperation with the Board of Education of the City of New York and the WPA, operated centers for continuing education that offered courses in French, Italian, and Spanish. The Denver Public

Library in 1940 reported that an NYA project had grown into a library station in the Community Vocational Center, which served largely Spanish and Negro youth.[38]

New Deal Era Library Publications and Projects

Undoubtedly the most creative and valuable by-products of these federal programs were the bibliographical works and microfilm collections produced, notably by the Chicago Public Library Omnibus Project, which was active from 1940 to 1943. Two of the by-products of the overall Omnibus Project focused on the history of the immigrant communities in Chicago. The first, the "Bibliography of Foreign Language Publications," identified 1,400 newspapers and periodicals in thirty-four foreign languages, which were published in Chicago during the period from 1840 to 1940. The second was the Chicago Foreign Language Press Survey, which involved the translation, indexing, and microfilming of articles from newspapers of twenty-two different foreign language groups on the social, cultural, economic, religious, and political life of the national and ethnic groups in Chicago.[39]

Changes in Administration of Foreign Language Collections

The foreign language department, as an integral administrative unit for foreign language materials and services to immigrant clienteles, was initiated in some libraries. In others it underwent a variety of transformations, including incorporation into new or already existing divisions. The Queens Borough Public Library in 1928 announced the establishment of the Central Foreign Collection.

This change marked the third stage in the development of circulation services for foreign language books. The first stage had been the maintenance of permanent foreign language collections in the various branches, and the second stage had involved the transferal of these collections to a central reserve collection, from which individual branches were provided with foreign language books through deposit collections. The Buffalo Public Library in 1930 announced the opening of its Foreign Language Department, to be administered by "one who for some years held the position of Italian consul in Buffalo."[40]

On the other hand, the Providence Public Library in 1934 shocked the library community by announcing the discontinuance of its Foreign Department as a separate entity and its incorporation as the Foreign Language Division of the Reference Department in early 1935. The justification was all too apparent. "Taking into consideration the disappearing flow of immigrants into our country, the small number interested in foreign languages who use the Foreign Department as a reading room, and the growing circulation for foreign language books throughout the branches situated in areas of foreign born population, it has been decided to discontinue the Foreign Department as a department, continuing Central Library service through the Circulation Department and emphasizing branch service."[41]

Before 1924 the standard practice in libraries serving large immigrant clienteles had been to hire library assistants who were conversant in the language spoken in the neighborhoods served by local branches. These assistants were employed to help immigrants find materials in the library as well as to make home visits in the immigrant community. After 1924, the emergent trend was the employment of field representatives, whose primary duty was to go out into the community to establish contacts and relationships with both the inhabitants of the immigrant community and the professional agencies serving immigrant clienteles.

The Denver Public Library in 1927 reported that the field representative there had designed a library card giving the location of the main building and all branches as well as a short list of books on U.S. history and citizenship. The list was supplied to federal authorities to distribute to immigrants seeking to become naturalized citizens. The Cleveland Public Library in 1939 employed Elsa Z. Posell, an immigrant citizen, as a field representative to publicize library resources and services to social welfare agencies, labor unions, ethnic and national societies, and various professional organizations. As late as 1947, the Jersey City Public Library reported that its public relations director had attended the induction of new citizens at the Naturalization Court and explained the services of the library.[42]

Despite the shrinking number of immigrants and the changing composition of the immigrant tide, however, libraries continued unabatedly to strengthen their collections in the foreign languages of the earlier and especially the recent immigrants. They began to build collections in the languages of immigrants from the Western Hemisphere and from Asia. During a systematic effort to strengthen the collection of Yiddish books, the New York Public Library in 1927 discovered ironically that the most fruitful source of Yiddish literature was no longer Poland or the United States. The most fruitful sources were Latin American countries, where the eastern European Jews denied admittance to the United States had immigrated.

The New Orleans Public Library in 1939 announced that through the donations of the Pro Libro Espanol committee, the nucleus of an important collection of books and pamphlets on Latin America had been formed. The Enoch Pratt Free Library of Baltimore in 1941 expressed gratitude to a professor of Spanish literature at Johns Hopkins University for helping to develop the collection of Spanish books. Librarians noted that this newly updated collection was fulfilling the demand for novels on Latin American countries written in Spanish and Portuguese or in good English translations.

The Los Angeles Public Library in 1930 reported the building of a Japanese collection. This collection was made possible through the donations of a patron who had lived several years in Japan. Later, in 1938, the Los Angeles Public Library reported the strengthening of collections in not only Japanese but also Chinese and Spanish.[43]

Acquisition of Foreign Language Materials

Following the example set in the mid–1920s by world travelers Eleanor (Edwards) Ledbetter and Edna Phillips of the ALA CWFB, several libraries encouraged their librarians to purchase foreign language books in the country of their publication. In 1925, during one of her trips to eastern and southern Europe, Ledbetter purchased books in Croatian, Czech, Polish, Serbian, Slovak, and Slovenian for the Cleveland Public Library, and on a commission basis for other public libraries. The Denver Public Library in 1931 and the Brooklyn Public Library in 1932 reported that their librarians had purchased books in foreign languages abroad for their respective collections while traveling in England, France, Germany, eastern Europe, and Scandinavia.

During the Great Depression, the public libraries in both New York and Cleveland in 1934 remarked on the crippling effect of the high rate of foreign exchange and shrinking library budgets on the building of their respective foreign language collections. The New York Public Library in 1939 lamented the fact that all its efforts to strengthen foreign language collections had been thwarted by the new and unexpected expense of war-risk insurance for transatlantic shipments. This, coupled with the British and French embargo against German shipments and the total collapse of communications with established institutions, governmental bureaus, and book dealers in central and eastern Europe, together brought all such efforts to a virtual standstill.[44]

Reference Services

Reference services both for the adult immigrant community as well as for the general public called for familiarity with foreign languages and foreign cultures. The materials collected expressly for the immigrant community were now filling needs for the community at large.

In 1928, the St. Louis Public Library reported with pride that the Soulard Branch was able to supply the music to the national song of Bohemia for one of its patrons, who was to sing it on radio within the hour. The Detroit Public Library in 1929 reported that translating for General Motors and other automobile manufacturing companies was done by the public library. In 1933, the Los Angeles Public Library reported that librarians there had been kept busy translating suitable slogans and greetings for advertisers, newspaper writers, and other agents involved in publicizing and reporting the activities of the Olympic Games of 1932. The Los Angeles Public Library noted that it supplied information to motion picture studios on foreign customs in 1934, translated a letter from the Vatican in 1937, and supplied in foreign languages mottoes and greetings to manufacturers of greeting cards and proper foreign words to novelists and playwrights in 1938. Because of its proximity to Broadway and the headquarters of national and international businesses, the New York Public Library in 1931 commented that theater groups, film producers, and publishing house representatives were using their collections increasingly as a source from which to draw materials for productions, publications, and translations.[45]

Library Services for Children

Children's services programs after 1924 reflected most markedly the shift from Americanization to internationalism and cultural pluralism. The New York Public Library in 1927 reported that the Spanish-speaking storyteller at the 115th Street Branch captivated the interests of fathers and mothers as well as their children.

The Denver Public Library in 1928 displayed a Japanese friendship doll received as a gift from Japan to symbolize the "friendship link between American children and Japanese children." Later, in 1931, the Denver Public Library displayed a collection of Mexican artifacts received as a friendship gift from children of Mexico. Denver's own Eric Philbrook Kelly received the 1929 Newbery Medal for the best children's book for his *Trumpeter of Krakow*. He arranged for the display of the original trumpet to delight not only Denver children of Polish descent but also children of all national and ethnic groups represented in the city's population.[46]

The travel theme was a particularly popular way to introduce children to different countries, cultures, and languages. In 1929, the Los Angeles Public Library sponsored a Passport Reading summer program. That same year, the Rice Branch of the Cleveland Public Library sponsored a World Cruise Travel Club. This activity afforded children the opportunity to dress in the costumes of different national and ethnic groups and to listen to a talk by librarian May (McDaniel) Sweet, a nationally recognized expert on Italian literature who had recently returned from a trip to Italy.

In 1931, the Boston Public Library and also the Denver Public Library sponsored an Around the World in Books reading program, where children received passports on which were written the names of the books they read and reported on orally. The St. Louis Public Library in 1931 compiled a list entitled "World Friendship through Children's Books." In 1935, the Buffalo Public Library reported that translations of Mark Twain's *The Adventures of Huckleberry Finn* had been purchased in Dutch, Finnish, French, German, Lettish, Norwegian, Russian, Serbian, Swedish, and Ukrainian.[47]

The Children's Crusade for Children, sponsored by author Dorothy (Canfield) Fisher, was the most notable event of 1940 in children's services in the public libraries of metropolitan New York. This crusade grew out of the concern of Vermont children for the plight of homeless European children, both refugees and displaced persons, who came to Vermont in 1939. The Vermont children sent the contents of a penny bank to Fisher with instructions to use the money to help the more unfortunate children who could not come to America.

Fisher, in turn, took the idea to leading educators in both public and private schools. Small collection cans were placed in classrooms throughout the five boroughs of New York and in the New York, New Jersey, and Connecticut suburbs. Similarly, the Treasure Chest campaign, sponsored in New York in 1945, carried the theme of concern for international issues forward by raising money for children's books to be selected by American children and sent to children in war-torn Europe.[48]

Adult Immigrant Services

The promotion of internationalism pervaded adult services in public libraries as well. In 1929, the Cleveland Public Library established an International Mind Alcove, which was stocked with books on international affairs and on the customs, art, culture, government, and politics of foreign nations and peoples. By 1933, the New York Public Library reported that the recognition of the Soviet Union by the United States stimulated a demand for Russian grammars and manuals of Russian business correspondence. In addition, the wave of anti-Semitic sentiment abroad in Europe had intensified the desires of patrons to gain familiarity with Jewish literature and with the so-called Jewish question in Germany.

In 1943, the Cleveland Public Library opened the Intercultural Library to display exhibits on cultural backgrounds of Clevelanders and to provide an appropriate setting for bringing together various national and ethnic groups for dialogues. That same year, the Chicago Public Library noted that the phenomenon of Americans learning foreign languages, especially Spanish, Russian, and Chinese and other Oriental tongues, was widespread among "forward-looking students."

The New York Public Library in 1944 reported the activities of the East and West Association, which was chaired by Pearl Buck. The library cooperated in a joint effort "to foster an understanding through books, music, and art of the culture of other countries." By 1945, the Carnegie Library of Pittsburgh had established a Public Affairs Room and reported that twenty-six different national and ethnic groups contributed to the first exhibit of arts and crafts held there.[49]

Lecture series, educational forums, book fairs, and film festivals were arranged and presented by libraries to encourage internationalism and the mingling of native- and foreign-born citizens. In 1927, the Los Angeles Public Library instituted a lecture series in modern languages, which continued into the 1940s. Professors from the University of California at Los Angeles gave many of the lectures in Spanish, French, and German. Lectures in Italian were given under the auspices of the Dante Alighieri Society, and lectures in Yiddish were given under the auspices of the Jewish Culture Society.

In 1929, the Brooklyn Public Library sponsored lectures and art exhibitions for Italian immigrants "to break down the barrier of fear towards our institutions that seems to exist among the foreign element." That same year, the Cleveland Public Library branch housed in the Alta House settlement sponsored an Italian book fair, which received favorable comment in the Italian newspapers of not only Cleveland but also New York, Philadelphia, and even Rome.

The Denver Public Library in 1929 coordinated the mounting of exhibits of antiques from the Denver Art Museum in each library branch. The exhibit for each library branch featured arts and crafts typical of the national or ethnic community it served. Polish, Russian, Austrian, and Czechoslovakian artifacts were displayed at the Globeville Branch, while Jewish and Dutch artifacts were displayed respectively at the Dickinson Branch and the Decker Branch.[50]

In 1935, the Chicago Public Library reported the biweekly meetings of a forum at the Toman Branch, which served a primarily Czechoslovakian clientele. Years later, in 1946, the Chicago librarians announced that the Informational Films program, which had begun during World War II, was being replaced by a series of documentary films on the peoples of the world. Attracting large attendance from various ethnic and national groups throughout the Chicago area, the film series "was designed to emphasize the similarities among the peoples of the world as a contribution to inter-cultural understanding."[51]

ALA Committee on Work with the Foreign Born

Publicity for library work with immigrants was a particularly strong emphasis of the ALA CWFB, especially under the leadership of Eleanor (Edwards) Ledbetter, during the mid-1920s. Ledbetter and her successors as chair of the ALA CWFB encouraged cooperation with the foreign language newspaper press, which ironically was fighting for its own survival. In a desperate attempt to hold their readership, many foreign language newspapers were beginning to publish articles in parallel columns of English alongside the foreign language of the immigrant community.

Advertisement of Library Materials and Services for Immigrants. From the 1930s through 1948, the ALA CWFB increasingly encouraged libraries to take advantage of technological advances in nonprint communications, notably radio, for library publicity, although the print media, including signs, flyers, and brochures, were not to be abandoned. In 1941, Italian-born radio announcer Lisa Sergio addressed the joint meeting of the ALA CWFB and the Adult Education Round Table on "The Importance of Interpreting America."[52]

Most public libraries relied on a combination of print and nonprint media for publicity. In 1925, the Boston Public Library reported that patrons were taking advantage of the public showers, which were located in the same building as the Mount Pleasant Branch. After they had finished their showers, library patrons were greeted by a cheery sign that read: "After the shower, why not a book? The library is just around the corner!" In 1928, the Los Angeles Public Library began a series of weekly half-hour book talks aired by a local radio station.

As late as 1935, the Enoch Pratt Free Library of Baltimore reported that the same information on children's reading that appeared in local newspapers was broadcast over the radio in programs sponsored by the library, the Child Study Association, and the Jewish Educational Alliance. In 1931, the Buffalo Public Library acknowledged the assistance of local radio stations in announcing library news. Later, in 1940, the Buffalo Public Library noted with pride that the scrapbook of the library's Public Relations Committee contained 224 items, which totaled eighty-nine columns of library news clipped from local English and foreign language newspapers. While libraries throughout the country were experimenting with radio and moving picture show advertising, the Brooklyn Public Library in 1933 admitted its ambivalence. The library commented that "the 'movies' and the radio have a great deal to do with forming habits diametrically opposed to those necessary to the reader."[53]

Cooperation among Libraries

From 1924 onward, the ALA CWFB worked to build cooperative networks for the sharing of information and expertise at the national, international, local, and state levels. The committee sought to establish continuing education opportunities, including classes within the curricula of library schools and series of programs and workshops at state and national library association conventions. Although examples of international library cooperation were infrequent, a notable example occurred, in 1930, at the Enoch Pratt Free Library of Baltimore, where Margaret Demchevsky, library organizer of the Ministry of Education, Bulgaria, spent two days studying the branch system.[54]

Cooperation between local libraries working with immigrant clienteles was more commonly reported. During the late 1920s, the ALA CWFB reported that a traveling expert in the cataloging of foreign language books who was employed by the Detroit Public Library had been borrowed by the Cleveland Public Library. The Chicago Public Library had distributed extra copies of its catalog cards to the Milwaukee Public Library.

In 1926, the Los Angeles Public Library sent a questionnaire concerning cataloging practices for foreign language books to several large eastern and northern libraries. The results of the survey showed that the Foreign Department of the Los Angeles Public Library was growing rapidly in comparison with these libraries and that its cataloging practices were standard. The Foreign Department librarian at the Providence Public Library was granted a nine-month leave of absence in 1931 to "study foreign languages at Boston University" and to "supplement this by practical experience in several of the branches of the Boston Public Library situated in the centers of foreign born populations." The arrival of several hundred German Jewish refugees in 1939 prompted the Enoch Pratt Free Library of Baltimore to publish a pamphlet on learning English, Americanization classes and activities, vocations, and educational opportunities. The pamphlet was shared with the Free Library of Philadelphia and later adopted for use with the refugee community in Philadelphia.[55]

Cooperation in Services to Immigrants

Cooperative efforts at the state and regional levels usually involved the co-ordination of the work of state library commissions and the committees of the state library associations, which were responsible for providing and improving library service to the immigrant community. The most dynamic of the cooperative ventures of this type occurred between the Massachusetts Free Public Library Commission and the Massachusetts Library Club's Committee on Work with New Americans, later called the Committee on Interracial Service. Together, they maintained a statewide traveling library collection of foreign language books. Although not as extensive or intensive, other statewide efforts of this nature were reported by public libraries in Michigan, New Jersey, New York, and Pennsylvania.[56]

Both the cooperative efforts at the state level and the transformations in library service at the local level began in the immigrant neighborhoods themselves and eventually affected citywide library administrative patterns. The constant shifting of centers of population and the changing makeup of urban neighborhoods directly affected immigrant branches.

Immigrant branches, which were originally established for one particular national or ethnic group, were often devoid of a single patron who spoke the language represented prominently in its collection. These same branches were suddenly surrounded by a new community of immigrants who clamored for books in languages that were either not available at all or available in insufficient quantities to meet the demand. In 1930, the librarian of the Brownsville Branch of the Brooklyn Public Library noted that "many of the Jewish people have prospered and risen in the social scale. They have gradually acquired a right sort of Americanization. Most of these have moved into East Flatbush for more breathing space and a plot of ground of their own. Many of those remaining are poor and less ambitious readers."[57]

As early as 1928, the St. Louis Public Library had noticed that in former Bohemian neighborhoods where church announcements and sermons had been delivered in Czech, English was now the language most often heard. Later, in 1937, St. Louis librarians reported that Americanization teachers in the day and evening programs were educating foreigners away from reading at all in their native languages.

By 1945, the St. Louis Public Library used its collection of fiction in foreign languages less frequently than during the first two decades of the twentieth century. The librarians there concluded that with the decline in immigration, the number of readers of foreign languages had also declined. They observed that "the second-generation Americans read their fiction in English."[58]

The Chicago Public Library in 1943 pondered the eventuality that "the maintenance of foreign language sections as such in American public libraries will tend to diminish in importance, although the significant literature in any language and any field will always receive due attention as additions to the library's general resources." In 1947, the Queens Borough Public Library renamed its Foreign Collection. The new Language Department would not only emphasize the inclusion of audiovisual materials as well as books, but also draw attention to the unit as an intercultural and interracial resource.[59]

Second-Generation and Subsequent Generation Immigrants

The reading habits of the American immigrant community were affected by the rapid assimilation of the second and subsequent generations. In 1930, the Chicago Public Library reported the results of a survey that documented a "growing indifference among our foreign-born patrons toward the periodical literature in their native languages." Six years later, in 1936, Chicago librarians discovered that this phenomenon was true as well for other types of foreign language materials. They noted that "the circle of readers interested in keeping up a knowledge of the literary products of their native tongues is obviously contracting, chiefly, perhaps, because of immigration restrictions and the rapid assimilation of the foreign-born and their succeeding generations in this country into American ways of life and habits of thought." One year later, in 1937, the Chicago Public Library admitted that "this branch of public library service is definitely on the decline."[60]

In 1939, the Foreign Language Department of the Detroit Public Library reported that

the character of the reading done is considerably different from that of the days when the reading circle was largely composed of recent immigrants. We are now dealing more frequently with the second generation and certain language-minded Americans: the older recreational literature, with a flavor of national sentiment, is less in demand. The patronage now is made up of intellectuals representing various foreign races and their local organized groups. Their attitude toward America is clearer, more searching, while at the same time they are endeavoring to understand the upheavals and group demands in other parts of the world.

Similar observations had been made in 1936 by the Los Angeles Public Library, where a survey had revealed "a decided trend toward the greater cultural rather than recreational use of foreign books."[61]

Continuing Education for Libraries Working with Immigrants

In the 1930s and into the 1940s, under the leadership of Edna Phillips, the ALA CWFB began to address the library needs of Filipino and Mexican immigrants. The Round Table for Work with the Foreign Born, held at the 1930 ALA conference in Los Angeles, featured as keynote speaker Emory Stephen Bogardus, the eminent sociologist and professor at the University of Southern California. He addressed the group on the background and future of immigration from Mexico and the Philippines.[62] Phillips and the ALA CWFB embraced Bogardus's progressive attitude toward immigration.

The Los Angeles Public Library in 1941 reported that the disruption in travel in and trade with Europe during World War II had drawn public attention increasingly to Latin America. That same year, the Enoch Pratt Free Library of Baltimore reported its cooperation with the Good Neighbor program sponsored by the U.S. Department of State and the Pan-American Union. The library promoted and supported a series of public lectures by South and Central American leaders in literature, education, and diplomacy.[63]

Services for Refugees and Displaced Persons

Beginning in the early 1930s and continuing after World War II, the plight of European refugees and displaced persons not only aroused deep-seated emotions among librarians but also created a new, highly visible clientele. In 1934, the New York Public Library noted the increase in refugee borrowers and commented that "book selection is manifestly complicated by the widespread interests of a cultivated group and by the increased cost of foreign books."

By 1938, New York librarians commented that refugees from central Europe "almost immediately upon arrival seek the Library for information about social and economic conditions, and for help generally in adjusting themselves to their new surroundings." That same year, the New York Public Library noted that the district of Washington Heights had been dubbed the Fourth Reich, since more than five thousand refugees had settled there.

In 1939, the Newark Public Library commented that educated refugees attended the evening school classes long enough to gain some facility with the English language and then dropped out because the general work was far too elementary for them. Public libraries in Chicago in 1938, Baltimore in 1939, and New Orleans in 1941, reported on their services offered and publications prepared to assist refugees. The Queens Borough Public Library as late as 1948 reported cooperation with the American Jewish Joint Distribution Committee to secure books for displaced persons.[64]

The employment of refugees and displaced persons was problematic throughout the United States, but most particularly in New York and other large urban centers, where a majority of them clustered. During the early 1940s, the ALA CWFB worked in close contact with the ALA Committee on Refugee Librarians, both chaired by Jennie Maas Flexner, readers' adviser with the New York Public Library. Together, they assumed as their mission to identify, retrain if necessary, and place refugee librarians in suitable positions for which they qualified in American libraries.[65] In 1942, the New York Public Library stressed the fact that "refugees from Hitler's brutality have become some of the Library's most loyal readers. Their curiosity about things American seems insatiable. Both parents and children are rapidly becoming Americanized and read mostly books in English. The war has possibly speeded up the process of Americanization and given them an added impetus to become assimilated."[66]

Although finding employment opportunities for refugees in general, and refugee librarians specifically, was quite difficult, libraries across the country reported some successful matches of refugee talent and library needs. In 1941, the Providence Public Library appointed as a cataloger a refugee from Czechoslovakia with experience and training in Europe and at Simmons College in Boston. The New York Public Library in 1942 received assistance from clerical workers supplied by the National Refugee Service.[67]

Censorship and Patriotism during World War II

The fact that library censorship had occurred during World War I was manifested in the concerns voiced by librarians across the nation, when the entry of the United States into World War II was imminent. These concerned librarians implored their colleagues not to tolerate violation of the First Amendment right to free speech. In 1936, well before World War II began, the Chicago Public Library had reported censorship attempts, ironically, by Russian and Polish immigrant groups, who objected to the contents of certain books declared to be either communistic or pornographic. In 1938, the Detroit Public Library reminded its community that "censorship and timidity are as impractical as gullibility and easy acceptance. May we not hope that integrity and independent judgment may be enhanced if we face realities unemotionally and observe loyalty to our own individual vision."[68]

After World War II began, all libraries collecting materials in European languages experienced censorship from outside their walls, censorship literally beyond their control. In 1939, the New York Public Library reported with dismay the fact that French and German periodicals were received with some blank pages bearing the single word "censored" printed across the center, instead of the article that was clearly listed in the table of contents. In other cases, entire paragraphs were omitted from articles.

In fact, many libraries had successfully resisted censorship efforts, even during World War I. This was made clear by the Providence Public Library in 1940: "[I]t is to be hoped that the attempted censorship of library shelves of the last war will not be repeated in this one. . . . It called for courage to resist those articulate self-appointed censors who attempted to rid library shelves of any printed matter concerned with the enemy, even his history, his art or his literature. Similar vision and fortitude may be required during the months or years ahead."[69]

After the United States entered World War II, public libraries throughout the country became not only the clearinghouse for war information for the general public, but also the agency where immigrants desiring employment in the war-related industries turned for certification. In 1940, the public libraries of Cleveland and Philadelphia both assisted foreign-born citizens in locating the names of steamships in which they had landed. This vital information was needed to apply for citizenship. Even citizens, both native- and foreign-born, needed these certificates in order to be eligible for employment in defense industries. The Enoch Pratt Free Library of Baltimore in 1941 reported a flurry of queries about where to obtain birth certificates. In 1942, the Buffalo Public Library supplied 3,560 certificates that proved certain names appeared in specific city directories with a place of residence.[70]

The Detroit Public Library in 1942 coordinated the distribution and routing of information released daily by various governmental and civilian wartime agencies. The library helped to prove that since European political boundaries had changed so drastically, most immigrants could not possibly be classed as enemy aliens.

The Los Angeles Public Library established a Wartime Information Desk, which opened 18 December 1941, within two weeks of the bombing of Pearl Harbor by the Japanese. Margaret Gabriel Hickman of the Foreign Department, formerly chair of the ALA CWFB, was given responsibility for organizing this service.

The Louisville Free Public Library in 1943 followed suit by establishing a War Information Center as a division of the Reference Department. The increased interest in the study of foreign languages prompted by wartime conditions was reported by the public libraries in Pittsburgh in 1944 and in Baltimore as late as 1945.[71]

Treatment of Japanese-Americans during World War II

With one notable exception, the public library community was strangely silent on the topic of the internment of Japanese-Americans during the course of World War II. In keeping with the pattern of exclusion and exceptions for Oriental immigrants, first-generation Japanese immigrants were not allowed to become naturalized citizens. Their children, however, were American citizens at birth. A further irony was that many American citizens of Japanese descent were interned along with their parents.

In 1942, the Publicity Committee of the ALA Section for Library Work with Children sponsored a symposium that addressed the issue of library service to Japanese-Americans on the Pacific Coast during wartime. Zada Taylor, children's librarian of the Los Angeles Public Library, presented a talk entitled "War Children on the Pacific." She shared her experiences in Los Angeles as well as responses from children's librarians in Fresno, Pasadena, San Diego, and San Francisco.

Taylor also shared reactions from Japanese-American students, American citizens by right of their birth, about their evacuation to and experiences at the Manzanar internment camp in eastern California near Death Valley. Ironically, the responses of the Japanese-American students were uniformly understanding of the treatment they received given the circumstances, particularly in the aftermath of the bombing of Pearl Harbor. Responses from the children's librarians were a mixed bag, however, ranging from sympathy for the internees and questioning of the need for such drastic action to total agreement with the decision to isolate the Japanese immigrant community for the sake of national security. The ALA CWFB made no official statement regarding the internment of Japanese-Americans.[72]

After World War II, public libraries, particularly those in large urban centers, reported increasingly the changing nature of their immigrant clienteles, both according to places of origin and educational levels. The New York Public Library in 1945 reported cooperation with the Committee for Refugee Education, which sponsored classes held in branches, and commented that "with new immigration quotas assigned, it is expected that this need to teach English to the foreign-born will become as great as in prewar years." That same year, the cooperation of the Aguilar Branch of the New York Public Library and the United Neighborhood Houses resulted in the establishment in East Harlem of the Aguilar Lounge for young people fourteen to seventeen years of age, mainly Puerto Ricans, Native Americans, and African Americans. The Chicago Public Library in 1946 noted the phenomenon of war brides seeking to combat nostalgia for their European homelands by reading books in their native tongues, including Belgian, Danish, Dutch, French, Hungarian, Italian, Polish, and Russian.[73]

All these changes were, as always, reflections of what was transpiring in American society at large. Nowhere was the change more apparent than in library work with the immigrant community. The cause of this fundamental reshaping of American society was the strict adherence to the National Origins Act of 1924, which reduced the former flood of European immigration to a mere trickle while increasing opportunities for immigration from throughout the Western Hemisphere. The effects on public library service to adult immigrants were a broadening of emphasis from exclusively immigrant education to the more inclusive concept of adult education and the inculcation of a spirit of tolerance and internationalism as opposed to provincialism and Americanism.

Disbanding the ALA CWFB

The ALA CWFB had witnessed these changes and tried constantly to adapt to them. As early as 1928, there was a move to upgrade from committee to section status, but it was deferred while the ALA executive staff considered, but never decided upon, the feasibility of creating at ALA headquarters a department for work with the foreign born.

By 1935, the ALA CWFB members began to question the appropriateness of the phrase "work with the foreign born," since the majority of their work was for the benefit of American-born children of foreign descent, and very rarely for the foreign born themselves. Consequently, there was a second call to upgrade from committee to section status and to consider a name change to the ALA Section for Interracial Service, although neither came to pass. The fact that in 1941 the ALA CWFB met jointly with the Adult Education Round Table was a further indication of the relatedness and overlapping of purpose of the organizations, but the former was never absorbed by the latter.

In 1945, since the emphases of the ALA CWFB had become internationalism and interculturalism, there was serious consideration given to a change in name to the ALA Committee on Intercultural Relations in the United States. Three years later, in 1948, the name of the ALA CWFB was officially changed to the ALA Committee on Intercultural Action. Although the ALA Committee on Intercultural Action existed from 1948/49 through 1956/57, at which time its duties and responsibilities were dispersed throughout the already existing ALA divisions, its proceedings were never recorded, its activities never chronicled.[74]

CONCLUSION

The fate of the ALA CWFB represented in microcosm the fate of library service to immigrants throughout the country. Its mission to Americanize the foreign born was eventually subsumed by the movement to educate the adult community. Finally, the committee found its niche within the movement to internationalize the citizenry of the United States.

The evolution of the ALA CWFB was indicative as well of the public library. Throughout this evolutionary process of trying to serve the needs of the immigrant community, the American public library began to come to grips with its inchoate mission to empower people to become full participants in the dynamics of a pluralistic society.

NOTES

1. Maldwyn Allen Jones, *American Immigration* (Chicago: University of Chicago Press, 1960), 279; John Higham, *Send These to Me: Immigrants in Urban America*, rev. ed. (Baltimore: Johns Hopkins University Press, 1984), chap. 2: "The Politics of Restriction," 29–70 passim; and Maxine Seller, *To Seek America: A History of Ethnic Life in the United States* (Englewood, NJ: Jerome S. Ozer, 1977), 217–19.

2. Jones, *American Immigration*, 177–83; and Seller, *To Seek America*, 217–18.

3. European emigrants represented 1,942,470, or 54 percent of the total of 3,595,472 immigrants entering the United States in the twenty-five-year period from 1924 through 1948. Calculated using the table "Immigrants, by Country: 1820 to 1970," in U.S. Department of Commerce, Bureau of the Census, *Historical Statistics of the United States: Colonial Times to 1970*, part 1, Bicentennial edition (Washington, DC: GPO, 1975), 105.

4. Jones, *American Immigration*, 278.

5. Ibid., 287–79; and Seller, *To Seek America*, 255.

6. *Historical Statistics of the United States*, part 1, 107.

7. Jones, *American Immigration*, 289; and Higham, *Send These to Me*, 57.

8. Jones, *American Immigration*, 290; Seller, *To Seek America*, 245–55; and John Bodnar, *The Transplanted: A History of Immigrants in Urban America* (Bloomington: Indiana University Press, 1985), 22–23, 70–71.

9. *Historical Statistics of the United States*, part 1, 107.

10. Jones, *American Immigration*, 291–93.

11. Ibid., 289–90. For accounts on Canadianization of immigrants, see Mrs. Norman Lyle, "Report of the O.L.A. [Ontario Library Association] Committee on Books for the Foreign Born," *Ontario Library Review* 15 (May 1931): 165–68; George H. Knight, "Our Library Problem," *Ontario Library Review* 16 (Nov. 1931): 48–49; and A. Lustig, "A Newcomer to Canada Looks at the Library," *Ontario Library Review* 26 (May 1942): 194–96.

12. Jones, *American Immigration*, 293–97; and Seller, *To Seek America*, 255–63.

13. Jones, *American Immigration*, 279–80; and Seller, *To Seek America*, 263–65.

14. *Historical Statistics of the United States*, part 1, 105.

15. Jones, *American Immigration*, 281.

16. Jones, *American Immigration*, 280–83; and Seller, *To Seek America*, 263–65.

17. Jones, *American Immigration*, 283, 300–303.

18. Ibid., 303–5; Higham, *Send These to Me*, 170–71; and Seller, *To Seek America*, 235–36.

19. Jones, *American Immigration*, 283–84; and Seller, *To Seek America*, 264.

20. Jones, *American Immigration*, 284–85; and Seller, *To Seek America*, 264.

21. Jones, *American Immigration*, 285–86; and Higham, *Send These to Me*, 61, 64.

22. Jones, *American Immigration*, 299–300, 305–6; Higham, *Send These to Me*, 170–71; and Seller, *To Seek America*, 249–50.

23. Jones, *American Immigration*, 297–98, 307. See also Will Herberg, *Protestant, Catholic, Jew; An Essay in American Religious Sociology* (Garden City, NJ: Doubleday, 1955).

24. Jones, *American Immigration*, 306; and Bodnar, *The Transplanted*, 198–201.

25. Jones, *American Immigration*, 298–99; Seller, *To Seek America*, 232; and John Bodnar, "Schooling and the Slavic-American Family, 1900–1940," in *American Education and the European Immigrant: 1840-1940*, ed. by Bernard J. Weiss (Urbana: University of Illinois Press, 1982), 87–91.

26. Carnegie Library of Pittsburgh, AR 1925, 11; and St. Louis Public Library, AR 1927/28, 80. See also "A Hot Bed of Citizenship," *WLB* 2 (June 1924): 246–48; and Vera

Morgan, "Expanding the Small Library's Contact with New Americans," *ALA Bulletin* 22 (Sept. 1928): 474–75.

27. *Libraries and Adult Education: Report of a Study Made by the American Library Association* (Chicago: ALA, 1926), 7–10, 172–76 (quote, 173). See also "Libraries and the Adult Foreign Born," *Interpreter Release Clip Sheet* no. 13 (18 Oct. 1926): 1–3.

28. Cleveland Public Library, AR 1924/25, 26, AR 1926, 28 (quote), AR 1928, 91–92.

29. Detroit Public Library, AR 1926/27, 12.

30. American Library Association, *A Survey of Libraries in the United States*, 4 vols. (Chicago: ALA, 1926–1927). See also Cleveland Public Library, AR 1924/25, 31; and *WLB* 2 (Oct. 1924): 298.

31. ALA, *A Survey of Libraries in the United States*, 3:218–59.

32. William M. Randall, "What Can the Foreigner Find to Read in the Public Library?" *Library Quarterly* 1 (Jan. 1931): 79–88; and Detroit Public Library, AR 1931/32, 9.

33. Eleanor E. Ledbetter, *The Polish Immigrant and His Reading*, Library Work with the Foreign Born (Chicago: ALA, 1924); May M. Sweet, *The Italian Immigrant and His Reading*, Library Work with the Foreign Born (Chicago: ALA, 1925); Alison B. Alessios, *The Greek Immigrant and His Reading*, Library Work with the Foreign Born (Chicago: ALA: 1926); and Melitta D. Peschke, *The German Immigrant and His Reading*, Library Work with the Foreign Born (Chicago: ALA, 1929). See also ALA CWFB Minutes, *ALA Bulletin* 18 (Aug. 1924): 249–50, *ALA Bulletin* 19 (July 1925): 220–21, and *ALA Bulletin* (Oct. 1926): 399–400.

34. *Reading Service to the Foreign Born*, compiled by the Committee on Work with the Foreign Born of the American Library Association (Chicago: ALA, 1929). See also Constantine Panunzio [Associate Director of the Foreign Language Information Service], "The Immigrant and the Library," *LJ* 49 (15 Nov. 1924): 969–73; "The Foreign Language Information Service," *LJ* 49 (15 Nov. 1924): 981; "Foreign Language Press Publicity," *LJ* 52 (1 June 1927): 603; and John Palmer Gavit, "Through Neighbors' Doorways," *Survey Graphic* 29 (Sept. 1940): 471–72, which explains the origins and development of the Foreign Language Information Service. The list of dealers, originally published in the pamphlet, was reprinted later as "Dealers in Foreign Books," *Pennsylvania Library Notes* 14 (July 1934): 438–41. Other articles on cataloging foreign language books, particularly those written in nonroman alphabets, were published during this period. These included "Cataloging Foreign Books, Seattle Plan," *Libraries* 32 (May 1927): 240–41; F. E. Sommer, "Books in Foreign Script in the Public Library," *LJ* 59 (15 Nov. 1934): 892–93; and Vi-Lien Wong, "Chinese Collections in American Libraries," *LJ* 60 (15 June 1935): 527–28.

35. Brooklyn Public Library, AR 1927, 38; Buffalo Public Library, AR 1932, 17; St. Louis Public Library, AR 1931/32, 42; Los Angeles Public Library, AR 1931/32, 21-22; and Cleveland Public Library, AR 1932, 1.

36. See, for example, the following bibliographies of languages other than Romance languages: Anthony J. Klancar, "Recent Serbian and Croatian Books," *Booklist* 33 (Mar. 1937): 222–23; Arthur Prudden Coleman, "Recent Polish Books," *Booklist* 33 (May 1937): 286; Ida M. Fritz, "Recent German Books," *Booklist* 34 (15 Nov. 1937): 115–16; Nadine Kovediaeff, "Recent Russian Books," *Booklist* 34 (15 Dec. 1937): 159–60; Evelyn R. Andrews, "Finnish Books," *Booklist* 34 (15 Feb. 1938): 238–39; A. B. Korman, "Yiddish Books," *Booklist* 34 (1 Apr. 1938): 292–93; Celia Udell, "Dutch Books," *Booklist* 34 (1 July 1938): 390–91, "Danish Books," *Booklist* 35 (15 July 1939): 385, "Norwegian Books," *Booklist* 36 (Sept. 1939): 20; Sol Matz, "Bohemian (Czech) Books," *Booklist* 35 (Aug. 1939): 391–92; Cecile F. Houghton, "Swedish Books," *Booklist* 36 (1 July 1940): 415–16; Augusta Markowitz, "Hungarian Books," *Booklist* 37 (1 Mar. 1941): 295–97; Lydia W.

Masters, "Armenian Books," *Booklist* 37 (15 Apr. 1941): 393–95; Alison B. Alessios, "Greek Books," *Booklist* 37 (15 July 1941): 554–56. See also ALA CWFB Minutes, *ALA Bulletin* 28 (June 1934): 363, (Sept. 1934): 723–31, *ALA Bulletin* 30 (May 1936): 420, *ALA Bulletin* 31 (Sept. 1937): 612, *ALA Bulletin* 32 (Sept. 1938): 640–41, (15 Oct. 1938): 984–85, *ALA Bulletin* 33 (Sept. 1939): 618, *ALA Bulletin* 34 (15 Sept. 1940): 582–83, *ALA Bulletin* 35 (15 Oct. 1941): 620; and Margery Quigley, "Encouraging Use of Foreign Books," *WLB* 14 (Jan. 1940): 392. Similar bibliographies, all prepared by foreign language experts, many of them members of the ALA CWFB, and the ALA CWFB itself, appeared in *LJ*. These included Ruth Cowgill, "Some Foreign Books of 1927 and 1928," *LJ* 53 (15 June 1928): 539–41; ALA CWFB Scandinavian Book Review Committee, "Danish Books for Libraries," *LJ* 58 (15 Feb. 1933): 173–74, "Norwegian Books for Libraries," *LJ* 59 (1 Feb. 1934): 117–18; Theodora B. Scoff and Michel S. Abourjaily, "Arabic Books for Libraries," *LJ* 59 (Aug. 1934): 609–10; Sarah Lawson and Anne Kallio, "Finnish Books," *LJ* 60 (1 Jan. 1935): 32–33; Greta Linder, "Swedish Books for American Libraries, 1932–33," *LJ* 60 (1 May 1935): 401–2; and Mary B. McLellan, "Contemporary Fiction in Polish," *LJ* 61 (15 Feb. 1936): 154–55.

    37. ALA CWFB Minutes, *ALA Bulletin* 34 (15 Sept. 1940): 582–83, *ALA Bulletin* 35 (15 Oct. 1941): 620, *ALA Bulletin* 36 (15 Sept. 1942): 128, (15 Oct. 1942): 675; and Queens Borough Public Library, AR 1943/44, 8.

    38. Queens Borough Public Library, AR 1937, 45; and Denver Public Library, AR 1939/40, 29–30.

    39. Alex Ladenson, "Chicago Public Library Omnibus Project," *LJ* 67 (1 Oct. 1942): 828–31.

    40. Queens Borough Public Library, AR 1928, 32; and Buffalo Public Library, AR 1930, 12. See also Edith Wirt, "English Speaking Readers in the Foreign Literature Division, Cleveland Public Library," *Libraries* 36 (July 1931): 305–6; and Margaret Hickman, "Why a Foreign Department in an American Public Library," *LJ* 57 (1 Apr. 1932): 327–29.

    41. Providence Public Library, AR 1934, 12. See also ALA CWFB Minutes, *ALA Bulletin* 34 (Aug. 1940): 224–25; and Karl Brown, "What Sells the Library," *LJ* 65 (15 Sept. 1940): 748–49.

    42. Denver Public Library, AR 1927, 18; Cleveland Public Library, AR 1939, 1; and Jersey City Public Library, AR 1945/47, 16. See also Elsa Z. Posell, "The Librarian Works with the Foreign Born," *ALA Bulletin* 35 (July 1941): 424–30.

    43. New York Public Library, AR 1927, 38; New Orleans Public Library, AR 1939, 25; Enoch Pratt Free Library of Baltimore, AR 1940/41, 46, AR 1942/45, 14–15; and Los Angeles Public Library, AR 1929/30, 19, AR 1937/38, 13. See also Ruth Cowgill, "Tendencies Today in Some of the European Literatures," *ALA Bulletin* 22 (Sept. 1928): 473; and Louis J. Bailey, "Standards and Tests in Evaluating Easy English Books for Adults," *ALA Bulletin* 22 (Sept. 1928): 473–74.

    44. ALA CWFB Minutes, *ALA Bulletin* 18 (Aug. 1924): 250, *ALA Bulletin* 20 (Oct. 1926): 400; Cleveland Public Library, AR 1924/25, 96, AR 1934, 1–2; Denver Public Library, AR 1931, 6; Brooklyn Public Library, AR 1932, 27; and New York Public Library, AR 1934, 13, AR 1939, 67.

    45. St. Louis Public Library, AR 1927/28, 79; Detroit Public Library, AR 1928/29, 11; Los Angeles Public Library, AR 1932/33, 14, AR 1933/34, 17, AR 1936/37, 14, AR 1937/38, 13; and New York Public Library, AR 1931, 77.

    46. New York Public Library, AR 1927, 64; and Denver Public Library, AR 1928, 14, AR 1929, 12, AR 1931, 12. See also Jean Lyman, "The Library Needs of the Foreign

Child," *WLB* 5 (May 1931): 581–83; and Irene Smith, "Human Side of Library Work with Foreign-Born Children," *LJ* 58 (1 Nov. 1933): 865–68.

47. Los Angeles Public Library, AR 1928/29, 33; Cleveland Public Library, AR 1929, 52; Boston Public Library, AR 1931, 46; Denver Public Library, AR 1931, 12; St. Louis Public Library, AR 1930/31, 59; and Buffalo Public Library, AR 1935, 21.

48. New York Public Library, AR 1940, 100–101, AR 1945, 97.

49. Cleveland Public Library, AR 1929, 24, AR 1942/43, 2; New York Public Library, AR 1933, 42, AR 1944, 86; Chicago Public Library, AR 1943, 25; and Carnegie Library of Pittsburgh, AR 1945, 6–7. See also Grace W. Wood, "Autobiographies of Foreign-Born Americans," *LJ* 49 (1 May 1924): 420; Mary B. McLellan, "Recent Aids to Inter-Racial Service," *LJ* 59 (1 Apr. 1934): 303–5; Edna G. Cleve, "Our Foreign-Born Americans," *WLB* 9 (Dec. 1934): 181–87; Josephine Butkowska Bernhard, "Suitable Books for Foreign-Born Readers," *Booklist* 31 (Jan. 1935): 149–52; and Agnes Camilla Hansen, "Books to Cultivate Tolerance," *LJ* 64 (1 Oct. 1939): 729–31.

50. Los Angeles Public Library, AR 1926/27, 36, AR 1929/30, 19, AR 1933/34, 17, AR 1940/41, 19; Brooklyn Public Library, AR 1929, 24–25; Cleveland Public Library, AR 1929, 40; and Denver Public Library, AR 1929, 13–14.

51. Chicago Public Library, AR 1935, 42, AR 1946, 22.

52. ALA CWFB Minutes, *ALA Bulletin* 18 (Aug. 1924): 250, *ALA Bulletin* 19 (July 1925): 220, *ALA Bulletin* 20 (Oct. 1926): 400, *ALA Bulletin* 30 (Aug. 1936): 827–28, *ALA Bulletin* 35 (Sept. 1941): 157–58; and Lisa Sergio, "The Importance of Interpreting America," *ALA Bulletin* 35 (1 Oct. 1941): 486–89.

53. Boston Public Library, AR 1924/25, 82; Los Angeles Public Library, AR 1927/28, 20; Enoch Pratt Free Library of Baltimore, AR 1926/35, 80; Buffalo Public Library, AR 1931, 28, AR 1940, 16; and Brooklyn Public Library, AR 1933, 30. See also "Branch Libraries Make Friends with Their Community," *The Library* 4 (June 1932): 95–96.

54. ALA CWFB Minutes, *ALA Bulletin* 19 (July 1925): 220, *ALA Bulletin* 20 (Oct. 1926): 400; and Enoch Pratt Free Library of Baltimore, AR 1930, 25.

55. ALA CWFB Minutes, *ALA Bulletin* 20 (Oct. 1926): 562; Los Angeles Public Library, AR 1925/26, 12; Providence Public Library, AR 1931, 20–21; and Enoch Pratt Free Library of Baltimore, AR 1938/39, 47.

56. Massachusetts Library Club, Committee on Work with New Americans, "Bilingual Dictionaries and Histories of the United States in Foreign Languages," *MLCB* 15 (June 1925): 42–43, which was reprinted as "Bilingual Dictionaries and United States Histories in Foreign Languages," *LJ* 50 (15 Dec. 1925): 1037–38; Massachusetts Library Club, Committee on Inter-Racial Service, French Book Review Committee, "Recent French Books," *LJ* 60 (15 Feb. 1935): 166–67, (1 Sept. 1935): 677–78, *LJ* 61 (15 May 1936): 411–12, (Aug. 1936): 609, *LJ* 62 (1 Oct. 1937): 741–42, *LJ* 63 (1 Dec. 1938): 929–31, *LJ* 64 (15 Oct. 1939): 796–99, and *LJ* 65 (1 Nov. 1940): 917–20; and Massachusetts Library Club, Committee on Inter-Racial Service, "New Americans and Americanization Workers," *LJ* 60 (15 Oct. 1935): 808–9. See also Elizabeth V. Briggs, "Service to Foreign Readers in the Small Library," *Michigan Library Bulletin* 21 (Dec. 1930): 315–17, reprinted in *LJ* 57 (1 Apr. 1932): 324–27, which treats cooperative efforts in Michigan; Maud I. Stull, "Inter-Racial Services Needed by Libraries," *LJ* 58 (1 Sept. 1933): 707, which treats cooperative efforts in New Jersey; "A Foreign Language Center," *LJ* 65 (15 Nov. 1940): 961, which treats cooperative efforts in New York; and Susan Himmelwright, "Work with the Foreign-Born: Pennsylvania Libraries," *Pennsylvania Library Notes* 14 (July 1934): 433–38, which treats cooperative efforts in Pennsylvania.

57. Brooklyn Public Library, AR 1930, 33.

58. St. Louis Public Library, AR 1927/28, 80, AR 1936/37, 22, AR 1944/45, 8. See also Ettie Lee, "Social Values in Studying English," *ALA Bulletin* 24 (Sept. 1930): 512.

59. Chicago Public Library, AR 1943, 24; and Queens Borough Public Library, AR 1946/47, 23. Attitudes such as those expressed by the Chicago Public Library in 1943 were addressed by Mary B. McLellan, Librarian in Charge of Work with the Foreign Born at the Hartford (CT) Public Library, in "There's Still Work to Be Done with the Foreign Born," *LJ* 70 (Aug. 1945): 676–77. McLellan's article sparked one reader to offer a counterpoint, to which McLellan returned a rapid repartee. See Ralph Charles Wood, "Not Foreign Born," *LJ* 70 (15 Sept. 1945): 764; and Mary B. McLellan, "A Matter of Interpretation," *LJ* 70 (1 Nov. 1945): 986.

60. Chicago Public Library, AR 1930, 31, AR 1936, 34, AR 1937, 46–47.

61. Detroit Public Library, AR 1938/39, 7; and Los Angeles Public Library, AR 1935/36, 15.

62. ALA CWFB Minutes, *ALA Bulletin* 24 (Sept. 1930): 511–12, which includes Bogardus's address entitled "Mexicans and Filipinos in the United States," *ALA Bulletin* 27 (15 Dec. 1933): 819–20, (Oct. 1933): 473, *ALA Bulletin* 36 (15 Oct. 1942): 675, *ALA Bulletin* 39 (15 Oct. 1945): 401, and *ALA Bulletin* 40 (15 Oct. 1946): 386.

63. Los Angeles Public Library, AR 1940/41, 19; and Enoch Pratt Free Library of Baltimore, AR 1940/41, 21, 42.

64. New York Public Library, AR 1934, 89, AR 1938, 13 (quote), 87; Newark Public Library, AR 1939, n.p.; Chicago Public Library, AR 1938, 38, 42; Enoch Pratt Free Public Library of Baltimore, AR 1938/39, 44, 47; New Orleans Public Library, AR 1941, 9; and Queens Borough Public Library, AR 1947/48, 20. See also "Visitors from Many Lands," *The Library* 4 (Mar. 1932): 67–68; Mary B. McLellan, "Babel and the Loan Assistant," *WLB* 7 (Feb. 1933): 363–65; Helen Hirt MacLean, "Library Aid for Refugees," *WLB* 13 (June 1939): 683, 685; Natalie Schretter, "What Books for the Newcomer?" *WLB* 15 (Sept. 1940): 24–27; Ilse Bry, "Reading for Refugees," *LJ* 65 (1 Nov. 1940): 903–6; New York Public Library, "Does It Deserve What It Gets?" *ALA Bulletin* 35 (July 1941): 421; Francis Wetmore, "Library Work with Foreign Born," *Illinois Libraries* 25 (Jan. 1943): 49–50; Bertha Morse Rosche, "Strangers in a Strange Land," *Illinois Libraries* 26 (May 1944): 163–65; and Rudolph H. Heimanson, "The Library in the Americanization of the Immigrant," (master's thesis, Pratt Institute, 1953).

65. New York Public Library, AR 1940, 78; and ALA Refugee Librarians Committee Minutes, *ALA Bulletin* 35 (15 Oct. 1941): 644–46, *ALA Bulletin* 36 (15 Oct. 1942): 675, *ALA Bulletin* 37 (15 Oct. 1943): 371–72, *ALA Bulletin* 38 (1 Oct. 1944): 367–68, *ALA Bulletin* 39 (15 Oct. 1945): 388. See also Rudolf Hirsch, "The Foreigner in Library Service," *WLB* 14 (Sept. 1939): 50–51, 56; Jennie M. Flexner, "Readers' Advisory Work with the New Émigré," *LJ* 66 (July 1941): 593–95; and Franklin F. Hopper, "Jennie M. Flexner" [Obituary], *LJ* 70 (1 Jan. 1945): 37.

66. New York Public Library, AR 1942, 85 (quote).

67. Providence Public Library, AR 1941, 16; and New York Public Library, AR 1942, 91–92.

68. Chicago Public Library, AR 1936, 11; and Detroit Public Library, AR 1937/38, 8.

69. New York Public Library, AR 1939, 62; and Providence Public Library, AR 1940, 10.

70. Cleveland Public Library, AR 1940, 2–3; Free Library of Philadelphia, AR 1940, 43; Enoch Pratt Free Library of Baltimore, AR 1940/41, 33; and Buffalo Public Library, 1942, 18.

71. Detroit Public Library, AR 1941/42, 2–3; Los Angeles Public Library, AR 1941/42, 4; Louisville Free Public Library, AR 1942/43, 1; Carnegie Library of Pittsburgh, AR 1944, 4; and Enoch Pratt Free Public Library of Baltimore, AR 1942/45, 5.

72. Zada Taylor, "War Children on the Pacific: A Symposium Article," *LJ* 67 (15 June 1942): 558–62.

73. New York Public Library, AR 1945, 91; and Chicago Public Library, AR 1946, 23. See also Mary Prescott Parsons, "Libraries and Foreign Born Readers, 1942," *ALA Bulletin* 36 (15 Sept. 1942): 28–31.

74. ALA CWFB Minutes and ALA Council Proceedings, *ALA Bulletin* 22 (Sept. 1928): 473–75, *LJ* 53 (Aug. 1928): 669–70, *ALA Bulletin* 23 (Aug. 1929): 269, *ALA Bulletin* 27 (Mar. 1933): 151–52, *ALA Bulletin* 29 (Sept. 1935): 731–33, (Sept. 1935): 560, *ALA Bulletin* 30 (May 1936): 420, (Aug. 1936): 617, *LJ* 63 (1 Sept. 1938): 644, *ALA Bulletin* 32 (15 Oct. 1938): 984–85, *ALA Bulletin* 33 (Sept. 1939): 618, *ALA Bulletin* 34 (15 Sept. 1940): 582–83, *LJ* 66 (1 Sept. 1941): 714, *ALA Bulletin* 35 (Sept. 1941): 157–59, (15 Oct. 1941): 620, *ALA Bulletin* 39 (15 Oct. 1945): 401, *ALA Bulletin* 40 (15 Oct. 1946): 386, *ALA Bulletin* 41 (15 Oct. 1947): 401–2, and *ALA Bulletin* 42 (15 Sept. 1948): 69–70, (15 Oct. 1948): 464.

6

The Librarian as Social Worker: Eleanor (Edwards) Ledbetter, 1870–1954

As the flood of immigrants from Europe and all other sources swelled Cleveland's population from 160,146 inhabitants in 1880 to 560,663 in 1910, the proportion of the city's inhabitants classified as foreign-born rose accordingly, from one-tenth to over one-third. Cleveland's foreign-born population in 1910 constituted a city unto itself larger than any other in the state of Ohio except Cincinnati, and equaled or surpassed in size only twenty-eight other cities in the entire country.[1]

The Cleveland Public Library, from its inception in 1869, had acquired foreign language books in response to the successive waves of immigrants to Cleveland. By 1878, the annual report of the Cleveland Public Library included statistics for German book acquisitions. These were followed in successive annual reports by the addition of statistics for Czech books in 1897, Italian books in 1898, Hebrew and Yiddish books in 1902, Finnish and Polish books in 1905, Slovenian books in 1908, Hungarian books in 1909, and Croatian books in 1910. At the end of the period of mass immigration to Cleveland, the 1915 annual report for the Cleveland Public Library reported acquisitions statistics for books in twenty-three foreign languages.[2]

William Howard Brett, then librarian of the Cleveland Public Library, observed two interrelated phenomena that had vast implications for the delivery of library service to Cleveland's immigrants. Brett observed that the city's immigrants, for reasons of economy and convenience, tended to congregate in residential neighborhoods near their places of employment and, in many cases, to segregate themselves along ethnic lines. This pattern of settlement thus permitted the maintenance of Old World social and cultural patterns that, in turn, attracted other immigrants of the same ethnic or national groups through the process of chain migration.[3]

Eleanor (Edwards) Ledbetter, 7 June 1938. Photo courtesy Cleveland Public Library Archives.

ethnic neighborhoods

131

& branch lbs

In recognition of the permanence of these residential patterns, the Cleveland Public Library fostered a policy of erecting branch libraries in these so-called foreign districts scattered throughout Cleveland to provide library service to the immigrants living there. Often the leaders of the more established immigrant neighborhoods would petition the Cleveland Public Library for a branch, as in the case of the leaders of the burgeoning Czech community in southeast Cleveland. Brett, in response to their request, solicited funds for this purpose from Andrew Carnegie, the immigrant philanthropist, who granted the capital needed to build the branch.

The Broadway Branch, named from its location at the intersection of East 55th Street and Broadway, opened for use in January 1906.[4] Four years later, in 1910, Eleanor (Edwards) Ledbetter, a forty-year-old widow, was appointed the third librarian of Broadway Branch. Her charge was to minister to the educational and recreational needs of mainly Czech, Polish, German, and Slovenian immigrants as well as smaller concentrations of other nationalities and ethnic groups living in the environs of the branch.[5]

EARLY YEARS

Prior to her arrival in Cleveland, Eleanor Ledbetter had spent the first thirteen years of her professional career serving brief stints as librarian, library organizer, and cataloger in academic and public libraries in Massachusetts, New York, Indiana, Texas, and, eventually, Ohio. During her longest tenure as special cataloger at the University of Texas, she married Dancy Ledbetter, gave birth to their son and only child, and suffered the loss of her husband, all within the course of four years.[6]

Commenting on these years of "roving librarianship," Marion (Moore) Coleman, Ledbetter's biographer and a scholar of Polish bibliography, surmised that "in all these years any true home or any sense of appointed destiny apparently eluded Eleanor, but in Cleveland they caught up with her."[7] Granted, a thorough examination of Ledbetter's resume of professional experiences prior to her arrival in Cleveland reveals nothing to indicate either experience with immigrants in general or, more to the point, a familiarity with their library and educational needs.

It was apparent almost immediately to her colleagues in the Cleveland Public Library system, her patrons at the Broadway Branch, and, undeniably, to Ledbetter herself, that her niche had been found, a channel for her energies discovered. Ledbetter immersed herself in the duties and responsibilities of her new post at the Broadway Branch with a total devotion comparable only to that of the penitent eager to expiate the "sins" of wandering and apparent lack of professional direction.

LIBRARY WORK WITH IMMIGRANTS IN CLEVELAND

The obvious reality that the Broadway Branch served a largely immigrant clientele did not alter Ledbetter's approach to library service. For Ledbetter,

L's

"community library service" ideal

library service to immigrants was merely a natural extension of what she defined as "complete community service."[8] Ledbetter elaborated upon her views on library service to immigrants. "It is not a philanthropy, not an exhibition of noble generosity on our part, not a condescension; it is just a straightforward necessary part of extending the service of the library, the use of books, and reading, to the whole community."[9] Her philosophy of community library service was undoubtedly cultivated during her training in Melvil Dewey's New York State Library School.[10]

Social Work Approach to Library Work with Immigrants

In order to put her philosophy of service into action, Ledbetter's first objective was to sell the library to the immigrant neighborhood rather than to wait for the neighbors themselves to discover the library. Ledbetter's staff included immigrants or first-generation Americans who spoke German and various Slavic languages used by the Broadway Branch's clienteles. She and her staff made personal visits to individual homes and workplaces.[11]

After the home and the workplace, the three initial targets in her publicity campaign were the church, the public and parochial schools, and the press. Ledbetter defined these three as the "universal agencies to be enlisted in work with the foreign born."[12]

Complete Community Service

Incorporating "the human touch" into her task of surveying the community, Ledbetter created a bond of mutual and lasting trust between librarian and immigrant.[13] "Complete community service," as Ledbetter defined it, required that the librarian "must know the community, must study its component parts, its industries, its recreations, its connections with the rest of the world, until she can penetrate the veil of the accustomed and the habitual, and visualize the possibilities of response in the untouched life beneath the surface, and then bring forward the books which appeal to the possibilities thus discerned."[14]

Outreach Services

Home visits, for example, served many purposes, not the least of which was to meet the immigrant women, who seldom left their homes, and to elicit their support and cooperation in the solution of discipline problems caused by their children. The most difficult discipline problems involved older boys and young men from fourteen to eighteen who did not attend public or parochial schools and consequently loitered in and around the Broadway Branch, causing disturbances. Their "roughness, ignorance and uncouthness," observed Ledbetter, "make them really objects of pity, though, unhappily, that is not the sentiment they most often inspire."[15] Ledbetter, who was preoccupied by the maintenance of good discipline, always accompanied her staff on home visits involving discipline problems. A mother herself, she knew instinctively that the surest way to gain the respect and trust of immigrant mothers was to demonstrate concern for the well-being of their offspring. She explained that "a home visit makes the needed change in behavior; the mother invariably thanks us for having come to them, and these visits accomplish a double end in winning their friendship. In a foreign neighborhood each new friend is the beginning of a geometrical progression."[16]

The other equally beneficial purpose for these home visits, in terms of library publicity, was to distribute finding lists. The women and older immigrants could send the lists back to the library, by way of their children and younger members of the community, marked with the items they desired.[17] Ledbetter observed that the elderly immigrants and foreign-born mothers seldom learned English sufficiently to be proficient or to transact business outside the confines of the close-knit Broadway neighborhood. She realized that the provision of books in their foreign tongues and the access to them provided by the finding lists were balms against isolation and homesickness.

Immigrant Branches

In 1911, a new administrative policy of the Cleveland Public Library, designed to make foreign language books even more accessible to the patrons of the Broadway Branch and other branches in immigrant neighborhoods, went into effect, thus increasing the usefulness of these finding lists. Selected branches in immigrant communities scattered throughout Cleveland would have sole responsibility for the on-site circulation as well as intersystem loans of books in one or sometimes two of the immigrant languages used primarily by the patrons of a particular branch.

The Broadway Branch was assigned, not surprisingly in view of its major clienteles, sole responsibility for the Czech and Polish books of the Cleveland Public Library system. Other branches assumed the responsibility for books in Italian, Slovenian, Croatian, Hebrew, and Yiddish, the other major foreign languages spoken by Cleveland's immigrants.[18] One year after this transfer of Czech and Polish books, a new sign was placed at the main entrance to the library. It proudly proclaimed that the Broadway Branch was a Free Public Library in five languages: English, Czech, Polish, Slovenian, and German, the latter language serving as a lingua franca for the Slavic peoples.[19]

Advertising Library Service to Immigrants

Placards advertising the library hours and the availability of books in foreign languages and easy English were placed in shops and grocery stores where, according to Ledbetter, "no better place can be found from which to start a bit of useful gossip about the library." The foremen at manufacturing plants in the Broadway neighborhood were persuaded to place placards near the time clocks and to pass out circulars in suitable languages when the men checked out from work. Circulars were distributed as well by priests and parishioners after church services, displayed prominently at exhibits in neighborhood festivals, and sent home by children either from the library or the school.[20]

Cooperation with the Foreign Language Press

Ledbetter was fervently earnest in her endeavors to elicit the support of the foreign language press. Realizing that the foreign language newspapers were the primary link between the native lands of her patrons and their adopted home in Cleveland, Ledbetter used the immigrant press as a primary source for advertising the Broadway Branch.

She understood as well that the editors of the foreign language newspapers were quite influential, giving their readers not only what the readers themselves wanted to read but also what the editors wanted them to read. Since numerous Czech and Polish newspapers, in particular, vied for the readership of the residents of the Broadway Branch community, Ledbetter habitually sent material to rival newspapers rather than concentrating on one newspaper, whose readership was often circumscribed.[21]

It was important that all of the newspapers, reflecting the wide range of opinions of the immigrant community, regarded the library as a friendly, helpful place, free of discrimination and bias. Ledbetter commented that "the foreign language newspapers are almost invariably edited by men of good general intelligence, who are vitally interested in the progress of their race. The library needs no explaining to them. . . . They are valuable allies."[22]

Lists of new books, book reviews, and news items were prepared by Ledbetter in English and then sent to the different newspapers. Editorial staffs then translated them into the appropriate languages and published them regularly in the foreign language newspapers of Cleveland, including the Czech newspapers *Svet*, *American*, and *Americky Delnicky Listy*; the Polish newspapers *Polonia w Ameryce*, *Jutrzenka*, and *Wiadomosci Codzienne*; and the Slovenian newspaper *Clevelandska Amerika*. She also provided articles and other news items to the Slovenian newspaper *Glas Naroda*, published in New York City, and served as English language editor of the *Serbian Herald*, based in San Francisco.[23]

All these articles and news items were meticulously clipped and preserved in scrapbooks so that Ledbetter could gauge the amount and tone of the coverage given the library by various newspapers. In one year alone, Ledbetter reported that a total of 545 inches of column space on library news appeared in the Czech papers and 516 in the Polish.

All of the clipped articles and news items preserved in Ledbetter's scrapbooks represented goodwill for the Broadway Branch and its librarian. Indeed, as Ledbetter proudly observed, almost all of the clippings contained "the addition of a paragraph or more in which the names of Mrs. Ledbetter and the Broadway Library appear prominently, the editor apparently not considering it complete otherwise."[24]

Increased Usage of Broadway Branch by Immigrants

Understandably, such wholehearted efforts to publicize the Broadway Branch were fruitful. Upon completing its tenth year of service in 1916, during Ledbetter's sixth year as librarian, the Broadway Branch's ledgers had recorded 1,228,085 visitors, had issued 1,749,980 books, and had registered over 30,000 borrowers representing at least twenty nationalities. Ledbetter reflected with justifiable pride that "such an influence in the life of a community cannot be measured." She continued that "it is the testimony of all persons in a position to take a large view, such as teachers, clergymen, bankers, merchants, and policemen, that in this ten years the library has been an influence of enormous potency in raising the whole standard of education and culture, and of life in general, in this neighborhood."[25]

Cooperation with Parochial Schools

Ledbetter's visits to the parochial schools, operated by the Roman- and Byzantine-rite Catholic and Eastern Orthodox churches in the Broadway neighborhood, confirmed her suspicion that the pupils enrolled in these schools were, without exception, from homes where a foreign language was the only language freely spoken. As a consequence, the foreign language was used at first in the lower grades, with the acquisition of English coming with progress in school. In direct contrast to the public schools, assumed by the general public to be the universal "melting pot," the parochial schools attended by hundreds of thousands of children of foreign-born parents were segregated by ethnic or national group.

Ledbetter understood that in order to improve teaching methods in the parochial schools, particularly with regard to instruction in English, she must win the confidence of the teachers, primarily nuns in teaching orders. Accordingly, she organized continuing education classes for the nuns and secured qualified teachers for them. The classes, held either at the Broadway Branch or, by special request, at the convents, provided the opportunity for the nuns both to improve their overall teaching skills and to acquire normal school credentials.

Ledbetter's activities in this regard gained national recognition by the Polish Sisters of St. Joseph, one of the principal teaching orders staffing the Cleveland parochial schools. She was invited to address a convention of nuns at the motherhouse of their order at Stevens Point, Wisconsin, on the topic of "how the library can help the Sisters improve their teaching." Ledbetter regarded this as a signal honor of far-reaching importance since the sisters taught, at that time, a total of 225,000 children in parochial schools in seven states.[26]

Cooperation with Public Schools

As a corollary to her work with the parochial schools, Ledbetter spared no energy in cultivating a healthy working relationship with the public schools of Cleveland. The principal responsibility for Americanizing the immigrant community, through instruction in English and preparation for citizenship, had been shouldered by the public schools and night schools.[27]

By 1916, Herbert Adolphus Miller, sociologist and recognized authority on immigrant assimilation, had conducted a survey of educational opportunities for immigrants commissioned by the Cleveland Foundation. He discovered that the schools had accomplished only to a limited degree their mandate to teach the foreign-born inhabitants of Cleveland the rudiments of the English language and to assist them to become naturalized citizens. Miller concluded his study with the rueful observation that "Cleveland is one of the most foreign cities in the United States." He based his conclusion on the findings that the majority of the foreign population of Cleveland could not speak or read English and that nearly one-third of all the men of voting age were ineligible to vote.[28]

The schools obviously needed the cooperation and support of other public and private voluntary agencies. The settlement houses, various social welfare organizations, and the public library had roles to play in the Americanization process that would prepare the immigrants for a fuller participation in the political and social life of Cleveland and the nation. The value of the public library as a provider of the books needed to aid immigrants in their efforts to Americanize themselves was recognized officially by the Cleveland Board of Education in 1916. The board recommended that at least one class period per night school session be devoted to a visit to the local branch library.[29]

Cooperation with Evening Schools

By providing space in the Broadway Branch for English and citizenship classes, easy books in the English language for beginners, and instructional sessions with the local night schools, the Broadway Branch was contributing to the eradication of the stumbling blocks to immigrant assimilation.

During her work with the night schools, Ledbetter was dismayed by the dearth of materials suitable for teaching immigrants the English language. The only books in easy English were designed almost exclusively for children, not adults needing a basic command of English in the workplace, and books in immigrant languages about American history, government, and customs, for immigrants who would never learn English well enough to be proficient, were virtually nonexistent. The discovery and promotion of materials in these categories would be a lifelong occupation.[30]

Undoubtedly it was in connection with her visits at the neighborhood public schools that Ledbetter made the acquaintance of Herbert Adolphus Miller, the author of the Cleveland Foundation survey on educational opportunities for immigrants. Miller, who must have found Ledbetter's rapport with the schools and the Broadway community in general refreshing, would have a profound impact on her career.

Attitude toward Immigrants and Their Americanization

Miller and Ledbetter were both adherents of the tenets of cultural pluralism as defined and expounded upon by Horace M. Kallen.[31] Representative passages from *"cultural pluralism" as a rejection of "Anglo-conformism"*

the works of Ledbetter and Miller reveal dramatically the similarity in their views regarding immigrant assimilation and the role of Americanization programs in this process. Miller expressed his devotion to the cause of cultural pluralism and prophesied its ultimate triumph over the tyranny of oppression and the concomitant "oppression psychosis" that drove European immigrants to America.[32]

Ledbetter viewed immigrants simply as Americans who had not yet learned to speak English. She never doubted their desire to be Americanized. "For myself, I have long ceased to think of anyone at all as 'a foreigner.' I may say: 'She does not speak English,' precisely as I say: 'She does not knit,' but I do not feel that she is any different on that account."[33]

The viewpoints of both Ledbetter and Miller demonstrate that neither had any qualms about Americanization per se. They both wanted the foreign born and the native born to share a common language and to participate fully in the democratic process as citizens. They believed that learning English would lead naturally to a desire for citizenship status.

Granted, the timing of the immigrants' learning English would vary depending on the educational attainment of immigrants in their native lands as well as their contact with English-speaking Americans in the workplace and outside the confines of the immigrant community. Ledbetter observed, for example, that foreign language books were read primarily by the immigrant generation, to a lesser degree by the second generation, and hardly at all by the third generation.[34]

Leaders of the immigrant community in Cleveland were in agreement that Americanization was desirable and that no arbitrary time restraints or compulsions should be or, furthermore, needed to be, placed on the immigrants.[35] Lack of citizenship status, it must be remembered, was only problematic for the immigrant generation. All children of immigrants born after their parents' arrival in the United States would automatically become citizens with all the rights and privileges of native-born Americans.

For these reasons, therefore, Ledbetter and Miller, as well as the immigrant community as a whole, believed that the concept of America as the melting pot was fundamentally flawed. If the fires that heated the pot could eliminate the baseness of various peoples without disturbing the originality inherent in them, Ledbetter and Miller both would have fanned the flames and stoked the fire. Miller purveyed the essence of their attitudes toward Americanization quite succinctly when he said that "each nationality has developed distinctive virtues, as well as vices; and true Americanization must conserve the virtues and eliminate the vices."[36] For Ledbetter and Miller alike, if the purification process of the melting pot meant uniformity or, more precisely, conformity as desired by the Anglo-conformists, it was too great a price to pay for the loss of diversity.

Exposes like Herbert Adolphus Miller's regarding the ineffectiveness of the Americanization programs of Cleveland's public schools carried in their aftermath a backlash of nativism, which was exacerbated by the entrance of the United States into World War I. A general hysteria spread among native-born Clevelanders, who began to question the loyalty of the unnaturalized foreign born, people who *[handwritten: how nativism hoped to use libraries (in WWI)]*

segregated themselves in neighborhoods throughout the city, and to characterize everything of immigrant origin as "un-American."

Cleveland Americanization Committee

In early 1917, Cleveland's mayor, Harry L. Davis, in an attempt to stem this tide of nativist hysteria, appointed his Advisory War Committee, which in turn spawned a network of subcommittees to coordinate, finance, and supervise the city's war-relief work. Davis's challenge to the subcommittees "to make Cleveland worth fighting for" was translated into, among many activities, programs for the distribution of food and clothing and the provision of housing, the organization of a speakers' bureau, supervision of draft boards, and, not surprisingly, the promotion of Americanization classes for immigrants.

To accomplish the all-important goal of Americanization, the Committee on the Teaching of English to Foreigners was appointed. Later, the committee was renamed the Cleveland Americanization Committee to reflect a change of mission to include preparation for citizenship as well as the teaching of English. Harold T. Clark of the Cleveland Chamber of Commerce was appointed as its first chair. The Cleveland Americanization Committee was charged with the coordination of the activities of sixty-eight local organizations involved with Americanization as well as given the responsibility for serving as liaison with state and federal Americanization programs.

The most pressing problem facing the Cleveland Americanization Committee at its inception was to allay the natural suspicions of immigrants, who had read, with understandable alarm, editorials in Cleveland's newspapers chastising them for maintaining foreign and thus "un-American" ways. Clark and the other members of the Cleveland Americanization Committee realized that the immigrants resented the arbitrary compulsion inherent in such attitudes on the part of many native-born Clevelanders, especially since that was precisely the attitude the immigrants had come to America to avoid. There were indeed both a surprising lack of knowledge among native-born Americans in general of immigrants and their backgrounds and, conversely, feelings of antagonism on the part of the immigrants for the aloofness of native-born Americans as well as their failure to recognize immigrant contributions and potential.[37]

Recognizing the contribution of the Cleveland Public Library through its immigrant branches, the Cleveland Americanization Committee sought the continued support of the branches in the provision of books in foreign languages and English as well as space for citizenship classes to aid in the Americanization process. The work of Ledbetter and other librarians at immigrant branches was singled out by the Cleveland Americanization Committee. The committee avowed that "no more effective social workers can be found than the librarian at these branches."[38] It was not surprising that in March 1918, Harold T. Clark approached the Cleveland Public Library's librarian, William Howard Brett, and vice-librarian, Linda Anne Eastman, with regard to obtaining the services of Ledbetter. Her talents in the area of community survey were already well known and recognized in Cleveland.[39]

In October 1918, when Ledbetter had completed the first six months and was beginning her final four months of work with the Cleveland Americanization Committee, Clark resigned as chair. Raymond Moley of Western Reserve University, who had developed the content and teaching methods of the citizenship component of the committee's work, was elected chair. As Ledbetter had found support and friendship in Harold T. Clark and Herbert Adolphus Miller, she also found a kindred spirit in Raymond Moley, an ardent advocate of the philosophy of cultural pluralism.

The Cleveland Americanization Committee promulgated the philosophy of cultural pluralism as an antidote for the hysteria of nativism and the sway of Anglo-conformist ideology. Moley, Ledbetter, and the other members of the Cleveland Americanization Committee recognized that

the problem of Americanization is far different from the so-called "melting pot" idea. The "assimilation" of the "foreigner" into American life means to some people the acquisition by the foreigner of a set of American ideals and customs and the putting off of the customs and ideals which he brought here. . . . [T]he difficulty with this type of Americanization is that it assumes that the making of an American is merely a matter of changing a few externals. It assumes that a man can set aside the manifold habits and affections that are the result of generations of foreign civilization, and adopt another code in a short time. It overlooks the fact that the deepest and most permanent characteristics of a human being are very difficult to change and that while the English language may be learned and American externals may be adopted, the foreigner remains foreign in thought and habit. However we may regard this impossibility of changing human nature in a few years, we must face it as a common truth. . . . It is the new infusions brought by the immigrant that will give us the very richness and diversity that we need. Hence the beginning of Americanization is a recognition by Americans of the value of the newcomer.[40]

Harold T. Clark and his successor, Raymond Moley, employed Ledbetter as well as sociologist Charles Wellsley Coulter and Americanization teacher Huldah Florence Cook to survey the immigrant communities of Cleveland for the Cleveland Americanization Committee. Their charge was to write detailed studies "to give the native born a sympathetic understanding of the backgrounds of the foreign-born, their political aspirations and social gifts ready for this country to make use of." Put another way, their task was no less than that of "introducing Cleveland to itself, and helping to make the municipality a community in the best sense of that expressive word."[41]

From 1918 to 1920, Ledbetter, Coulter, and Cook produced a total of seven pamphlets on as many ethnic groups. The pamphlets, all available for sale at a modest price, included studies of the Czechs, Yugoslavs, and Slovaks by Ledbetter, studies of the Poles, Italians, and Lithuanians by Coulter, and a study of the Hungarians by Cook.[42]

Forty years later, Marion (Moore) Coleman, Ledbetter's biographer, would consider the era in which Ledbetter wrote her pamphlets for the Cleveland Americanization Committee. She was "struck not only with the great amount of sound information, soberly presented, that they contain, but equally by the total absence of the feverish, 'quickie Americanization' spirit which . . . informed so much of the stuff that was written in those days of inflamed Americanism." Contemporary historians still marvel at Ledbetter's understanding of immigrant culture and regard her studies as primary sources for the history of ethnic communities in Cleveland.[43] Toward the end of her tenure with the Cleveland Americanization Committee and before returning to her duties at the Broadway Branch, Ledbetter began to work concurrently with Herbert Adolphus Miller, who had been recently appointed head of the Immigrant Heritages Division of the Carnegie Foundation Study on the Methods of Americanization, on a similar writing project but with a national scope.[44]

Shortly thereafter, Ledbetter wrote Linda Anne Eastman, who had been appointed librarian of the Cleveland Public Library after William Howard Brett's tragic death. Ledbetter explained that she was resigning her duties and returning to work at the Broadway Branch. She mentioned that her decision to resign was precipitated by a conversation she had had with Helen Horvath, a local Americanization teacher, regarding the outlines of the work that Dr. Park (presumably Robert Ezra Park, a Carnegie Foundation associate) wanted done for the Carnegie Foundation study. Horvath, an immigrant herself, had reacted negatively to the nature of many of the questions proposed by Park, finding them patronizing and offensive to the immigrants for whom the questions were designed.[45]

Although Ledbetter's letter to Eastman was written on Cleveland Americanization Committee stationery, it is more likely that Ledbetter, who had at that time already completed the assignments given her by the Cleveland Americanization Committee, was resigning from the Carnegie Foundation study. There was apparently a fine line between the role of the social worker called for in the Cleveland Americanization Committee's work and the role of the professional investigator called for by the Carnegie Foundation study.

For Ledbetter, the work of the former project helped her gain a more informed acquaintance with her immigrant patrons at the Broadway Branch, while the latter project, requiring more probing into the intimate lives of immigrants, had less applicability to her own situation. There is no indication that Ledbetter regretted any of the work she did for the Cleveland Americanization Committee, but rather she found the Carnegie Foundation study's tactics too personal and potentially offensive to the immigrants she was assigned to interview.[46]

By the close of the hostilities in November 1918, most of the subcommittees of the Mayor's Advisory War Committee turned their attention to the needs of returning soldiers. By the summer of 1919 the subcommittees began to disperse, and by December of the same year the Mayor's Advisory War Committee itself ceased to exist.

Established in July 1919, the Cleveland Americanization Council carried on the Americanization activities and programs of the Cleveland Americanization Committee. The activities and programs of the Cleveland Americanization Council, like its predecessor, received national recognition. Linda Anne Eastman, as a member of the Executive Board of the Cleveland Americanization Council,

ALA CWFB

continued to advocate the library's role in the Americanization process and to promote Ledbetter's studies of the Czechs, Yugoslavs, and Slovaks of Cleveland until the council, too, disbanded in the summer of 1920.[47]

ALA COMMITTEE ON WORK WITH THE FOREIGN BORN

Ledbetter shared the varied experiences garnered in her work with immigrants in Cleveland with other librarians and social workers throughout the nation. Her first significant contribution to the library literature was *Winning Friends and Citizens for America; Work with Poles, Bohemians, and Others*, published in 1918 by John Foster Carr of the Immigrant Publication Society of New York. Impressed by the work that Ledbetter had accomplished in the immigrant neighborhood surrounding the Broadway Branch, Carr was anxious that her methods and philosophy, quite similar in many particulars to his own, be broadcast to libraries in communities throughout the country and especially in cities with large concentrations of immigrants.[48]

The same year as the publication of this pamphlet, the Committee on Work with the Foreign Born of the American Library Association was organized, with John Foster Carr appointed its first chairman. During the second year of its existence, in 1919, Ledbetter was appointed to the committee, due to Carr's influence and his obvious admiration for her work at the Broadway Branch as well as with the Cleveland Americanization Committee.[49] For the next nine years, from 1920 through 1926, she served as the chair of the Committee on Work with the Foreign Born. In this latter capacity especially, Ledbetter took full advantage of the opportunity it afforded to disseminate practical advice and to offer sound leadership. Ledbetter was acutely aware that library work with immigrants often proceeded without a sense of direction and without proper training of librarians entering the field. Under Ledbetter's leadership, the ALA CWFB became a national force for continuing education of librarians working with immigrant clienteles.[50]

Library Work with Immigrants in a Democracy

Ledbetter believed that "[t]he public library should be absolutely democratic in regimen and administration, giving equal service to the whole public regardless of the place of nativity. Where funds are insufficient, preference should be given to those portions of the community having least opportunity at their own command."[51] In support of this philosophical stance, she wrote revealing articles expounding upon the idea of the library as a democratic institution.[52]

In one article, for example, Ledbetter, in the face of certain criticism, related her views that the public library was not always as democratic as it was purported to be, particularly in its response to the immigrant community. Ledbetter, who had been in a position to hear complaints from librarians who justified the absence of books in immigrant languages in their libraries because of lack of funds, related the following anecdote:

An all too common civic condition was naively expressed by a librarian who said, "We have never done anything for the foreign born of our city because we have never had money enough to get all the books we need for ourselves." By "ourselves" she meant perhaps at most the 40 per cent which is accustomed to privilege, which looks for privilege as a right and which scarcely knows of the existence of the other 60 per cent. A library which takes this position has no claim to democratic standing. It is a class institution.[53]

Such strong sentiments were unusual for a branch librarian in Cleveland or anywhere else, and certain to be unpopular with library boards and library administrators, who controlled the purse strings and who had many diverse clienteles to please. In every aspect of library service, Ledbetter identified with her immigrant clientele completely and lobbied adamantly for their share of tax revenues. Could this outspokenness have accounted for the criticisms of her immediate superior? Bessie Sargeant Smith, supervisor of branches for the Cleveland Public Library system, called Ledbetter to task for her "derisive attitude towards almost any authority or regulation," "her naive egotism," and lack of a "sense of the system."[54]

Ledbetter apparently balked at any aspect of the system that might possibly serve to slight the immigrant patrons of the Broadway Branch. Her independence and wholehearted allegiance to the needs of the immigrants, rather than pleasing her colleagues in the system, once elicited the veiled criticism of none other than Linda Anne Eastman. Eastman commented that while Ledbetter's "work with the foreign born has been remarkable and her energy and interest have been given more and more to them, . . . in her contacts with her own countrymen [*sic*] she is perhaps not always so happy."[55] Philosophically and psychologically, then, Ledbetter was prepared to risk even the criticism of her colleagues in order to obtain the funds necessary to maintain the quality of service and provide the quantity of books needed by her patrons at the Broadway Branch.

Rights of Immigrants as Taxpayers

Ledbetter believed that the provision of library materials in foreign languages was essential if the library was to serve its immigrant taxpayers. "In order to provide the service which is the just due of all taxpayers, and which is an essential part of the educational and recreational functions of the public library, the immigrant people should be provided with reading matter which they can use, both in easy English books and in books and periodicals in their native tongues."[56]

Ledbetter's prior experiences with the night school classes in Cleveland had made her acutely aware of the paucity of books about America written in the languages of immigrants. Ledbetter corresponded widely with librarians from across the country about this problem and used the ALA CWFB as a clearinghouse to disseminate information on the availability of such publications from a variety of sources. She alerted librarians to the general publications of domestic publishers, including John Foster Carr's Immigrant Publication Society, the foreign language newspapers, and the Foreign Language Information Service. She recommended as well the topical publications of businesses, social welfare institutions, patriotic societies, religious organizations, and immigrant cultural organizations. The endeavors of state library associations, notably the New York State Committee on Work with Immigrants, and the efforts of individual librarians, specifically Jane Maud Campbell of the Massachusetts Free Public Library Commission, to secure financial support for immigrant publications were encouraged and applauded.

Ledbetter and the ALA CWFB were well aware that the expense involved in the publishing of books in immigrant languages was a major stumbling block to their production; the profits to be derived were minimal at best. Ultimately, even the limited success of the few publishing concerns willing to take the financial risk would be only temporary. The absence of new immigrants, due to the National Origins Act of 1924, as well as the inevitable death of immigrants of the first generation eroded their potential audience. Ironically, the publications produced were almost invariably directed toward immigrants who had been in the United States long enough to achieve economic stability, to establish an ethnic identity, and as a result, to attain political clout. Despite these seemingly insurmountable odds, Ledbetter used her position as chair of the ALA CWFB to encourage libraries, particularly those in cities with large immigrant communities, to buy the books produced by these largely philanthropic organizations.[57]

Since the supply of books in foreign languages, available from foreign as well as domestic publishers, was a continuing concern of librarians throughout the nation, the ALA CWFB acted as a clearinghouse for information on book buying and selection. Lists of twenty-five books for beginning collections in fifteen languages were compiled and distributed to correspondents writing for assistance. The committee, in turn, referred some requests to persons more qualified to offer suggestions and called for volunteers from the ranks of American librarians to assist with the fulfillment of others.[58]

Under the auspices of the ALA CWFB and the Cleveland Public Library, Ledbetter undertook two book-buying trips to southern and eastern Europe during the summers of 1923 and 1925. The ostensible purpose of these excursions, Ledbetter related, was "to visit European countries from which Broadway readers come, for purpose of study and better understanding." As she was always ready to combine business with pleasure, Ledbetter took on the added responsibility of establishing contacts with book sellers, publishers, and literati as well as placing orders on behalf of the Cleveland Public Library for books in Polish, Czech, Slovak, Lithuanian, Romanian, Serbian, Croatian, Slovenian, and Ukrainian. During her second European trip in the summer of 1925, Ledbetter extended her services as buying agent for books in these languages not only to the Cleveland Public Library but also to the public libraries of Indianapolis and Gary (IN), Detroit, Pittsburgh, and Lakewood (OH).[59]

During these summer vacations, Ledbetter visited libraries and special collections in Czechoslovakia, Poland, and Yugoslavia and was profoundly influenced by the experiences she shared with the Slavic peoples of these countries. When they learned of her plans to travel in their native lands, the foreign dignitaries in the United States who had visited with Ledbetter at the Broadway Branch arranged personal guided tours and formal introductions to local officials. Ledbetter was given the red-carpet treatment wherever she went.

Prior to her trip, Bedrich Stepanek, the Czechoslovakian minister to the United States, had written letters of introduction for her and sent ahead letters to officials in Czechoslovakia telling of her work with Czech immigrants in America. While in Czechoslovakia, she visited the public schools accompanied by Vojta Benes, inspector of schools for the Czechoslovakian Ministry of Education, whom Ledbetter knew from his visit to the United States to study American school methods. In Poland the secretary of the Polish-American Chamber of Commerce escorted her. In Ljubljana, Yugoslavia, the newspapers reported Ledbetter's presence and mission, and the officers of various Slovene cultural societies met with her and expressed their appreciation of what she was doing in Cleveland for Yugoslav immigrants.[60]

Her European travel experiences provided the basis for several articles that Ledbetter wrote for library and general interest periodicals. She shared her impressions of the public library of Warsaw, her commendation of the student travel excursions sponsored by the Czechoslovakian Ministry of Education as a means of promoting the unity of the Czech and Slovak peoples, and her fascination with Polish history, literature, and folklore. Her experiences were shared also in lectures at the Broadway Branch as well as the public and parochial schools of Cleveland.[61]

Education for Librarians Working with Immigrants

Ledbetter believed that education in immigrant cultures for library staff working with immigrants should not be neglected. "Assistants [i.e., library staff] should be trained for work with immigrants as a special field of library work, and encouraged in the study of racial understandings and of immigrant literatures and of the characteristics of immigrant cultures. Library schools should incorporate work along this line into their regular courses."[62]

It was Ledbetter's conviction that librarians entering the special field of library service with immigrants needed not only a uniform philosophical approach, which was, at least for Ledbetter, the model of librarian as social worker, but also adequate educational preparation, both formal and informal. Throughout her career at the Broadway Branch she found time to devote to teaching and lecturing on library work with immigrants.

As early as 1918, she gave a lecture entitled "The Library as an Americanization Agency" at the Immigrant Education Institutes held during the summer in the principal cities of New York State. From 1919 through 1922, during Herbert Adolphus Miller's tenure as professor of sociology at Oberlin College, Ledbetter regularly planned lectures and tours of immigrant neighborhoods in Cleveland for his students.

Ledbetter, of course, had the most remarkable admiration and respect for Miller, referring to him as "probably the best informed man in the country regarding immigrant backgrounds." Miller, on the other hand, realized that Ledbetter's experiences would add to the practical knowledge needed by the future sociologists and social workers under his tutelage. Ledbetter summed up this mutually advantageous relationship by commenting that "our intimate acquaintance enables us to plan a program in which the immigrant people are seen on their own ground and in their natural social relations." One of the highlights of these sessions with Miller's students from Oberlin was always attendance at a worship service at one of the immigrant churches of Cleveland. These visits, coupled with Ledbetter's inquisitiveness regarding the religious experiences of her patrons and her own religious convictions, found expression in several periodical articles written during this time period. Ledbetter wrote on Greek Catholics, Serbian Christmas celebrations, Easter services in immigrant churches, and Saint Sava, a thirteenth-century Serbian archbishop.[63]

Ledbetter gave a regular series of lectures on "Library Work with the Foreign Born" to the Western Reserve University Library School in Cleveland during the early twenties, and on several occasions presented similar lectures to the Carnegie Library School of Pittsburgh.[64]

In addition to frequent addresses to the American Library Association, the Ohio Library Association, and various civic and cultural organizations throughout Cleveland, Ledbetter made notable addresses at religious and social work conferences. She addressed the conference of the Department for Work with the Foreign Born of the Episcopal Church in 1921 on the topic "The Pressing Need of Human Contacts." She was guest speaker with the National Association of Social Workers in 1924, on the very eve of the imposition of immigration quotas in the United States, her topic being "Recent Development in Library Work with Immigrants." At the annual Conference on Children's Reading held in Grand Rapids, Michigan, in 1927, she addressed the conference attendees on the topic "Immigrant Parents and Their American Children."[65] It is apparent that Ledbetter viewed her activities in librarianship, social work, and religious service as being interrelated and complementary.

Publications. The ALA CWFB assumed the responsibility for providing informal avenues of education for librarians involved in work with the foreign born who might not have the time or opportunity for formal courses or access to experts in the various foreign literatures. Beginning in late 1921 and continuing through 1924, a series of articles was written to introduce librarians to various ethnic and national groups of immigrants, to discuss their particular library needs, and to provide a common understanding upon which to base Americanization programs and library activities for immigrants.

Each article in the series was written by a committee member with expertise and familiarity with a specific immigrant group and presented information on immigrants' backgrounds as well as their contributions to American society. The series, edited by Ledbetter as chair of the committee and published in the *Library Journal*, included in-depth articles on Yiddish, Polish, Japanese, Romanian, Greek, Czechoslovakian, and Italian immigrants.[66]

Ledbetter herself wrote the articles on Polish and Czechoslovakian immigrants, the groups with whom she had a special affection and affinity. She received laudatory reviews of them in the foreign language press of Cleveland, where huge concentrations of immigrants of these nationalities resided.[67] In addition to these articles, the ALA CWFB also published in *Library Journal* a directory of dealers in foreign language books. A bibliography of bibliographies of Slavic literatures compiled by Ledbetter was also published.[68]

The three articles on the Polish, Italian, and Greek immigrants were later revised, expanded, and published in pamphlet form by the ALA CWFB in its Library Work with the Foreign Born series. The rationale behind each pamphlet in the series was, according to Ledbetter, "to set forth those characteristics of a racial group which influence its receptiveness to library activities,—its possibilities and its limitations in the way of books and reading; to show what means have been found most effective in establishing contacts with its members; and to give general information about their literatures, with definite suggestions regarding choice of titles and methods of purchase." Ledbetter wrote the pamphlet entitled *The Polish Immigrant and His Reading.* She also wrote the introductions to the two remaining pamphlets published during her tenure as chairman, May M. Sweet's *The Italian Immigrant and His Reading* and Alison B. Alessios's *The Greek Immigrant and His Reading.*[69] Each of the pamphlets included a selective bibliography that demonstrated the compiler's familiarity with the literature of the immigrant group in question.

The bibliography accompanying Ledbetter's pamphlet on the Polish immigrant consisted of not only an annotated list of about two hundred Polish titles but also an additional list of translations into Polish from other languages. Ledbetter described the process of compiling the bibliography. "The titles in this list have been chosen from the most popular during a period of years in the Cleveland Public Library and from newer titles recommended by competent literary advisers and examined in Warsaw in the summer of 1923. The list thus compiled has been critically reviewed by His Excellency Dr. Wladyslaw Wroblewski, Minister of Poland to the United States, who authorizes a statement of his approval."[70]

International Recognition. Three years later, in 1928, at a dinner sponsored by the Cleveland post of the Polish Army Veterans Association, Ledbetter was presented the Sword of Haller cross from the Polish government for distinguished service to Poland. For these veterans, Ledbetter's publications on behalf of Polish immigrants were tangible evidence of her continuing concern for Polish immigrants in America. The medal, which she proudly wore at the round table meeting of the ALA CWFB during the last year of her tenure, was a symbol of the international as well as local impact that her work had had both at home and in Europe.[71]

The Library as a Community Center

Ledbetter believed that the library existed only for the community it served. She wrote that "in communities having considerable immigrant population, the library should be given prominence as a social institution, and should be made in actual fact a community center." Ledbetter recommended the free use of library rooms for clubs and public meetings and classes. She suggested that "libraries take the initiative in the public introduction of official representatives of European countries, such as consuls and visiting members of legations, and of distinguished European visitors of races locally represented. The public library is admirably situated as a place for informal public receptions which, in the entertainment of distinguished guests, may naturally bring together native and foreign born elements of the population, to the great increase of mutual respect and appreciation."[72]

Participation in Immigrant Organizations. Ledbetter's research for the Cleveland Americanization Committee pamphlets on ethnic groups in Cleveland had brought her into close contact with the immigrant patrons of the Broadway Branch. According to Ledbetter, this experience had "cemented her friendship with those groups."

She continued to cultivate this friendship through her attendance at activities sponsored by immigrant communities in the proximity of the Broadway Branch and throughout Cleveland, including dramatic performances, festivals, and church services. Ledbetter had learned through her home visits that only a very limited number of the foreign born could be seen during the workday; in order to develop a sympathetic understanding of immigrants and immigrant life, she had to share their Sundays and holidays.

Cultural Events for Immigrant Community. For Ledbetter the line between work time and private time was often blurred. She believed that "a librarian is a librarian even in her private time, and can not [*sic*] help representing her in-stitution."[73] Her attendance at cultural events in the immigrant community afforded her firsthand knowledge of the artistic, musical, literary, and oratorical talents that often remained, at best, untapped, and at worst, undiscovered. Ledbetter resolved that the Broadway Branch was the perfect setting for bringing these newly found talents to appreciative audiences of Clevelanders.

Lecture Series. In the winter of 1920, Ledbetter inaugurated a series of lectures on Slav Conditions of Today, which was delivered in the auditorium at the Broadway Branch. She considered these lectures "the crowning event of the year" and "Americanization work of the ideal sort," since they brought old and new Americans together on a ground of mutual interest. The lectures were followed by informal receptions that afforded the residents of the Broadway community the opportunity not only to meet Clevelanders from all parts of the city, but also to gain a deeper acquaintance with and respect for other members of their particular ethnic or national group.[74]

Ledbetter realized all too well that all immigrant groups did not act as one block; each group had its own idiosyncrasies as well as strengths, and even within the same ethnic group there was often a wide range of temperaments and opinions. The lectures and "entertainments" sponsored by the Broadway Branch served as a subtle means of "interpreting the various groups to one another." Ledbetter had learned that "between each two of them lies a gulf as deep and as wide as that which separates them from the American; and bridge-building is always in order."[75] As the lectures provided common ground on which to base a lasting understanding, the public library provided neutral territory for the expression of diverse ideas.

After the tremendously gratifying success of the inaugural series of lectures in terms of not only bringing people together but also introducing newcomers to the Broadway Branch, Ledbetter determined that a series of Slav Evenings would be an annual cultural event for the community. Approximately twelve lectures and entertainments were presented during the winter months from 1920 through 1930. She secured the wholehearted support of the Western Reserve Chapter of the Daughters of the American Revolution, who supplied refreshments at the receptions following these events. This relationship between the Broadway Branch and the conservative patriotic organization was ironical, in that DAR members presumably adhered to Anglo-conformist ideals, while Ledbetter promoted the ideals of cultural pluralism. Ledbetter, however, found no conflict of interest in the arrangement and, indeed, often referred to the cooperative effort as mutually beneficial.

Visits of International Scholars. Local groups were supplemented by visiting international scholars, including Boris Morkovin and Otakar Vocadlo, both of the University of Prague; Roman Dyboski, of the University of Krakow; and Sir Bernard Pares, head of the School of Slavonic Studies of the University of London. Visiting dignitaries included Bedrich Stepanek, Minister of Czechoslovakia to the United States, and consular officials from Cleveland and other major United States cities.[76] Ledbetter was particularly proud of the visit of A. Tresic Pavicic, minister of Yugoslavia to the United States. Ledbetter commented that his visit marked "the first time that any foreign minister has made an official visit and address in an American library, and it constitutes a milestone in the history of work with the foreign born, as a definite recognition of the value of the library to the immigrant."[77]

Ledbetter acknowledged the impact that such events had not only on the civic life of Cleveland but also in the creation of goodwill both in the United States and abroad for the American public library. For lovers of Slavic culture, the Slav Evenings were more than just the highpoint of the bleak winter months in Cleveland. The influence of the Slav Evenings, reasoned Ledbetter,

reaches beyond local community and beyond Cleveland. It touches the nation in helping to develop mutual understanding among the elements of our national population. From this mutual understanding comes a feeling of unity, and in the immigrant a sense of belonging to America and of being recognized as so belonging. Neither do we stop with a national influence; our evenings touch chords that vibrate internationally. Every time a Polish paper reviews a Russian concert or a Czech paper speaks with appreciation of a Slovenian program, a contribution is made to international relations.[78]

International Recognition of Local Efforts. Tangible evidences of international goodwill appeared in foreign publications as a direct result of the Slav Evenings. Descriptions of the Broadway Branch and its services to Czech immigrants appeared in a Czechoslovakian school methods textbook written by Vojta Benes, inspector of schools for the Czechoslovakian Ministry of Education. The Czech woman's periodical, *Rude Kvety*, published a feature article on the Broadway Branch written by Marie Majerova, editor and noted Czech author.[79]

National Recognition of Local Efforts. Ledbetter, both under the auspices of the ALA CWFB and on her own, publicized the library's Americanization programs indirectly through newspaper and periodical articles of general interest. In 1922

Broadway Branch, Cleveland Public Library, circa 1910. Photo courtesy Cleveland Public Library Archives.

Ledbetter wrote a very provocative article entitled "The Human Touch and the Librarian," for the popular periodical *Scribner's Magazine*.

Ledbetter's article, intended as a rebuttal to a previously published article by a disgruntled librarian, was selected by the editors of *Scribner's Magazine*, apparently from a huge assortment of rebuttals from other offended librarians, as the most appropriate rejoinder.[80] The disgruntled librarian in the article was an assistant in the periodical department of a large urban public library. She had complained that "at times it seems to me that a library is not a place of learning, not a place to increase the intelligence of the community, but rather a place for the poverty-stricken and the outcast."[81]

In Ledbetter's article she includes a story about giving counsel to a young student interested in pursuing librarianship as a profession. The student, related Ledbetter, "had intended to go into social work, but has had a vision of library work as social work, and has been sent to me to discuss it on that ground. I assure her that certainly it is the finest kind of social work, since it is constructive, and it has for the worker a wholesomeness which does not exist in those types of social work which deal always with the abnormal and frequently with the pathological."[82] The librarian as social worker was once again the model that Ledbetter used to publicize library work with immigrants.

Cooperation with the Foreign Language Information Service. In addition to this article, Ledbetter undertook two other publicity projects of significance during her period as chair of the ALA CWFB, the purpose of which was to bring the work of librarians working with immigrant clienteles to a general audience nationwide. To this end, news releases were provided regularly to the Foreign Language Information Service from 1924 to 1926, and a series of articles was written for the library column of the *Christian Science Monitor* from 1926 to 1928.

The cooperation between the Foreign Language Information Service and the ALA CWFB was based on a common understanding of the needs of immigrants and informed by a mutual advocacy of cultural pluralism. The Foreign Language Information Service was created in 1918 as an agency of the federal government, lost this affiliation within three years, and emerged as an independent agency by 1921.

Daniel Erwin Weinberg reported in his in-depth investigation of the Foreign Language Information Service that it "was perceived, and indeed perceived itself, as liberal," and although it was ardently committed to the Americanization process, saw its mission as "enlightened reform." Throughout its years of service from 1918 to 1939, the Foreign Language Information Service was driven by "a vision that not only had room for diverse kinds of men, but one that posited the absolute necessity for variety."

For the Foreign Language Information Service, then, as well as the ALA CWFB, there was a consensus of opinion that "rather than being melted, the foreign born have importantly shaped the character of [American] society."[83] Believing therefore that their missions were compatible, the two organizations worked closely together in order to avoid duplication of efforts.

Ledbetter, throughout her tenure as chair of the ALA CWFB, maintained lasting working relationships with officials of the Foreign Language Information Service, particularly with its associate director Constantine Panunzio, and Czechoslovakian bureau chief Sarka Hrbkova. Ledbetter furnished the Foreign Language Information Service with a series of general articles, prepared in the form of news releases, on libraries and library work. These were translated subsequently into immigrant languages and disseminated widely by the various foreign language bureaus of the Foreign Language Information Service to almost nine hundred newspapers published in the United States in seventeen foreign languages as well as English. One series of articles supplied by the ALA CWFB in 1926 was reportedly published 124 times in seven languages. In reciprocity for these news releases, the Foreign Language Information Service, through its various publications, particularly its periodical *The Interpreter*, drew their readers' attention to articles and publications produced by the ALA CWFB.[84]

Newspaper Journalism. From 1926 to 1928, concurrently with the Foreign Language Information Service writing project, Ledbetter was requested by the editor of the *Christian Science Monitor* to write a series of articles for its library column. All of the articles Ledbetter contributed were related to some aspect of library work with immigrants, and in their context Ledbetter made direct comparisons between librarianship and social work, as she had done in prior writings throughout her career.

In one article, for example, Ledbetter commented that "the successful agent in any phase of social work is the one who can actually get . . . the mental attitude of the subject, and working from that, frame his program to touch the spots where contact brings the spark of response." In other articles, she related case studies of various immigrants she had known. She gave the particulars of their experiences with, presumably, the Broadway Branch library, and offered insights into why these individual immigrants came to the library, what they read and for what purpose, and, in some cases, why they stopped coming to the library. She stressed the fact that considering the three classifications of social work—case work, family social work, and group service—"all three types exist in library relations with the public."[85]

BIBLIOGRAPHER AND TRANSLATOR OF FOREIGN LITERATURE

From 1922 until her retirement from the Cleveland Public Library, and particularly after her final year as chair of the ALA CWFB in 1928, Ledbetter concentrated all of her spare energies in the areas of Polish bibliography and Czech translation. The issue of language as it affected her work with immigrants had always been critical and, indeed, problematic for Ledbetter, who implied in her writings that she had a grasp of the rudiments of spoken German but never admitted to fluency in speaking any language other than English.[86]

Ledbetter understood that immigrants' retention of their native languages as well as religions were symbolic of their national and ethnic pride, especially for immigrants from countries where they had experienced political, religious, and cultural oppression. In recognition of the efforts of her immigrant patrons to maintain their native tongues even as they became more and more proficient in English, she longed to be able to communicate with her patrons in their native tongues.

Ledbetter was inspired by the experience of her friend and colleague Helen Horvath, a Hungarian-born Americanization teacher in Cleveland. Horvath had been politicized to learn to speak English perfectly because of the derisive comments of an American who ridiculed her foreign accent.[87] Following Horvath's example, Ledbetter began her own personal attempts at self-education in the Polish and Czech languages in response to an encounter she had with a multilingual butcher in the immigrant neighborhood surrounding the Broadway Branch. Ledbetter had commented as early as 1918 that "once I may have thought myself superior to any butcher, but this butcher commands four languages, while I have only one and though I acknowledge it with regret, I fear he is my superior in ready courtesy."[88]

During her trips to Europe in 1923 and 1925, she had hoped to practice speaking some of the Polish, Czech, and Slovene she had learned on her own, but found that most of the Slavs she met insisted on speaking to her in German. In Czechoslovakia, she toured the library of the Lobkovic family at their castle at Roudnice and amazed the guides with the knowledge of Czech literature she had gained working with Czech immigrants in Cleveland.

When Ledbetter's visit at the castle library drew to a close, the archivist promised her that he would resume his study of English in appreciation for the knowledge and interest she had exhibited on Czech literature and language. He also wanted to be able to speak English with Ledbetter whenever she visited again. Ledbetter was profoundly touched by the archivist's sensitivity and recalled this poignant experience in 1927. "Not to be outdone in courtesy, I responded that when I come again, I hope to be able to speak Czech with him, and as the carriage took me from the courtyard, we exchanged final greetings [in Czech] and I hoped with all my heart that I might go back some day and speak Czech!"[89]

Through daily contact with Czech and Polish immigrants and through intensive study on her own, Ledbetter did acquire a reading knowledge of Polish and Czech sufficient for the work she was to accomplish with regard to the literatures of these Slavic languages. Later, in 1927, while praising the accomplishments of the immigrant patrons of the Broadway Branch, she candidly confessed her own inadequacy.

I have myself studied Czech with considerable diligence, and for quite as much time as the average immigrant can give to English in his first two years in America; I read the Czech newspapers every day, but I am a long way from understanding all that they say. . . . If I were transported to Czechoslovakia tomorrow and had to work eight or ten hours a day for my living, and had available only Czech literature, I should have to give up reading. Now then can I expect the Czech immigrant to find rest and recreation in English?[90]

International Recognition for Translation of Czech Fairy Tales

Notwithstanding her feelings of inadequacy with regard to facility with foreign languages, Ledbetter delved into an in-depth study of Czech fairy tales and folklore. She had for many years advocated this form of literature as a medium for bridging the generation gap between immigrant parents and their American children. She believed that "the library has possibilities in this situation and through books and the development of the child's imagination, it can help to create a common background."[91]

With this conviction concerning the efficacy of fairy tales in the child's development as well as in the bridging of the generation gap, Ledbetter chose for translation into English the folktales of Czech author Bozena Nemcova, whose stories deal with the richness and variety of Czech country life. *The Shepherd and the Dragon: Fairy Tales from the Czech of Bozena Nemcova*, with woodcut illustrations by William Siegel, was published in 1930.

One year later, in 1931, the Czechoslovakian consul in Cleveland presented Ledbetter the gold medal of the Order of the White Lion from the Czechoslovakian government. She was honored for her work in three areas: (1) cultural work among Czechoslovak immigrants in America, (2) promoting, among Americans, an understanding of Czechoslovaks and appreciation of their culture, and (3) translation of Czech folktales.[92]

International Recognition for Bibliography of Polish Literature

Ledbetter's fascination with Polish bibliography had begun as early as 1922, with the publication, under the auspices of the ALA CWFB, of her two-part article, "The Polish Immigrant and the Library." In this initial offering could be discerned the tentative outlines for her major bibliography of Polish literature in translation, which would appear ten years later. As Marion (Moore) Coleman recalled in her biography of Ledbetter, "[I]t was a good start, but, as Eleanor herself at once saw, a start only, and we can imagine her from this time on, making a card for each new translation of a Polish literary work that she came upon."[93]

By 1924 Ledbetter had written an article entitled "Polish Literature in English" for *Poland* magazine, which was in turn reprinted in summary form for librarians in *Library Journal*. Ledbetter pointed out that translations of Polish literature into English were at that time comparatively few, with many Polish authors of the first rank being without representation. That same year the ALA CWFB published her pamphlet *The Polish Immigrant and His Reading*, with an extensive bibliography including English translations of Polish literature. This was the pamphlet for which, as has been noted earlier, she was decorated by the Polish government.[94]

Ledbetter's *Polish Literature in English Translation: A Bibliography with a List of Books about Poland and the Poles* was published in 1932 and marked the end of ten years' labor. Alliance College in Cambridge Springs, Pennsylvania, had offered the financial guarantee to the H. W. Wilson Company for its publication. Tadeusz Mitana, professor at Alliance College, a college affiliated with the Polish National Alliance, wrote the foreword. According to Mitana, the bibliography "is, to the best of my knowledge, the first and a wholly successful attempt at bringing together all important bibliographic items of Polish literature, history and art ever published in English."[95] Marion (Moore) Coleman, Ledbetter's biographer, was even more effervescent, recalling "the pioneer energy and enterprise [and] the vision it took to compile such a list . . . at that time . . . when one was laughed at for being concerned in any serious way about the literature of a Slavic people, Polish or any other."[96] Ledbetter, in her modest and self-effacing way, merely acknowledged that "this bibliography has been compiled to help the student find all the Polish literature that is available in English, however obscure or unobtrusive its hiding place."

Shortly after the publication of the bibliography, the Polish Academy of Literature awarded her its silver medal and presented her with a certificate indicating that she was named for this prestigious honor by the Polish Ministry of Education in recognition of her "sincere interest in our literature in foreign lands." Three distinguished and prolific Polish authors, Waclaw Sieroszewski, Leopold Staff, and Juliusz Kaden-Bandrowski signed the certificate. Although the wording of the certificate was not specific, Ledbetter herself believed that this honor was, at least partially, in recognition of the bibliography of Polish literature in English translation.[97]

FINAL YEARS AT BROADWAY BRANCH

The six years before Ledbetter's retirement in 1938 saw many occasions for Cleveland to honor her. A signal honor was bestowed upon Ledbetter in 1932, on the occasion of her twenty-third year as the librarian of the Broadway Branch. The *Cleveland Plain Dealer* declared her a "distinguished citizen." The honor was bestowed on Ledbetter "because for 23 years, as librarian of the Broadway Library, she has had a greater influence on untold thousands of Cleveland's East and South Sides than probably any ten other residents of this community; because if she ever ran for mayor or councilman, she would get the solid Czech, Slovak, and Polish vote, . . . because never in her history has she ever thought a 'foreigner' was somebody to be patronized . . . and because she is a serene kind of person who is sure anyone can learn greatly from those around him."[98]

Twenty-fifth Anniversary at Broadway Branch

Two years later, in celebration of her twenty-fifth anniversary at the Broadway Branch, she was feted with a reception attended by local dignitaries and library officials. Distinguished Clevelanders who had served under Ledbetter as library pages also attended. These included the Ohio state director of aeronautics, an outfielder for the Cleveland Indians, president of the League of Polish Organizations, chief clerk of the Grand Trunk Railway, lawyers, engineers, architects, and politicians.[99]

Retirement from Broadway Branch

When Ledbetter retired in 1938, after almost thirty years' service to the Cleveland Public Library, all of the major newspapers of Cleveland ran laudatory and appreciative editorials and news releases in her honor. The headlines of the columns in themselves were indicative of the respect, admiration, and affection of Clevelanders: "More than Librarian" proclaimed the *Cleveland Plain Dealer*, and "Mrs. Ledbetter, Librarian Friend of Broadway Neighborhood, Retires" announced the *Cleveland Press*. The *Cleveland News*, in the most familiar tone of all, heralded Ledbetter as "Eleanor of Broadway," and summed up for all of Cleveland that

when Eleanor Edwards Ledbetter announces she will quit her post at Broadway library after 30 years' service, that is unhappy news.

You can count on your fingers the Clevelanders who have done so much for their city in 30 years as Mrs. Ledbetter. . . . By affection and whole-souled interest, Eleanor Ledbetter has helped countless thousands who otherwise would have had drab lives.

She has taught strangers to love this city, yet to keep the pride of their homelands. Doubtless some agency will see that Cleveland has a place and time to honor Mrs. Ledbetter. That place should be big enough for thousands![100]

Even Bessie Sargeant Smith, her supervisor and oftentimes her nemesis as well, glowed with unrestrained fervor that "Mrs. Ledbetter's work at Broadway has been creative and constructive, especially in relation to the Bohemian and Polish citizens of the city. She continually studied her neighborhood and gave it understanding service. Her contribution to the work of libraries of the foreign born has been distinctive, not alone in the Cleveland Library but in the entire library world. She has been held in high esteem by her community and publicly honored by several nationalities, both in Europe and in Cleveland. We are proud and fortunate to have had her as a member of the Cleveland Public Library staff."[101]

LATTER YEARS

Ledbetter was undeniably glad of the opportunity afforded by her retirement to relax, travel, cook, garden, be a doting grandmother, and get more involved with church work, but in September 1938 after her retirement in July, the Broadway Branch was still very much in her thoughts. Concerned about the appointment of her successor at the Broadway Branch, Ledbetter wrote to Charles Everett Rush, then librarian of the Cleveland Public Library, who had succeeded Linda Anne Eastman upon her retirement during the same year as Ledbetter's. Ledbetter wrote that "naturally I am greatly interested in the naming of my successor. The Broadway neighborhood is definitely non-responsive to strangers. I have noticed in clergy, school principals and others who came among us that it takes at least two years for a friendly person to get sufficient footing to get ready to start."[102]

This expression of Ledbetter's continuing concern for the Broadway Branch, revealing the difficulties she must have had to face as a young librarian unfamiliar with the foreign districts of Cleveland, showed quite conclusively that Ledbetter was reluctant to give up her association with the immigrant community. She maintained her residence in southeast Cleveland, not far from the Broadway Branch, and continued to work on her bibliography of Polish literature in English translation. Toward the end of her life, Ledbetter passed on the mantle with regard to her bibliographic research to her friend Marion (Moore) Coleman, whom, ironically, Ledbetter never met in person. Coleman published the definitive bibliography of Polish literature in English translation, dedicated to the memory of Eleanor (Edwards) Ledbetter, in 1963, nine years after Ledbetter's death in her beloved Cleveland.[103]

THE LEGACY OF LEDBETTER TO LIBRARIANSHIP

Although the name of Eleanor (Edwards) Ledbetter may have receded into the oblivion of a bygone era, her legacy endures in the annals of the Cleveland Public Library and the ALA CWFB. More important, however, her abiding influence lives on in the descendants of Polish, Czech, German, and Slovenian immigrants. These immigrants, while strangers in a new land, were once welcomed at the entrance to the Broadway Branch by a sign that proclaimed Free Public Library in a language they understood.

NOTES

1. Josef J. Barton, *Peasants and Strangers: Italians, Rumanians, and Slovaks in an American City, 1890–1950* (Cambridge, MA: Harvard University Press, 1975), 11–14; David D. Van Tassel and John J. Grabowski, eds., *The Encyclopedia of Cleveland History*, Published in Association with Case Western Reserve University (Bloomington: Indiana University Press, 1987), s.v. "Immigration and Migration," by John J. Grabowski, 540–43; and Herbert Adolphus Miller, *The School and the Immigrant*, Cleveland Education Survey (Cleveland: The Survey Committee of the Cleveland Foundation, 1916; reprint, New York: Arno Press and the New York Times, 1970), 11.

2. CPL AR 1869, 9, AR 1878, 8, AR 1898, 17, AR 1902, 85–86, AR 1905, 26, AR 1908, 104–13, AR 1909, 92–102, AR 1910, 104–15, AR 1915, 94–98; Eleanor C. [i.e., E.] Ledbetter, "A Library for Bohemians," *Czechoslovak Review* (Sept. 1919): 258–60; and C(larence) H(enley) Cramer, *Open Shelves and Open Minds: A History of the Cleveland Public Library* (Cleveland: Press of Case Western Reserve University, 1972): 247–48.

3. John Bodnar, "Schooling and the Slavic-American Family, 1900–1940," in Bernard J. Weiss, ed., *American Education and the European Immigrant: 1840–1940* (Urbana: University of Illinois Press, 1982), 85–86; and Barton, *Peasants and Strangers,* 22.

4. Ledbetter, "A Library for Bohemians," 258–60, which also appeared in summary form in *LJ* 44 (Dec. 1919): 792–93.

5. The first and second librarians of the Broadway Branch were Charlotte A. Buss and A. G. Hubbard respectively, each serving a tenure of two years. See CPL AR 1906, 55–61, AR 1907, 48–55, AR 1908, 61–64, AR 1909, 53–56, AR 1910, 58–61.

6. Van Tassel and Grabowski, eds., *The Encyclopedia of Cleveland History,* s.v. "Ledbetter, Eleanor Edwards," 623; Edith A. Case, Personnel Supervisor, CPL, to Marion (Moore) Coleman, Alliance College, Cambridge Springs, PA, 5 Apr. 1962, Ledbetter Papers; Marion (Moore) Coleman, "Eleanor E. Ledbetter: Bibliographer of Polonica," *Polish-American Studies* 19 (Jan.–June 1962): 37; "Collects Slavic Literary Work;

Broadway Branch Library Head Makes It Factor in Americanization," *Cleveland Plain Dealer,* 9 Jan. 1926, Ledbetter Papers; Grace V. Kelly, "Broadway Librarian Quits Post," *Cleveland Plain Dealer,* 7 June 1938, Ledbetter Papers; Resume of Eleanor E. Ledbetter, Ledbetter Papers; and C. C. Williamson and Alice L. Jewett, eds., *Who's Who in Library Science* (New York: H. W. Wilson, 1933), s.v. "Ledbetter, Mrs. Eleanor E(dwards)," 263.

7. Marion (Moore) Coleman, comp., *Polish Literature in English Translation: A Bibliography* (Cheshire, CT: Cherry Hill Books, 1963), i (quote); and Coleman, "Eleanor E. Ledbetter, Bibliographer of Polonica," 37.

8. Ledbetter, *The Polish Immigrant and His Reading,* Library Work with the Foreign Born (Chicago: ALA, 1924), 3.

9. Ledbetter, "Recent Development in Library Work with Immigrants," in *Proceedings of the National Conference of Social Work (Formerly National Conference of Charities and Correction) at the Fifty-First Annual Session* (Chicago: University of Chicago Press, 1924), 588–89.

10. Williamson and Jewett, eds., *Who's Who in Library Service,* 263; Ledbetter, *The Polish Immigrant and His Reading,* 3; and CPL AR 1912, 78.

11. Ledbetter, *Winning Friends and Citizens for America; Work with Poles, Bohemians, and Others,* Library Work with the Foreign Born (New York: Immigrant Publication Society, 1918), 13–18, 23.

12. Ledbetter, *The Polish Immigrant and His Reading,* 11.

13. Ledbetter, "The Human Touch and the Librarian," *Scribner's Magazine* 72 (Oct. 1922): 450–55.

14. Ledbetter, "Recent Development in Library Work with Immigrants," 588.

15. Ledbetter, *Winning Friends and Citizens for America,* 28–30 (quote, 28).

16. CPL AR 1910, 60 (quote), AR 1913, 94.

17. CPL AR 1910, 59, AR 1913, 92-93; and Ledbetter, *Winning Friends and Citizens for America,* 15–16.

18. CPL AR 1911, 31–32; Cleveland Americanization Committee, *Americanization in Cleveland; An Account of the Work which Has Been Done in Cleveland to Develop and Maintain a City Morale,* issued by the Cleveland Americanization Committee of the Mayor's Advisory War Board (Cleveland: Economy Printing, 1919), [22–23]; Mary Catherine Nagy, "History and Relationship of the Rice Branch to Its Hungarian Patrons" (master's thesis, Western Reserve University, 1952), 10–11; Virginia Phillips, "Fifty-Six Years of Service to the Foreign-Born by the Cleveland Public Library" (master's thesis, Western Reserve University, 1957), 8, quoted in May Wendellene Butrick, "History of the Foreign Literature Department of Cleveland Public Library, 1925–72" (master's thesis, Kent State University, 1974), 9–10; and Butrick, ibid., 12.

19. CPL AR 1912, 76; and Ledbetter, *Winning Friends and Citizens for America,* 12.

20. Ledbetter, *Winning Friends and Citizens for America,* 13–14 (quote, 14); CPL AR 1911, 61, AR 1912, 77; and Ledbetter, "Channels of Foreign Language Publicity," *Christian Science Monitor,* 23 Mar. 1927, Ledbetter Papers.

21. Coleman, "Eleanor E. Ledbetter: Bibliographer of Polonica," 37; Ledbetter, *The Polish Immigrant and His Reading,* 11; and "Foreign Language Press Publicity," *LJ* 52 (1 June 1927): 603.

22. Ledbetter, *Winning Friends and Citizens for America,* 10–11.

23. CPL AR 1910, 59, AR 1911, 63, AR 1913, 95; CPL/BB AR 1922–23, 7, AR 1924-25, 10; and *LJ* 47 (1 Jan. 1922): 42. Titles were verified using *Newspapers in Microform: United States, 1948–1983,* Library of Congress Catalogs (Washington, DC: Library of Congress, 1984).

24. Nine scrapbooks of newspaper clippings, which are preserved in the Ledbetter Papers, are arranged accordingly: [1] 1906–1922; [2] 1913–1921; [3] 1922; [4] 1923; [5] 1924; [6, pt. 1] Jan.–Mar. 1925; [6, pt. 2] Mar.–Dec. 1925; [7] 1926; [8] 1927; and [9] 1928. See also, CPL/BB AR 1920-21, 4, AR 1921-22, 10, AR 1922–23, 7, AR 1924–25, 10; Ledbetter, *The Polish Immigrant and His Reading*, 12; and Ledbetter, "Channels of Foreign Language Publicity," Ledbetter Papers.

25. CPL/BB AR 1913, 91–92, AR 1914, 1, AR 1916, 3.

26. CPL AR 1912, 75, AR 1921–22, 9–10; ALA CWFB Minutes, *ALA Bulletin* 16 (July 1922): 228; Ledbetter, *The Polish Immigrant and His Reading*, 10; CPL/BB AR 1926, 2; Ledbetter, "Group Service to Immigrants," *Christian Science Monitor*, 29 June 1927, Ledbetter Papers; Ledbetter to Linda A. Eastman, Librarian, CPL, 17 Oct. 1931, Ledbetter Papers; and Coleman, "Eleanor E. Ledbetter: Bibliographer of Polonica," 37–38.

27. Barton, *Peasants and Strangers, 22–26.*

28. Miller, *The School and the Immigrant*, 21–22. See also, Ruth A. Elmquist, "The Education of the Immigrant in American Society: 1880–1915" (master's thesis, Drew University, 1982), Chapter 1: "The Language Experience," 6–18; and Chapter 2: "Education and the Adult Immigrant," 19–36.

29. Ledbetter, *Winning Friends and Citizens for America*, 16–18; "Americanization Work of the Cleveland Public Library," *CAB* 1 (18 Feb. 1920): 1; and Ledbetter, *The Polish Immigrant and His Reading*, 14.

30. Ledbetter, *Winning Friends and Citizens for America*, 16–20.

31. Horace M. Kallen, *Culture and Democracy in the United States: Studies in the Group Psychology of the American Peoples* (New York: Boni and Liveright, 1924; reprint, New York: Arno Press and the New York Times, 1970); Kallen, "The Meaning of Americanism," *Immigrants in America Review* 1 (Jan. 1916): 12–19; and Kallen, "Democracy versus The Melting-Pot," *Nation* 100 (18 Feb. 1915): 190–94, (25 Feb. 1915): 217–20.

32. Herbert Adolphus Miller, "The Oppression Psychosis and the Immigrant," *Annals of the American Academy of Political and Social Science* 93 (Jan. 1921): 142.

33. Ledbetter, *Winning Friends and Citizens for America*, 32.

34. Ibid., 14–15.

35. See, for example, Joseph Remenyi, "The Americanization Movement in Cleveland from the Viewpoint of One of the Leaders among the Hungarian-Born," *CAB* 1 (15 Jan. 1920): 1.

36. Herbert Adolphus Miller, "The True Americanization of the Foreign Child," *ALA Bulletin* 13 (July 1919): 130.

37. Van Tassel and Grabowski, eds., *The Encyclopedia of Cleveland History*, s.v. "Americanization," by Edward M. Miggins, 29, s.v. "Mayor's Advisory War Committee," 671; Cleveland Americanization Committee, *Report of the Work of the Cleveland Americanization Committee of the Mayor's Advisory War Board, July 1917–July 1918* (Cleveland: The Committee, 1918), [1]; Cleveland Americanization Committee, *Americanization in Cleveland*, [7–9]; and Cleveland Mayor's Advisory War Committee, *Cleveland in the War: A Review of Work Accomplished by the Mayor's Advisory War Committee and Work Proposed During the Great Period of Reconstruction* (Cleveland: Harris Printing and Engraving, 1919), [3].

38. Cleveland Americanization Committee, *Report of the Work of the Cleveland Americanization Committee*, [2]; CPL/BB AR 1917, 1; Cleveland Americanization Committee, *Americanization in Cleveland*, [26]; and "Friendly Words in Commendation of the Americanization Council and the Work Cooperating Agencies Are Doing for Americanization," *CAB* 1 (15 Dec. 1920): 1.

39. CPL/BB AR 1918, 1; Harold T. Clark, Chair, Cleveland Americanization Committee, to William H. Brett, Librarian, CPL, 14 Mar. 1918, Ledbetter Papers; William H. Brett to Harold T. Clark, 22 Mar. 1918, Ledbetter Papers; Linda A. Eastman, Vice-Librarian, CPL, to Harold T. Clark, 22 Mar. 1918, Ledbetter Papers; and Cleveland Americanization Committee, *Report of the Work of the Cleveland Americanization Committee*, [2].

40. Cleveland Americanization Committee, *Americanization in Cleveland*, [6–8]. See also, John F. Clymer, "The Americanization Movement and the Education of the Foreign-Born Adult, 1914-25," *American Education and the European Immigrant: 1840-1940*, ed. Bernard J. Weiss, 102; and Frank V. Thompson, *Schooling of the Immigrant* (New York: Harper and Brothers, 1920; reprint, Monclair, NJ: Patterson Smith, 1971), Chap. 10: "Schooling in Citizenship," by Raymond Moley, 327–62.

41. Cleveland Americanization Committee, *Report of the Work of the Cleveland Americanization Committee*, [2] (quote); Cleveland Americanization Committee, *Americanization in Cleveland*, [9]; and Cleveland Mayor's Advisory War Committee, *Cleveland in the War*, [13–15] (quotes).

42. The following studies of ethnic groups in Cleveland were published by the Cleveland Americanization Committee of the Mayor's Advisory War Committee: Eleanor (Edwards) Ledbetter, *The Jugoslavs of Cleveland, with a Brief Sketch of Their Historical and Political Backgrounds* (Cleveland: Cleveland Americanization Committee, Mayor's Advisory War Committee, 1918), Ledbetter, *The Slovaks of Cleveland, with Some General Information on the Race* (Cleveland: Cleveland Americanization Committee, Mayor's Advisory War Committee, 1918), Ledbetter, *The Czechs of Cleveland* (Cleveland: Cleveland Americanization Committee, Mayor's Advisory War Committee, 1919); Charles Wellsley Coulter, *The Italians of Cleveland* (Cleveland: Cleveland Americanization Committee, Mayor's Advisory War Committee, 1919), Coulter, *The Poles of Cleveland* (Cleveland: Cleveland Americanization Committee, Mayor's Advisory War Committee, 1919), Coulter, *The Lithuanians of Cleveland* (Cleveland: Cleveland Americanization Committee, Mayor's Advisory War Committee, 1920); and Huldah Florence Cook, *The Magyars of Cleveland, with a Brief Sketch of Their Historical, Political and Social Back Grounds* [*sic*] (Cleveland: Cleveland Americanization Committee, Mayor's Advisory War Committee, 1919).

43. Coleman, "Eleanor E. Ledbetter: Bibliographer of Polonica," 37; and Van Tassel and Grabowski, eds., *The Encyclopedia of Cleveland History*, s.v. "Ledbetter, Eleanor Edwards," 623.

44. CPL/BB AR 1918, 1; *LJ* 43 (Nov. 1918): 841; and CPL/BB AR 1920-21, 3.

45. Ledbetter to Linda A. Eastman, Librarian, CPL, 18 Jan. 1919, Ledbetter Papers; and CPL/BB AR Jan. 1919–Mar. 1920, 5. Thomas, Park, and Miller cited Ledbetter's manuscript "Study of the Jugo-Slavs" in William I. Thomas, Robert E. Park, and Herbert A. Miller, *Old World Traits Transplanted* (New York: Harper and Brothers, 1921; reprint, Montclair, NJ: Patterson Smith, 1971), 128.

46. Elaine Fain, "Books for New Citizens: Public Libraries and Americanization Programs, 1900–1925," in *The Quest for Social Justice; The Morris Fromkin Memorial Lectures, 1970–1980*, ed. by Ralph M. Aderman (Madison: University of Wisconsin, 1983), published for the Golda Meir Library of the University of Wisconsin-Madison, 268–69. Fain makes no distinction between Ledbetter's work with the Cleveland Americanization Committee and that with the Carnegie Foundation Study on Americanization Methods; in fact, she does not mention the latter association at all. She assumed that Ledbetter resigned from the Cleveland Americanization Committee because its approach was patronizing and offensive. Compare Ledbetter's favorable remarks concerning the work of the Cleveland

Americanization Committee, in Americanization Conference, *Proceedings [of the] Americanization Conference, Held under the Auspices of the Americanization Division, Bureau of Education, Department of the Interior, Washington, May 12, 13, 14, 15, 1919* (Washington, DC: GPO, 1919), 240.

47. Cleveland Americanization Committee, *Americanization in Cleveland*, [30]; "Ohio Gives Work Preference," *Americanization* 1 (1 Mar. 1919): 14; *CAB* 1 (15 Oct. 1919): 1, (11 Nov. 1919): 1, (15 Dec. 1920): 1, (18 Feb. 1920): 1, (18 June 1920): 1; and "Coordinating All Civic Agencies: Cleveland Plans to Eliminate Waste Effort," *Americanization* 2 (1 Nov. 1919): 8.

48. Ledbetter, *Winning Friends and Citizens for America*; and Carr, "The Library in Americanization Work," 60–61, which summarizes Ledbetter's approach to library work with immigrants. See also "Americanization by the Public Library," *Survey* 41 (18 Jan. 1919): 537-38; and "Libraries' Task," *Americanization* 1 (1 Mar. 1919): 11.

49. *ALA Bulletin* 12 (Nov. 1918): 405, 13 (Sept. 1919): 451, 14 (Oct. 1920): 380, 15 (Sept. 1921): 281, 16 (Sept. 1922): 504, 17 (Sept. 1923): 361, 18 (Sept. 1924): 418, 19 (Sept. 1925): 444, 20 (Nov. 1926): 668, and 21 (Nov. 1927): 513.

50. ALA CWFB Minutes, *ALA Bulletin* 16 (July 1922): 228–29.

51. Ibid.

52. Ledbetter, "Is the Public Library Democratic?" *ALA Bulletin* 16 (July 1922): 366-70; and Ledbetter, "Factors that Should Determine the Proportion of a Library's Book Fund to Be Spent for Reading of the Foreign Born," *ALA Bulletin* 22 (Sept. 1928): 475, which was summarized in *LJ* 53 (Aug. 1928): 670, and *Libraries* 33 (Nov. 1928): 476–77.

53. Ledbetter, "Is the Public Library Democratic?" 367.

54. "Annual Report on the Work and Qualifications of Eleanor E. Ledbetter," signed by Bessie Sargeant Smith, Mar. 1922, June 1928, and 10 Apr. 1934, Ledbetter Papers.

55. Linda A. Eastman, Librarian, CPL, to Charles F. D. Belden, Massachusetts Free Public Library Commission, 16 Dec. 1921, Ledbetter Papers. Ledbetter was considered as a replacement for Jane Maud Campbell, who had resigned her position as Secretary of Work with the Foreign Born with the Massachusetts Free Public Library Commission. Edna Phillips succeeded Campbell.

56. ALA CWFB Minutes, *ALA Bulletin* 16 (July 1922): 228.

57. ALA CWFB Minutes, *LJ* 48 (1 May 1923): 406, *ALA Bulletin* 17 (July 1923): 209–10, *ALA Bulletin* 20 (Oct. 1926): 399–400; and Eleanor E. Ledbetter, "Books in Immigrant Languages," *LJ* 50 (15 Jan. 1925): 73–75.

58. ALA CWFB Minutes, *ALA Bulletin* 17 (July 1923): 209, 18 (Aug. 1924): 249, 19 (July 1925): 220, and 20 (Oct. 1926): 399.

59. CPL/BB AR 1923–24, 8–10, AR 1924–25, 3; Bessie Sargeant Smith, Supervisor of Branches, CPL, to Ledbetter, 12 May 1923, Ledbetter Papers; ALA CWFB Minutes, ALA Bulletin 18 (Aug. 1924): 250 (quote); Ledbetter to Bessie Sargeant Smith, [1925], Ledbetter Papers; Linda A. Eastman, Librarian, CPL, to Ledbetter, 15 Apr. 1925, Ledbetter Papers; Grace Kerr, Chief, Book Order Department, Indianapolis Public Library, to Linda A. Eastman, 20 Apr. 1925, Ledbetter Papers; Ledbetter, Requests for Leave of Absence, dated June 20 until August 20, 1925, and also June and July 1925, Ledbetter Papers; "Foreign Books Bought Abroad for Use Here; Popular Librarian Returns from Trip to Add to Shelves of Branch Libraries in Cleveland," *Cleveland Press*, 12 Aug. 1925, Ledbetter Papers; "Collects Slavic Literary Work; Broadway Branch Library Head Makes it Factor in Americanization," Ledbetter Papers; ALA CWFB Minutes, *ALA Bulletin* 20 (Oct. 1926): 400; Louise Hunt, "Co-operation Among Libraries," *LJ* 51 (1 Oct. 1926): 828; and Ida M. Gurwell, "Chats with Cleveland Writers: Eleanor E. Ledbetter," *Cleveland Plain Dealer*, 13 Sept. 1931, Ledbetter Papers.

60. Martha Ann Aikin, "New-Old Lands Wait Arrival of 'American Lady'; Broadway Librarian Tells How Foreign Born Friends Arranged for Reception Abroad," *Cleveland Plain Dealer*, 7 Sept. 1923, Ledbetter Papers; Ledbetter, "A Gallant Institution: The Warsaw Public Library," *Poland* (Jan. 1924): 28; and Ledbetter, "Libraries and the Attitude of Tolerance," *Christian Science Monitor*, 24 Nov. 1926, Ledbetter Papers.

61. CPL/BB AR 1923–24, 8–10, AR 1926, 11; Coleman, "Eleanor E. Ledbetter: Bibliographer of Polonica," 38–39; Ledbetter, "A Gallant Institution: The Warsaw Public Library," 28–29, 52, 54; *LJ* (1 June 1924): 540; Ledbetter, "June in Czechoslovakia," *Survey Graphic* 52 (1 June 1924): 301-3; and Ledbetter, "The Girl Queen," *Poland* (Nov. 1926): 681–82, 708, 710–11, 714–15.

62. ALA CWFB Minutes, *ALA Bulletin* 16 (July 1922): 228–29.

63. *LJ* 43 (Nov. 1918): 841; CPL/BB AR Jan. 1919–Mar. 1920, 5–6, AR 1920–21, 4, AR 1921–22, 8 (quote); Ledbetter, "The Religion of the Rusins: The Greek Catholic Church in America," *Czechoslovak Review* (Jan. 1920): 14–19; Ledbetter, "My Serbian Christmas," *Survey Graphic* 49 (1 Dec. 1922): 306–9; Ledbetter, "Easter in the Karpathians," *Spirit of Missions* 85 (Apr. 1920): 209–15; and *LJ* 47 (1 Jan. 1922): 42.

64. CPL/BB AR 1921-22, 8, AR 1922-23, 7; and ALA CWFB Minutes, *ALA Bulletin* 19 (July 1925): 220.

65. ALA CWFB Minutes, *ALA Bulletin* 16 (July 1922): 228; Ledbetter, "Recent Development in Library Work with Immigrants," 587–93; CPL/BB AR 1927, 6; and "Library Is Rival of School, Opinion at Reading Meet; Voluntary Study by Foreign Born Children Is Biggest Aid; Helps Understanding with Their Parents," *Grand Rapids (MI) Herald*, 8 May 1927, Ledbetter Papers.

66. David Pinski and Jennie Meyrowitz, "Yiddish Literature," *LJ* 46 (1 Dec. 1921): 977–79; Eleanor (Edwards) Ledbetter, "The Polish Immigrant and the Library [Part I]," *LJ* 47 (15 Jan. 1922): 67–70, "The Polish Immigrant and the Library [Part II]," *LJ* 47 (1 June 1922): 496–98; Marion Horton, "Library Work with the Japanese," *LJ* 47 (15 Feb. 1922): 157–60; Josephine Gratiaa, "Roumanians in the United States and Their Relations to Public Libraries," *LJ* 47 (1 May 1922): 400–404; Margery Quigley, "The Greek Immigrant and the Library," *LJ* 47 (15 Oct. 1922): 863–65; Ledbetter, "The Czechoslovak Immigrant and the Library," *LJ* 48 (1 Nov. 1923): 911–15; and May M. Sweet, "Italians and the Public Library," *LJ* 49 (15 Nov. 1924): 977–81.

67. See, for example, the remarks of Thomas Siemiradski in the *Wiadomosci Codzienne (Polish Daily News)* of Cleveland, quoted in Ledbetter, "The Polish Immigrant and the Library [Part II]," 496; ALA CWFB Minutes, *ALA Bulletin* 18 (Aug. 1924): 250; Ledbetter, "Recent Development in Library Work with Immigrants," 590–91; and *LJ* 49 (1 Dec. 1924): 1044.

68. ALA CWFB, "Dealers in Foreign Books," 647-48; and Ledbetter, comp., "Slav Literatures: A List of Bibliographies," *LJ* 49 (1 June 1924): 553.

69. Eleanor (Edwards) Ledbetter, *The Polish Immigrant and His Reading*, Library Work with the Foreign Born (Chicago: ALA, 1924), 4 (quote); May M. Sweet, *The Italian Immigrant and His Reading*, Library Work with the Foreign Born (Chicago: ALA, 1925); and Alison B. Alessios, *The Greek Immigrant and His Reading*, Library Work with the Foreign Born (Chicago: ALA, 1926). The ALA CWFB also published in 1929 one other pamphlet in this series after Ledbetter's tenure, Peschke, *The German Immigrant and His Reading*, Library Work with the Foreign Born (Chicago: ALA, 1929).

70. Ledbetter, "Suggested List of Titles for a Beginning Collection in the Polish Language," in *The Polish Immigrant and His Reading*, 24–40 (quote, 24).

71. "Medal for Librarian; Mrs. Ledbetter to Be Decorated by Polish Group," *Cleveland Plain Dealer*, 21 Feb. 1928, Ledbetter Papers; "Poland Honors 5 Clevelanders; Haller

Crosses Bestowed at Vets' Banquet," *Cleveland Plain Dealer*, 21 Feb. 1928, Ledbetter Papers; and ALA CWFB Minutes, *ALA Bulletin* 22 (Sept. 1928): 475.

72. ALA CWFB Minutes, *ALA Bulletin* 16 (July 1922): 229.

73. CPL/BB AR Jan. 1919–Mr. 1920, 5 (quote), AR 1920–21, 3 (quote).

74. CPL/BB AR Jan. 1919–Mar. 1920, 5–7 (quotes, 6, 7), AR 1920–21, 3–4, AR 1921–22, 4–7.

75. Ledbetter, "Recent Development in Library Work with Immigrants," 592.

76. CPL/BB AR 1922–23, 6, AR 1923–24, 5–7, AR 1924–25, 7–10, AR Apr. 1, 1925–Dec. 31, 1925, 4, AR 1926, 11, AR 1928, 3, AR 1929, 5–6, AR 1930, 7; Ledbetter, "Is the Public Library Democratic?" 369; Ledbetter, "Recent Development in Library Work with Immigrants," 591; and Ledbetter, "Group Service to Immigrants—II," *Christian Science Monitor*, 3 July 1927, Ledbetter Papers.

77. CPL/BB AR 1923–24, 6–7.

78. CPL/BB AR 1924–25, 9.

79. CPL/BB AR Jan. 1919–Mar. 1920, 4, AR 1920–21, 5; and Martha Ann Aikin, "New-Old Lands Wait Arrival of 'American Lady'; Broadway Librarian Tells How Foreign Born Friends Arranged for Reception Abroad," Ledbetter Papers.

80. Ledbetter, "The Human Touch and the Librarian," *Scribner's Magazine* 72 (Oct. 1922): 450–55; *LJ* 47 (15 Oct. 1922): 888; and Robert Bridges, Charles Scribner's Sons, to Ledbetter, 20 Jan. 1923, Ledbetter Papers.

81. Elizabeth T. Kirkwood, "Life and the Librarian," *Scribner's Magazine* 71 (June 1922): 737–40 (quote, 738).

82. Ledbetter, "The Human Touch and the Librarian," 454.

83. Daniel Erwin Weinberg, "The Foreign Language Information Service and the Foreign Born, 1918–1939: A Case Study of Cultural Assimilation Viewed as a Problem in Social Technology" (Ph.D. dissertation, University of Minnesota, 1973), 20–22 (quotes, 20, 21), 261 (quote).

84. CPL/BB AR 1922–23, 6; Panunzio, "The Immigrant and the Library," 969–73; ALA CWFB Minutes, *ALA Bulletin* 18 (Aug. 1924): 250, *ALA Bulletin* 19 (July 1925): 220, *ALA Bulletin* 20 (Oct. 1926): 400, 563; Hrbek [i.e. , Hrbkova], "The Library and the Foreign-Born Citizen," 98–104; Ledbetter, "Books in Foreign Language," *Public Libraries* 27 (Dec. 1922): 599; Ledbetter, "Recent Development in Library Work with Immigrants," 589; *LJ* 51 (1 Nov. 1926): 979; *Libraries* 31 (Nov. 1926): 472; Ledbetter, "Foreign Language Press Publicity," 603; and Ledbetter, "Channels of Foreign Language Publicity," Ledbetter Papers. See also various issues published between 1924 and 1926 of *The Interpreter*, vol. 1 (1922)–vol. 9 (Nov.–Dec. 1930) [all published].

85. Ledbetter, "Helpful Magazines for Workers with Foreign-Born," *Christian Science Monitor*, 26 Jan. 1927 (quote), Ledbetter Papers; and Ledbetter, "Group Service to Immigrants," (quote), Ledbetter Papers. See also Ledbetter, "Some Immigrant Readers Considered," *Christian Science Monitor*, 2 Mar. 1927, Ledbetter Papers; and Ledbetter, "Types of Immigrant Readers Studied," *Christian Science Monitor*, 9 Mar. 1927, Ledbetter Papers.

86. Ida M. Gurwell, "Chats with Cleveland Writers: Eleanor E. Ledbetter," Ledbetter Papers.

87. Van Tassel and Grabowski, eds., *The Encyclopedia of Cleveland History*, s.v. "Horvath, Helen," 519–20; "Introducing the Library," *LJ* 26 (June 1921): 350–51, is an excerpt from the Cleveland Public Library Log Account of Americanization Work that recalls a visit to Horvath's High School of Commerce classes; Ledbetter, "Library for Bohemians," 260; Ledbetter, "Easter in the Karpathians," 215; Ledbetter, "Recent De-

velopment in Library Work with Immigrants," 589–90; Ledbetter, *The Polish Immigrant and His Reading*, 22; and Ledbetter, *Winning Friends and Citizens for America*, 4.

88. Ledbetter, *Winning Friends and Citizens for America*, 4 (quote).

89. Ledbetter, "The Lobkovic Library at Roudnice, Czechoslovakia," *Christian Science Monitor*, 27 Apr. 1927 (quote), Ledbetter Papers. See also Ledbetter, "Libraries and the Attitude of Tolerance," *Christian Science Monitor*, 24 Nov. 1926, Ledbetter Papers; and Ledbetter, "Czech Literature in American Libraries," *Christian Science Monitor*, 25 Jan. 1928.

90. Ledbetter, "Is the Public Library Democratic," 368 (quote); and Ida M. Gurwell, "Chats with Cleveland Writers: Eleanor E. Ledbetter," Ledbetter Papers.

91. Ledbetter, "Immigrant Parents and Their American Children," *Christian Science Monitor*, 25 May 1927 (quote), Ledbetter Papers. See also Ledbetter, "Library for Bohemians," 260; and Ledbetter, "Library Is Rival of School, Opinion at Reading Meet," Ledbetter Papers.

92. Bozena Nemcova, *The Shepherd and the Dragon; Fairy Tales from the Czech of Bozena Nemcova*, translated by Eleanor E. Ledbetter, illustrated by William Siegel (New York: Robert M. McBride & Company, 1930); S. H. Steinberg, ed., *Cassell's Encyclopedia of World Literature* (New York: Funk & Wagnalls, 1954), s.v. "Nemcova, Bozena," by R. Auty, 2: 1287; Van Tassel and Grabowski, eds., *The Encyclopedia of Cleveland History*, s.v. "Ledbetter, Eleanor Edwards," 623; "Edits Book," *Cleveland Press*, 22 Sept. 1930, Ledbetter Papers; *Libraries* 36 (May 1931): 235; Ida M. Gurwell, "Chats with Cleveland Writers: Eleanor E. Ledbetter," Ledbetter Papers; and "Medal of White Lion Is Given Librarian," *Cleveland Plain Dealer*, 12 Mar. 1931, Ledbetter Papers.

93. Ledbetter, "The Polish Immigrant and the Library"; and Coleman, "Eleanor E. Ledbetter: Bibliographer of Polonica," 38–39.

94. CPL/BB AR 1923–24, 10; Ledbetter, "Polish Literature in English," *Poland* (Apr. 1924): 229–33, 249, and in summary form, "Polish Literature in English," *LJ* 49 (1 Sept. 1924): 738–39; Ledbetter, *The Polish Immigrant and His Reading*; *LJ* 49 (1 Dec. 1924): 1044; "Medal for Librarian; Mrs. Ledbetter to Be Decorated by Polish Group," Ledbetter Papers; and "Poland Honors 5 Clevelanders; Haller Crosses Bestowed at Vets' Banquet," Ledbetter Papers.

95. Ledbetter, *Polish Literature in English Translation; A Bibliography with a List of Books about Poland and the Poles*, with a foreword by Tadeusz Mitana (New York: Published under the Auspices of the Polish National Alliance by H. W. Wilson, 1932), 3; *WLB* 6 (June 1932): 672; and CPL/BB AR 1931, 7, AR 1932, 3.

96. Coleman, "Eleanor E. Ledbetter: Bibliographer of Polonica," 36 (quote).

97. Ledbetter, *Polish Literature in English Translation*, 6 (quote); and "Poland Sends Medal to Broadway–E. 55 Librarian," [unidentified newspaper], [1932?], Ledbetter Papers.

98. "As a Distinguished Citizen, the Plain Dealer Presents Eleanor E. Ledbetter," *Cleveland Plain Dealer*, 7 Feb. 1932, Ledbetter Papers.

99. "Librarian of 25 Years to Be Honored at Party and Reunion," *Cleveland Plain Dealer*, 3 Dec. 1934, Ledbetter Papers; "Saluting Mrs. Ledbetter," *Cleveland Plain Dealer*, 10 Dec. 1934, Ledbetter Papers; and "All Neighborhood Honors Librarian; Mrs. Ledbetter, 25 Years at Broadway Branch, Given Party," [unidentified newspaper], [1934], Ledbetter Papers.

100. CPL/BB AR 1938, 8; "More Than Librarian," *Cleveland Plain Dealer*, 8 June 1938, Ledbetter Papers; "Mrs. Ledbetter, Librarian Friend of Broadway Neighborhood Retires," *Cleveland Press*, 7 June 1938, Ledbetter Papers; and "Eleanor of Broadway," *Cleveland News*, 7 June 1938, Ledbetter Papers. For other tributes, see also "Veteran Librarian Resigns," *Cleveland News*, 7 June 1938, Ledbetter Papers; "A Rich Life," Cleveland Press,

8 June 1938, Ledbetter Papers; and Grace V. Kelly, "Broadway Librarian Quits Post," Ledbetter Papers.

101. Sargeant Smith's comments are found in Eleanor E. Ledbetter, CPL Resignation Form, 20 May 1938, Ledbetter Papers.

102. Grace V. Kelly, "Broadway Librarian Quits Post," Ledbetter Papers; "Mrs. Ledbetter, Librarian Friend of Broadway Neighborhood, Retires," Ledbetter Papers; and Ledbetter to Charles Everett Rush, Librarian, CPL, 25 Sept. 1938, Ledbetter Papers.

103. Coleman, "Eleanor E. Ledbetter: Bibliographer of Polonica," 39–41; Coleman, Marion (Moore), comp., *Polish Literature in English Translation: A Bibliography* (Cheshire, CT: Cherry Hill Books, 1963); and "Mrs. Eleanor Ledbetter" [Obituary], *Cleveland Plain Dealer*, 21 July 1954.

7

The Librarian as Educator: Edna Phillips, 1890–1968

Leadership in the Americanization movement was not forthcoming from the federal government. This was due primarily to the rivalry between the short-lived Division of Immigrant Education of the Bureau of Education within the U.S. Department of the Interior, representing the educational factor in the Americanization equation, and the Bureau of Naturalization within the U.S. Department of the Interior, representing the naturalization factor. Even after the demise of the Division of Immigrant Education of the Bureau of Education in 1919 and the emergence of the Bureau of Naturalization as the winner by default for federal control of the Americanization process, leadership remained where it had always been, at the local and state levels.[1]

The statewide Americanization effort of Massachusetts was representative of that of the more than thirty states enacting legislation that facilitated the establishment of and financial support for evening school programs in Americanization during the decades surrounding World War I.[2] In 1919, the Americanization program in Massachusetts was further strengthened by administrative changes mandated by the Act of Consolidation of State Departments. Immigrant education was, from that point on, firmly entrenched within the Massachusetts State Department of Education as its Division of University Extension. Under the auspices of this division, John Joseph Mahoney and Charles Michael Herlihy were charged with the responsibility for the supervision of evening school programs statewide.

The same 1919 act was also responsible for the establishment of the Division of Public Libraries. The Division of Public Libraries was, in actuality, new only in name, having offered on a continuing basis library service to public libraries throughout Massachusetts since its establishment, in 1890, as the Massachusetts Free Public Library Commission, the first state library commission. In keeping with the long tradition of service begun under its former name, the governing board of

Edna Phillips, circa 1952. Photo by Ken McLean, Norwood, MA. Courtesy Morrill Memorial Library, Norwood, MA.

the Division of Public Libraries, then chaired by Charles Francis Dorr Belden, director of the Boston Public Library, retained the designation Massachusetts Board of Free Public Library Commissioners. Along with this administrative restructuring, the responsibility for the supervision of school libraries throughout the state was added to its original charge of assisting small libraries in communities and villages with a tax valuation of $1,000,000 or less.[3]

The personnel of the Division of Public Libraries, specifically Jane Maud Campbell, secretary for Library Work with Foreigners, and the Division of University Extension, specifically Mahoney and Herlihy, worked in close cooperation with each other. In theory, their missions to serve the educational needs of adult learners, both foreign- and native-born, were supplementary and complementary; in practice, their joint educational programs presented a united front in Americanization work in Massachusetts. In an era when such sentiments were widely broadcast and well received by the American public at large, it was understandable that the education of the immigrant in the English language was viewed as being tantamount to providing for the defense of the nation.

The year 1922 was a transitional year for Americanization personnel in the Massachusetts Department of Education, in both the Division of University Extension as well as the Division of Public Libraries. That year Herlihy succeeded Mahoney as the state supervisor of Adult Alien Education and Mary Louise Guyton replaced Herlihy as assistant supervisor. The position of secretary for Library Work with Foreigners was vacant during the entire year. Belden, who served as both the director of the division and chairman of the Board of Free Public Library Commissioners, searched for a suitable replacement for Jane Maud Campbell, who had resigned effective December 1921 to accept the directorship of a public library in Virginia.[4]

Belden's task was not an easy one. He was justifiably anxious to secure a librarian of Campbell's stature to carry on the innovative programs of library work with immigrants already in place, notably the system of traveling libraries of foreign language and easy English books circulated upon request throughout Massachusetts. It is also not difficult to imagine Herlihy's anxiety, since school and public libraries provided invaluable resources and services to supplement the adult immigrant education programs sponsored by the Division of University Extension.

EARLY YEARS

In February 1923, after an extensive nationwide search lasting over a year, a suitable candidate, Edna Phillips, a native of Newark, New Jersey, was secured as Campbell's replacement. Phillips's educational background included some advanced study in art, but no college degree. Her training in librarianship was acquired through a summer school course taught under the auspices of the New Jersey Public Library Commission and, from 1913 to 1914, two years of experience as a library assistant at the Madison (NJ) Public Library. The knowledge gained from these two experiences was sufficient for her to pass the civil service examination and secure her first position as a librarian in the community of

she succeeded Campbell (ch. 3)

Edgewater, New Jersey. Edgewater was located in the densely populated north-eastern section of New Jersey, where industrial and manufacturing plants employed large numbers of immigrants.

Service in Europe during World War I

Phillips served in Edgewater from 1914 to 1918, when she, like many patriotic young women during the World War I era, answered the call of duty and volunteered her services to the American armed forces in Europe and in the United States. Under the auspices of the Young Men's Christian Association, Phillips served a tour of duty as a canteen operator in France and Germany, from April 1918 through May 1919, as well as back home at the ports of debarkation in Newport News, Virginia, and Hoboken, New Jersey, until November 1920.

Service in East Orange, New Jersey

In January 1921, she began her two-year tenure as librarian in East Orange, New Jersey, located in the heart of the state's industrial belt, where the majority of the foreign-born population resided. In late 1922, Phillips was faced with the dilemma of choosing between two promising positions that she had been offered. Refusing the position as librarian for the American University in Beirut, Lebanon, Phillips apparently viewed an opportunity for international service closer to home as more attractive in the long run.

MASSACHUSETTS FREE PUBLIC LIBRARY COMMISSION

Phillips thus brought to her new post as secretary for Library Work with Foreigners in the Division of Public Libraries years of library experience with immigrant clienteles and the added dimension provided by international travel and social service. She began what would be a ten-year professional commitment to the Division of Public Libraries amid the high hopes and expectations of her associates in the Massachusetts Department of Education. As in any successful match between employer's expectations and employee's qualifications, Phillips was chosen as much, if not more, for her philosophy of library service to immigrants as for her library experience per se. Undoubtedly Phillips was as candid in her employment interviews as she was a few years later, in 1929, when she addressed a group of librarians at a convention of the New Hampshire Library Association.[5]

At that meeting, one of numerous occasions on which she would address librarians and educators on Americanization-related topics, Phillips revealed her philosophy of library work with immigrants. Phillips believed that librarians should eliminate all barriers between themselves and their immigrant clienteles and thus create an openness that encouraged dialogue and the mutual exchange of ideas.[6]

Phillips made her point perfectly clear that the intent of Americanization was to bring culturally diverse immigrants into the mainstream of Anglo-Saxon America without depriving them of their heritages. Her support of the 1924 National Origins *cultural pluralism*

Act in principle and practice placed her squarely in the restrictionist camp, but this was for social and economic rather than racial or cultural reasons. "As I look toward the future, I believe this idea of inter-racial exchange will be the element that grows. 'Americanization' as the process of bringing the newcomer into sympathetic relations with the older stock, will diminish as the foreigners become adjusted, and as the new immigration policy begins to be felt."[7]

Phillips elaborated upon her position with regard to immigration restriction and urged the librarians in her audience to lend a sympathetic ear to her justification for this conservative stance. "Perhaps you share my belief that restricted immigration is a wise policy. While I thoroughly believe that differences between people are individual to a much greater degree than racial, I have had many opportunities both in New Jersey and in Massachusetts to see the difficulties that arise when there are more newcomers than conditions can care for in employment and housing and schools."[8]

Phillips espoused the view that there are "[t]hree things of prime importance . . . the libraries can do for the foreign-born: Help them to learn English by supplying books in easy form for adult beginners; help them to know America by offering books that reflect its life; preserve their racial culture by offering books in their native language."[9] She concluded by noting that to provide "the basic service of the library in a foreign community" requires "knowledge of the races locally represented; an energetic, sympathetic, and adaptable program for recruiting new readers; enlisting the cooperation of all constructive agencies; developing the support of an informed public opinion; and . . . spending a suitable proportion of the book fund on books for foreign readers and those working with them."[10]

The selection of Phillips as Campbell's replacement thus revealed a conscious move on the part of the Division of Public Libraries away from the liberal settlement-worker-like advocacy of Campbell and toward a more conservative stance in keeping with national immigration policy. Throughout Phillips's tenure with the Division of Public Libraries, the focus of its program with immigrants was education for Americanization, pure and simple. The model of the librarian as educator informed her approach to library work with immigrants.

Americanization Work with the Division of Public Libraries

Phillips's educational work with the Division of Public Libraries and Herlihy's with the Division of University Extension reflected a national trend toward viewing the educational factor of the Americanization process as not only the exclusive territory of the non-English-speaking foreign-born adult, but also the territory of the illiterate native-born adult. Herlihy, who served during the 1924/25 term as president of the Department of Immigrant Education of the National Education Association, founded in 1920 as a forum for state and local Americanization program directors, saw the birth of the adult education movement in United States during his presidency. In 1924, the Department of Immigrant Education was renamed the Department of Adult Education in recognition of the expansion of its mission to include all adult illiterates regardless of their origins.[11]

the librarian as educator (of adults)

As Phillips began her duties with the Division of Public Libraries, she knew instinctively that she would indirectly come under the scrutiny of adult educators and librarians throughout the nation, who looked to Massachusetts, along with other states with large immigrant populations, for leadership in this burgeoning field. Within two years, Phillips, along with her colleagues in the Divisions of Public Libraries and University Extension, viewed with justifiable pride the results of a national survey conducted in 1925 by Herlihy for the U.S. Bureau of Education. Herlihy's study showed that while Massachusetts was one of thirty-four states to enact legislation favoring the establishment of evening schools for adults, it was one of only twenty-seven states to furnish leadership for adult education within state departments of education. Further testimony of Massachusetts's progressive stance on adult education, for both immigrants and native-born Americans, were the statistics showing it to be one of only twenty-four states to provide financial aid to local school districts and one of only fourteen states to conduct special teacher-training courses for adult educators.[12]

Written concurrently with Herlihy's survey but appearing a few months earlier, in November 1924, Phillips's appropriately titled article, "Encouraging the Foreign Reader," was published in *Library Journal*. Her article shared with the national library community the accomplishments of public and school libraries in immigrant communities comprised of mainly Italian, French Canadian, and Polish laborers. These immigrant laborers were employed throughout Massachusetts in the factories and mills, stone quarries, the Connecticut River Valley farms, and the cranberry bogs of Cape Cod.[13] The article served as a report card not only for library service to immigrants established during Campbell's tenure, but also for the accomplishments of the first two years of Phillips's tenure with the Division of Public Libraries.

Phillips quoted statistics based on the 1920 federal census to document the progress that had occurred in the field of education for adult illiterates, both foreign- and native-born. This progress had been brought about by the close cooperation between the Division of Public Libraries, under her supervision and Campbell's before her, and the Division of University Extension, under Herlihy's supervision and Mahoney's before him. She made the distinction between foreign-born adults, the immigrants themselves, and adults of foreign stock, the American-born descendants of immigrants. "A significant commentary on the work of the Massachusetts evening schools and libraries is afforded by the statistics on illiteracy in the 14th Census. The Commonwealth is fourth in number of adult foreign-born; fourteenth in percentage of illiteracy among the foreign-born; fifth in percentage of number of adults of foreign stock; and thirtieth in percentage of illiteracy among adults of foreign stock." Phillips commented further that the state of Massachusetts, through its Division of University Extension, absorbed half the cost of instruction and supervision for the evening school classes operated for adult immigrants by local public schools and that enrollment had increased in five years' time from 3,000 to 32,000.[14]

These impressive statistics showed, according to Phillips, that "both divisions believe firmly in the joint action of library and schools." Phillips closed her article with the prediction "that many states of the Union having large foreign populations will find the method adopted by Massachusetts the most effective in developing this form of adult education." She revealed as well the more liberal attitude toward the process of Americanization espoused by both divisions in stating that "the policy of these classes is to teach English, to encourage the alien in becoming informed and fitted for citizenship, but not to force it."[15]

Phillips's article served a twofold purpose: (1) to affirm the commitment to adult education shared by the Divisions of Public Libraries and University Extension, and (2) to promote the Massachusetts model of statewide cooperation between the public library and the evening school as an ideal to emulate nationwide. The article placed before the national library community her agenda for the provision of statewide library service to the immigrant communities in Massachusetts.

Massachusetts Library Club Committee on Work with New Americans

In addition to her work with the Massachusetts Department of Education, her agenda for library work with immigrants required the coordination of local library efforts with immigrants through the Massachusetts Library Club Committee on Work with New Americans. The committee was established at Phillips's instigation in the spring of 1924, barely one year after her arrival in Massachusetts.

Phillips's primary responsibility as secretary for Library Work with Foreigners of the Division of Public Libraries was to small towns and villages with limited revenues for library service. In addition, through the MLC Committee on Work with New Americans, which she chaired throughout her tenure, she was able to offer assistance to libraries in the more prosperous cities and communities where large foreign-born populations resided.[16]

Also during the productive year of 1925, Phillips published the article "Contribution of the Public Library to Adult Education," which presented the results of her national survey on library service to immigrants conducted for the U.S. Bureau of Education. Appearing in *School Life*, a periodical sponsored by the Bureau of Education, Phillips's article informed Americanization personnel specifically and adult education personnel in general of the resources and services available in public libraries to assist them in their tasks.[17]

Phillips outlined the work of the Division of Public Libraries as well as the accomplishments of the MLC Committee on Work with New Americans and closed with recommendations for the improvement of library service for illiterate foreign-born and native-born adults. These recommendations served as a mental checklist for Phillips by which she evaluated herself and the services she implemented throughout the remainder of her tenure with the Division of Public Libraries.

Indeed, all of her activities with the Division of Public Libraries could be viewed as five strategies for implementing literacy programs for adults in Massachusetts. The five strategies were: (1) promoting literacy programs at state and national meetings, (2) encouraging more state library associations to investigate ways to fulfill the needs of illiterate adults and to appoint more literacy specialists to their staffs, (3) providing lists from various governmental agencies to assist public libraries in the purchase of suitable materials, (4) advocating that a fair share of library budgets be allocated to the purchase of books in easy English for adult beginners and supplementary collections in foreign languages, and (5) informing individual library directors and state library associations on the topic of illiteracy.[18]

ALA Committee on Work with the Foreign Born

It was undoubtedly the enthusiastic reception of Phillips's vision of library service to immigrants that prompted her appointment to the ALA Committee on Work with the Foreign Born during the 1925/26 term. She was invited to address the ALA at its fiftieth anniversary conference, in October 1926, in Atlantic City (NJ) on the topic "The Place of Service to the Foreign-Born in the Small Library."

After a one-year hiatus during the 1926/27 term, Phillips returned to the ALA CWFB as its newly elected chair during the 1927/28 term and continued to serve in this capacity for the next six years.[19] Phillips's agenda as chair of the ALA CWFB was a reflection at the national level of what she was accomplishing at the state, local, and regional levels in Massachusetts and New England in the areas of public library service to immigrants and immigrant education.

Traveling Libraries of Foreign Books

Phillips carried on the highly successful services planned and implemented by Campbell, notably the traveling libraries of books in twenty-nine foreign languages. These traveling collections included not only contemporary and classic foreign language titles, but also new titles on American history and civics to help immigrants prepare for citizenship. Alberto Pecorini's *The Story of America* in Italian and Polish, which was written and translated at the urging of Campbell and published by the Colonial Dames of Massachusetts, was often included in the traveling collections. Supplementing the foreign language books were books in easy English for the adult beginner.

Adding her own personal touch to an already established routine, Phillips incorporated into the traveling library service marketing techniques for attracting immigrant readers; these techniques had been pioneered by the ALA CWFB. Each traveling library included a brief newspaper notice, which the librarian receiving the collection was instructed to forward to the editor of the local foreign language newspaper for translation and publication. The notice advertised the Division of Public Libraries' services for foreign-born residents of Massachusetts and described the nature of the books included in the traveling collection, to which the local librarian could add the address of the public library with its hours of opening.

The traveling library service had naturally fallen off during the intervening year of 1922 between Campbell's resignation and Phillips's employment. At the end of her first ten months of service, Phillips reported in the 1922/23 annual report of the Division of Public Libraries an increase of 75 collections added to the 190 collections already in the circuit. This represented "the largest increase reported since the foreign work was started [in 1913]."[20]

Phillips envisioned the traveling library service of the Division of Public Libraries as but one component in its overall mission to serve as a "clearing house for information useful to librarians active in foreign work." As such, the Division maintained card files, classified by language. There were lists of dealers in foreign language books as well as the names and addresses of foreign societies and their secretaries. Lists of foreign language newspapers included not only the names of their editors but also the general nature or political slant of individual publications. Librarians were supplied the names and addresses of foreign language experts to assist in cataloging and transliteration, and to recommend books for library purchase, both in foreign languages and easy English.[21]

The provision of advice in the selection and acquisition of books in foreign languages and easy English was the most time-consuming task associated with Phillips's responsibilities with the Division of Public Libraries. Phillips once commented with characteristic good humor, alluding undeniably to her native state of New Jersey, that "an ideal compiler of such information would need the persistence of a pneumatic drill and a hunger for getting results of a New Jersey mosquito."[22]

Consultation on Library Americanization Programs

Phillips provided advice via correspondence and mailings of mimeographed lists on collection development and maintenance, advertising foreign language collections, and gaining an understanding of racial and ethnic groups through reading. She participated in statewide institutes, workshops, and round table discussion groups and addressed local, regional, and state library associations. She also found time for on-site visits to individual libraries. During the first two years of her tenure alone, Phillips consulted with Massachusetts librarians on the selection and maintenance of collections in a variety of foreign languages, including Armenian, Czech, Chinese, Finnish, French, Greek, Italian, Polish, Portuguese, Swedish, and Yiddish.[23]

Phillips included in her bibliographies materials not only in foreign languages but also in what she referred to as the "simplest" English. These lists, which served as selection aids, were circularized throughout Massachusetts and bordering New England states to libraries, patriotic and philanthropic organizations interested in Americanization, foreign societies, and unions with large foreign-born memberships. Phillips's lists included a wider variety of new titles that were being published in response to the lobbying efforts of library organizations, notably the ALA CWFB, and individual librarians throughout the country in touch with the needs of immigrant clienteles.

These new titles were on practical subjects, such as domestic affairs, industry, civics, and history, and included a wide selection of English primers, all critically examined by Phillips herself. All of these lists included, as a standard feature, books of interest to Americanization teachers. Phillips also frequently shared bibliographies compiled by well-known experts in given foreign languages, notably college professors and librarians working in foreign language departments in major public libraries, whom Phillips knew personally through their association with the ALA CWFB.[24]

One list that was particularly notable for its usefulness and timeliness was circulated on a state, regional, and national basis. In 1923, during her first year with the division, Phillips compiled a bibliography of books for immigrants and Americanization teachers. One year later, in 1924, the list, entitled "Adult Education Through the Library: Books for New Americans," was revised, mailed to 290 libraries by the Division of Public Libraries, and provided in a quantity of eight hundred copies to the Division of University Extension for distribution to Americanization personnel. Later that same year, the list received national publicity when it appeared in *Wilson Library Bulletin* under the title "Library Aids in Naturalization."

Two years later, in 1926, the list, identified as the second revised and enlarged edition, was published in pamphlet form as *Easy Books for New Americans, with a Reading List for Americanization Workers*, by the American Library Association which, one year later, in 1927, published a third revised edition. In each successive edition of this helpful bibliography, Phillips always gave credit to Herlihy and Guyton, of the Division of University Extension, for their advice and expertise.[25]

Travels in Europe and Asia

Traveling under the auspices of the Division of Public Libraries and the ALA CWFB as its chair, Phillips used her vacations on two occasions, in 1925 and 1927, to gain knowledge of the homelands from which many immigrants to the United States had come. She made contacts with book dealers and purchased books, photographs, and native handicrafts for exhibits and displays. In 1925, Phillips traveled extensively in Italy, where she attended the International Book Fair in Florence. Her firsthand exposure to the European book trade and publications, particularly children's books, was shared with Massachusetts librarians in the bibliographies she compiled and distributed under the auspices of the Division of Public Libraries.

Notable examples were bibliographies of children's books in Italian to introduce American-born children of immigrant Italians to the heritage of their parents. A spin-off of these bibliographies was "A Musical Story Hour for Italian Children," a lesson plan for teachers, with suggestions for musical accompaniment. This lesson plan was furnished to 177 communities having Italian residents, and on request to the Massachusetts State Parent-Teacher Association. Later, Phillips used this lesson plan as a model for designing story hours for children of other cultural heritages.

The national library community benefited from Phillips's 1925 Italian travels as well through her bibliography, "Children's Picture Books from Other Lands," published in *Publishers' Weekly* later that year. This bibliography included recommended titles in German, Italian, Polish, Romanian, and Serbian that she had personally examined and purchased for the traveling library collections of the Division of Public Libraries.

The concern shown by Phillips for the welfare of Italian immigrants in Massachusetts and throughout the United States was not unappreciated in Italy. The city of Ravenna conferred upon Phillips, in 1925, the Dante Medal "for interest and activity in caring for Italian immigrants and in promoting sympathetic understanding between Italy and the United States."[26]

In 1927, Phillips's vacation to Turkey and Greece was equally advantageous both to her individually and, in turn, to the library community in Massachusetts and the United States. Through conversations with the ministers of education in Greece and Turkey, Phillips learned that "the departments of education in both countries are alive to the importance of book circulation as part of their education program."

Phillips was impressed as well by the quality of the educational efforts of American educational institutions there. Sponsored by independent boards in the United States and the Young Women's Christian Association and the leadership of their respective administrators, these institutions had begun to provide rudimentary library service to both nationals and American residents.

Phillips wrote about her impressions, especially emphasizing the need for gifts of books to these developing educational institutions and programs and the American library community's collective responsibility in fulfilling this need, in an article entitled "American Book Service in Greece and Turkey," which was published in *Library Journal*. Phillips revealed her total commitment to international library service when she concluded that "those who know good book service in America will realize how vital a part the right books well administered play in furthering inter-racial relationships."[27] As a corollary to this support of international exchange among libraries, Phillips worked diligently as chair of the ALA CWFB to encourage the compilation of bibliographies of works that "other nations regard as the best books in English about their countries."[28]

Cooperative Book Reviewing

Phillips, through the coordination of the activities of the Division of Public Libraries and the MLC Committee on Work with New Americans, developed and implemented programs in the areas of cooperative book reviewing and bibliographic instruction for Americanization teachers. This fruitful relationship affected the library community in Massachusetts, through the cosponsorship of state, regional, and local meetings and the medium of the *Massachusetts Library Club Bulletin*. In turn, the American library community benefited from the bibliographies and articles published in major library periodicals and addresses at library conferences, notably meetings of the ALA CWFB.

The MLC Committee on Work with New Americans functioned in effect as the publicity agent for the Division of Public Libraries. The MLC committee wrote articles describing the local public library services and resources available to the immigrant community as well as those available through the Division of Public

Libraries, which were published in the major Polish, French, and Italian newspapers read throughout Massachusetts.[29]

As a selection tool for public libraries serving immigrant clienteles, the MLC Committee on Work with New Americans published in the *Massachusetts Library Club Bulletin*, in 1925, a bibliography entitled "Bilingual Dictionaries and Histories of the United States in Foreign Languages." The bibliography included recommended titles "in languages most called for in the Commonwealth," including Arabic, Armenian, Finnish, French, German, Greek, Italian, Lithuanian, Polish, Portuguese, Russian, Swedish, and Yiddish. The bibliography was reprinted later that year in *Library Journal*, since it filled a similar need for libraries throughout the United States.[30] Three years later, in 1928, the MLC committee published in the *Massachusetts Library Club Bulletin*, a list of "Dealers in Foreign Books" to assist libraries in the acquisition of these and other foreign language titles.[31]

MLC French Book Review Committee

In December 1926, in response to the needs of a large French Canadian population in Massachusetts, the French Book Review Committee, a subcommittee of the MLC Committee on Work with New Americans, was formed. The committee's purpose was to review current French books, both fiction and non-fiction, as to their suitability for public library purchase. The inspiration for such a group was undoubtedly the Book Review Club of Greater Boston. Composed of librarians in the Boston area, the Book Review Club was already supplying the Division of Public Libraries with lists of recommended titles for purchase.

The French Book Review Committee members met monthly at Phillips's apartment for their reviewing sessions. Phillips compiled bibliographies of recommended titles as a result of their deliberations, which were distributed throughout Massachusetts and New England by the Division of Public Libraries. Many were published for nationwide consumption in *Library Journal*.[32]

The practice of cooperative book reviewing took hold in Massachusetts. It gained such popular support that, in 1927, within a year of the formation of the French Book Review Committee, Phillips was requested to write an article for *Survey* magazine. Her article described the concept and how it had been applied in Massachusetts in library work with the immigrant community.[33] The success of the French Book Review Committee encouraged Phillips to form similar subcommittees within the ALA CWFB for reviewing books in the Scandinavian, German, and Polish languages. The ALA CWFB compiled bibliographies using the cooperative book reviewing method that appeared in *Library Journal*, *American-Scandinavian Review*, and *Poland* throughout the 1930s. These bibliographies were produced while Phillips was chair both of the MLC Committee on Work with New Americans and the ALA CWFB.[34]

Americanization of Adults in Evening Schools

Cooperation between librarians and Americanization personnel manifested itself as well in the area of bibliographic instruction for the Americanization teachers throughout Massachusetts. Within months of assuming her position with the Division of Public Libraries, Phillips had established a lasting rapport with Herlihy and Guyton in the Division of University Extension.

The 1922/23 annual report of the Massachusetts Board of Free Public Commissioners commented that Herlihy had encouraged Americanization teachers throughout the state to confer with Phillips in planning their classes. The annual report for the following fiscal year, 1923/24, noted that Herlihy had addressed Massachusetts librarians at the Springfield meeting of the Massachusetts Library Club, held in October 1924, on the need for cooperation and collaboration between public libraries and evening schools.[35]

Thus a division of labor was established. Phillips addressed groups of Americanization teachers under Herlihy's supervision, mainly meetings sponsored by the Massachusetts Association of Americanization. Herlihy addressed groups of librarians working with immigrant clienteles under Phillips's supervision, mainly meetings sponsored by the MLC Committee on Work with New Americans.

National Survey of Library Work with Immigrants

In 1925, Phillips reported in her national survey of library work with immigrants, which she conducted for the U.S. Bureau of Education, the tangible result of these collaborative efforts. Librarians and Americanization supervisors had agreed on a standard program or series of lesson plans for introducing evening school students to the resources and services of the public library. These plans would be revised over the years and widely distributed throughout Massachusetts and neighboring New England states by the Divisions of Public Libraries and University Extension.[36] Under the leadership of Phillips and Herlihy, the MLC Committee on Work with New Americans and the Massachusetts Association of Americanization Teachers engaged in statewide cooperative book reviewing. In May 1926, these two organizations met jointly with the Boston International Institute of the Young Women's Christian Association, of which Phillips was a member of the board of management. Another pattern was thus set for joint annual meetings with these and other organizations interested in Americanization, notably the Massachusetts Federation of Women's Clubs, to exchange ideas and to review and recommend books published within the year on immigration- and Americanization-related topics.[37]

The MLC committee, in addition to its programs of a cooperative nature, sponsored regularly scheduled workshops at various locations throughout Massachusetts. The workshops were occasions to discuss specific issues of interest to librarians working with immigrants, and included group discussions and consultation hours devoted to the problems involved in the cataloging, classification, and processing of foreign language materials.[38]

ALA CWFB Publications

The success of Massachusetts's public library programs and evening school Americanization classes for immigrants was made readily apparent, in 1929, when the ALA CWFB, under Phillips's leadership, published a handbook entitled *Reading Service to the Foreign Born*, "the first offered on the subject." Of the seven articles included in the handbook, three were directly related to library and Americanization efforts in Massachusetts.

The first article was a list of dealers in foreign books based on the list compiled by the MLC Committee on Work with New Americans. The second, entitled "Program to Coordinate Work in Adult Education by Libraries and Schools," was the standardized lesson plan for introducing the public library to immigrants in Americanization classes. This plan was written as a joint effort between Phillips, in the Division of Public Libraries, and Mary Louise Guyton, who replaced Herlihy in the Division of University Extension. The third article, a list entitled "National Organizations That Promote Americanization and Inter-Racial Understanding," was compiled by the chair of the Department of Americanization of the Massachusetts Federation of Women's Clubs.[39] The standardized lesson plan was later revised and published in January 1932 in the *ALA Bulletin* as "A Plan for Cooperation in Work with Racial Groups."[40]

The remaining four articles and bibliographies addressed specific areas of interest to librarians and Americanization teachers working with immigrants. "The Approach to the Foreign Born Reader," by Eleanor (Edwards) Ledbetter of the Cleveland Public Library, emphasized techniques for immigrant community analysis, foreign language press publicity, and bridging the generation gap between immigrant parents and their American children. "Lists for Americanization Workers," compiled by the ALA CWFB, was a classified bibliography, arranged by language group, of books of interest to Americanization supervisors and teachers. "Cataloging Foreign Literature" by Adelaide F. Evans, Chief of the Catalog Department of the Detroit (MI) Public Library, offered practical advice on cataloging and processing books in foreign languages, including suggestions on transliteration. "Racial Organizations with Educational Programs," a list compiled by Marion Schibsby of the Foreign Language Information Service, identified key organizations and presented brief annotations outlining their particular slants toward the Americanization process.[41] Although the majority of the contents of the handbook were reprints and revisions of previously published material, the compilation of the disparate articles and bibliographies created a handy compendium for both librarians and Americanization personnel.

The last three years of Phillips's tenure with the Division of Public Libraries, from 1930 through 1932, were tinged with irony and marked a turning point in her career in library work with immigrants. The drastically reduced influx of immigrants from Europe was having two interrelated effects on the Americanization process. First, immigrant customs and traditions transferred to the New World were harder to maintain without the infusion of immigrants from the homelands in Europe. Second, as a consequence, this stabilizing effect on the immigrant community allowed for the concentration of Americanization efforts on second and third generations of the immigrant community rather than on newcomers only.

MLC Committee on Inter-Racial Service

The emphasis in library and educational endeavors was no longer immigrant education, but adult education. The overarching concern was no longer the issue of foreign-born versus native-born, but the promotion of interracial unity and cohesion among American citizens. No more tangible evidence of this revolution in educational philosophy, as it was applied to librarianship specifically, could be found than the fact that early in 1930, the name of the MLC Committee on Work with New Americans was changed to the MLC Committee on Inter-Racial Service.[42]

Phillips, as chair, justified the change of emphasis implied in the name change to the Massachusetts Library Club membership. She reasoned that library service for the foreign born in Massachusetts "comprises also reading service to second generation foreigners, to Americanization workers in connection with their racial background reading, and to clubs and individuals studying inter-racial matters. Many groups among the foreign-born in Massachusetts are now becoming sufficiently adjusted and self-dependent to share leadership in cultural service undertaken by Americans for other races."[43]

Tercentenary of the Massachusetts Bay Colony Celebration

The year 1930, which began with this rededication of Massachusetts librarians to the ideals of Americanization and library service to the immigrant community, was to be a year of celebration for Massachusetts citizens in all walks of life. Massachusetts, which traced its beginnings back to the Massachusetts Bay Colony founded in 1630, pulled out all the stops for its Tercentenary Celebration.

One of the key components of the celebration was the recognition of the contributions of the various ethnic and racial groups to Massachusetts. Elizabeth (Lowell) Putnam, a well-known supporter of conservative causes and a pioneer in prenatal care, was appointed the chair of the Committee on Racial Groups of the Tercentenary. The committee's charge was to oversee the publication of appropriate pamphlets; the planning and promotion of significant social events, including a gala exposition opening; and the mounting of displays and exhibits, all to pay tribute to the Bay State's immigrant heritage.[44]

Putnam, who knew Phillips both personally and professionally, wanted her assistance in the implementation of this ambitious project. Initially Phillips was assigned to work with a subcommittee of the leaders of the "smaller racial groups" of Massachusetts to highlight their contributions. As the magnitude of the overall project unfolded, Putnam was determined that Phillips would assume the position of vice-chair of the committee. Phillips was excited about the possibilities of such an undertaking but reluctant to take on such a time-consuming task. On 2 June 1930, Phillips wrote Belden formally requesting his permission on behalf of the

Massachusetts Board of Free Public Library Commissioners to allocate more of her time to the tercentenary project. "The Division's part in the exposition of racial contributions to civilization means that we are being connected with what I believe to be the most important event in the cultural life of the foreign-born of which I have heard in Massachusetts. Plans are under way to have the racial leaders of the Commonwealth now serving on this committee asked to become a permanent committee following the exposition's close. This would be a most strategic connection for the Division's foreign representative."[45]

Belden was persuaded to allow the reallocation of Phillips's time to accommodate her responsibilities with the Tercentenary Celebration, which, by all accounts, was considered a tremendous success. Phillips's personal touch was most evident in the organization of the numerous meetings with the various ethnic and racial groups participating in the events of the year. The high point of the festivities was the Exposition of Racial Contributions to Civilization, which was held at Symphony Hall in Boston for ten days and evenings in July 1930.

Phillips wrote reports on the contributions to American life of the Italians, Poles, French, Swedes, Greeks, and Armenians, and coordinated the publication of a souvenir pamphlet entitled *Historical Review: Contributions to Civilization of the Armenians, French, Germans, Greeks, Italians, Letts, Lithuanians, Poles, Russians, Swedes, Syrians, Ukrainians*. After the celebration ended, the Committee on Racial Groups of the Tercentenary became a permanent committee, and was renamed the Inter-Racial Citizens' Committee of Massachusetts.[46]

Elimination of Phillips's Position with the MFPLC

In October 1931, after surviving the whirlwind of activities of the Tercentenary Celebration, the Division of Public Libraries experienced a very personal tragedy in the death of Belden. He had been the driving force behind the provision of library service to the immigrant community in Massachusetts and the undisputed mentor of both Campbell and Phillips. Belden's death seemed to portend the ominous changes within the Division of Public Libraries that would drastically alter Phillips's career.[47]

During the 1931/32 fiscal year, the Massachusetts Department of Education, along with all other state departments, experienced a 5 percent cut in its budget. The Division of Public Libraries bore this cut and later a voluntary further 3 percent reduction. Since an amelioration of the financial situation in Massachusetts and throughout the United States as a whole was not seen to be forthcoming, further cuts were projected for the 1932/33 fiscal year.

This disastrous turn of events posed a major dilemma for Edward H. Redstone, Belden's successor as director of the Division of Public Libraries. In the 1931/32 annual report of the division, Redstone reported that the board had made the difficult decision "to abolish the position of Supervisor of Work with Racial Groups because this curtailment, however regrettable, appeared to [be] the one which would work least injury to libraries and the public."[48]

Massachusetts State House, circa 1930, where the offices of the Massachusetts Free Public Library Commission were located during the tenure of Edna Phillips. Photo courtesy Boston Public Library, Public Relations Department.

The board's decision to eliminate Phillips's position was perhaps the only viable option available to them under the circumstances. Nevertheless, the board's encomium to Phillips, which was included in the 1931/32 annual report of the Division of Public Libraries, belied the wisdom of such a move. "For nearly ten years Miss Edna Phillips has been supervisor of library work with foreigners. Throughout this period she has shown an intelligence, devotion, and enthusiasm that have stimulated interest and won the cooperation both of librarians and of the various racial groups in the Commonwealth."[49]

The library community of Massachusetts, in whose interests this momentous administrative decision had been made, was not convinced. Subsequent to the elimination of her position with the Division of Public Libraries, Phillips resigned as chair of the MLC Committee on Inter-Racial Service, whose members, in their statement of appreciation for her visionary leadership and dedication to library work with immigrant groups, written in 1934, a little over a year later, still lauded Phillips as one who "brought the ardor and courage of the explorer to her work; she dared to challenge the unknown."[50]

A tribute by Galen W. Hill, chairman of the Book Review Club of Greater Boston, was published in the December 1932 issue of *Library Journal*. Hill's comments were on behalf of the librarians throughout the state who had grown to respect and rely on Phillips's expertise. Hill reminded the *Library Journal*'s readership that "the personal visits of Miss Phillips, her suggestions as to the use of the books already in the library, her lists of titles for future purchase, and her hints as to methods of contact under given conditions, have been invaluable." Also, with a touch of irony, Hill recognized that "in representing the library in contacts with other agencies interested in the foreign-born, Miss Phillips has created a new realization of and respect for public libraries. The group meetings which she has organized in various cities have made many citizens realize for the first time the importance of the library in civic problems."[51]

Whether Phillips was prepared for the elimination of her position or not, she accepted the decision of the board with the personal sense of satisfaction that she had accomplished a great deal and with the philosophical resolve to forge ahead in her search for library-related work elsewhere. Phillips expressed these sentiments in a candid letter to Putnam, her friend and former associate during the Tercentenary Celebration, in October 1932, the last month of her employment with the Division of Public Libraries.

The Board of Free Public Library Commissioners are convinced that the need for cutting expenses of our Division, and lessened immigration, make it necessary to abolish my position November 30. From the point of view of the work, as well as my own, I am very sorry that this must be done because I feel that in our industrial centers there are still thousands of foreigners untouched by library service, and for some time to come there will still be need for work such as this.

As for my own view of it—I feel this finishes one cycle of my life and that now I will begin another and plan that it shall be an even better one.[52]

Almost a year later, in August 1933, Phillips again wrote Putnam, but this time in a much more jubilant tone. Phillips wrote that she was presently "cataloging the private library of an explorer and big game hunter." Commenting on the interim that had elapsed since their last correspondence, Phillips confided to Putnam that "one good feature, at least, of leaving Massachusetts is this opportunity to have a year with my family." Phillips had good news to share as well. "A fellowship has been awarded me for the coming academic year at Columbia, for work in adult education through the library, with special reference to less privileged readers. Doing post graduate work when I have never had any undergraduate work, will have me on tiptoes."[53]

GRADUATE STUDY IN ADULT EDUCATION

The Carnegie Fellowship in Adult Education made it possible for Phillips to pursue her lifelong interest in reading habits and the improvement of the reading skills of adults, both foreign- and native-born.[54] Her research was based largely upon the foundational studies in reading of Douglas Waples and Ralph Winfred Tyler and funded by a grant from the American Association for Adult Education. The project was a collaborative effort initially with Elizabeth C. Morriss, former director of Adult Elementary Education in Buncombe County, North Carolina. Later, Marion V. Morse, former union superintendent of Schools, Berkshire County, Massachusetts, joined them. The justification for their study, entitled *An Experimental Reading Study in the Joint Library–Adult Elementary Education Field*, was the fact that, based on statistics compiled by the U.S. Office of Education, "there are in the United States at least twelve million men and women in whose lives reading does not function effectively."[55]

Phillips, who had worked with immigrant education in Massachusetts, and Morriss, who had worked with native-born adults in North Carolina, were anxious to find out through an experimental study if the reading needs of the foreign-born adults were similar to those of native-born whites and blacks. Their most instructive finding demonstrated that the needs of at least three basic groups of adult beginners in reading must be addressed: African Americans, native white Americans, and new Americans.[56] These three groups shared the goal of literacy, but due to different backgrounds and experiences, each group would need its own reading materials.

The remainder of Phillips's career in library work with immigrants was shaped and molded by these experiences and discoveries while at Columbia University. Her professional energies, from this point on, were focused on the importance of literacy training for the adult American, foreign-born and native-born, and the improvement of reading skill. Phillips demonstrated this professional concern in her annotated bibliography entitled "The Use of Books," a list of books for the adult educator working with students to improve their reading and study skills. This bibliography was published in *Library Journal* in November 1934, shortly after Phillips had accepted the position of librarian of the Sawyer Free Library in Gloucester, Massachusetts. With the exception of this bibliography, Phillips was not active in publication during her 4½-year tenure at Gloucester, from 1934 to 1939.[57]

LIBRARY SERVICE IN NORWOOD, MASSACHUSETTS

In April of 1939, Phillips accepted the position of librarian of the Morrill Memorial Library in Norwood, Massachusetts, a suburb of Boston. Phillips, who was entering the final stage in her career in librarianship, would serve as Norwood's librarian for over twenty-three years. Although the education of immigrants would remain an abiding interest for Phillips during her tenure in Norwood, her energies were now being redirected to the improvement of cultural relations between and among racial and ethnic groups in local communities throughout the United States. Her primary concern would be the integration of library work with immigrants into the an overall library program that would fulfill the reading needs of all segments of the community.[58] In this regard, on her return to Massachusetts, Phillips had renewed her ties with the Massachusetts Library Club, being particularly active in the promotion of Friends of the Library organizations throughout the state.[59]

Renewal of ALA CWFB Affiliation

Phillips also reestablished her affiliation with the ALA CWFB. The current chair of the ALA CWFB was Harland Abbott Carpenter, a fellow Massachusetts librarian who had served with Phillips on the MLC Committee on Inter-Racial Service. In 1940, Carpenter invited her to address the ALA CWFB at its round table meeting during the Cincinnati annual conference of the ALA. Phillips addressed the group on the topic "Integrating Racial Service with General Library Administration." This event served as a milestone marking Phillips's formal reentry into the field of library and educational work with immigrants.[60]

Phillips's professional activities, particularly her addresses to library groups on the subjects of reading instruction and the improvement of reading and study skills, were reported regularly in the national library periodicals. Her interest in library staff development surfaced as well in the early 1940s during her tenure in Norwood. Her article "Staff Progress Measurement," an evaluative checklist designed to be used by individual library staff members as an "annual self-measurement device," was published in the December 1942 issue of *Wilson Library Bulletin*.[61]

With her visibility within the library community having been reestablished, Phillips was the logical choice for reappointment to the ALA CWFB. Beginning her second tenure as chair of the ALA CWFB during the 1944/45 term, Phillips succeeded Jennie Maas Flexner, who had, in the interim, succeeded Harland Abbott Carpenter.[62]

ALA CWFB Service during World War II

The momentous changes occurring in American society as a result of the entry of the United States into World War II affected the activities of the ALA CWFB as well. Transition and transformation marked the period from 1939 to 1945. European immigration, which had been reduced to a mere trickle by the imposition of the quota system put into place by the National Origins Act of 1924, virtually ceased during the war.

A critical shortage of labor occurred in the United States during World War II due to two factors: the redirection of American manpower away from domestic industrial and agricultural enterprises and toward support for the war effort overseas, and the lessened immigration from Europe. Since immigration from areas throughout the Western Hemisphere was unaffected by the 1924 immigration legislation, the importation of migrant laborers from Mexico was seen as the most viable solution to meet this labor shortage.[63]

ALA CWFB Service to Mexican Migrant Laborers

The ALA attempted through its CWFB to provide library service for these Mexican migrant laborers, who were contracted in the mid-1940s to work in railroad construction camps and on farms throughout the United States. Carl H. Milam, executive director of the ALA, requested Phillips to conduct a study of the labor situation with regard to Mexican migrants and to report on the feasibility of providing library service to them on a national basis.[64]

In June 1945, Phillips sent Milam a two-page memorandum outlining her findings. Phillips had previously consulted with officials of the War Manpower Commission, the War Food Administration, and the U.S. Railroad Retirement Board; representatives of individual railroads hiring migrant laborers; and librarians and educators with experience working with them. She reported to Milam that 75,000 Mexican migrant laborers were expected in the United States in July 1945, within a month of his receipt of her memorandum. Thirty-two railroads, covering an area "from Maine to Florida and from coast to coast," had been assigned quotas of 100 to 12,750 laborers. By harvest time, later in the summer of 1945, 75,000 Mexican migrant laborers were expected for work on farms, mostly in the West and Midwest, with more than half this total to be employed in California.

Phillips reminded Milam that "the temporary nature of the labor quotas, and the contingents not always being stationary even while they are here, present special problems in devising ways to serve them." Phillips suggested that the most feasible setting for the provision of library service to the migrant laborers was in the railroad construction and farm labor camps themselves. She called attention to work already in progress with migrant laborers in Ohio under the supervision of Edith Wirt, head of the Foreign Literature Department of the Cleveland Public Library and member of the ALA CWFB. Phillips recommended the continued support of such efforts as well as the establishment of library service points in other labor camps throughout the United States. "The ALA Committee on Work with the

Foreign Born is very much interested in the development of such camp service, and in the start of service to camps not now receiving it. The Committee suggests that libraries and library extension agencies in the area of such camps desiring to explore the possibility, get in touch with camp supervisors of the railroads at which these men are located, especially such fixed camps as those employed in freight houses and railroad shops. Similar contacts might well be made for camps employing farm labor."[65]

Phillips's memorandum including this recommendation was distributed to all U.S. library extension agencies that might possibly be in a position to provide library service to migrant labor camps. In the minutes of the ALA CWFB for October 1946, Phillips reported that her memorandum "brought a good deal of correspondence and some assistance in bettering reading facilities for the Mexicans doing wartime work here." Although Phillips had envisioned ALA financial support for the development of library service to migrants, she hid her disappointment admirably when she concluded the ALA CWFB minutes with the statement that "the felicitous end of the war changed the whole labor situation. Since then there has not been further need to develop the project."[66]

Shift from Americanization to Internationalization

During the three-year period from October 1945 through October 1948, the ALA CWFB under Phillips's leadership accelerated the process of its transition from an organization promoting programs for the Americanization of immigrants into an organization working for the improvement of international and intercultural relations.[67] Beginning in October 1946, Phillips reported to the ALA CWFB membership that negotiations were underway with ALA officials to bring about these changes.[68]

Concurrently with her efforts to bring about the shift of emphasis from Americanism to internationalism within the library community at the national level, Phillips held an identical philosophical stance with regard to her work at the state level with the Massachusetts Library Association, formerly the Massachusetts Library Club. Under the auspices of the Library Council of the United Nations Association of Massachusetts, organized in 1946, Phillips sought the support of librarians "to seek, and to demonstrate, concrete ways in which libraries can carry out in their communities the purpose of the council, which is to further understanding and support of the United Nations."[69]

Final Years of the ALA CWFB

By October 1948, the transition period had come to a close; the transformation was complete.[70] Phillips reported to the ALA CWFB membership that during the Atlantic City (NJ) Conference of the ALA, the ALA council had approved, based on the recommendation of the Committee on Boards and Committees, that the name of the ALA CWFB should be changed to the ALA Committee on Intercultural Action. The new committee would have four basic functions: (1) to foster tolerance and understanding among cultural groups; (2) to promote an appreciation for diversity among racial and ethnic groups; (3) to support the aims and work of the United Nations, especially UNESCO; and (4) to disseminate widely information on race, group dynamics, and techniques for handling potential violence due to racial friction.[71]

Phillips was elected to be the chair of the newly formed committee and served from 1948–1949 through 1949–1950. Under Phillips's leadership, the principal activity of the new Committee on Intercultural Action was the "shipment of food or clothing packages to librarians in need, in the countries serviced by CARE."[72] Although the Committee on Intercultural Action was appointed and presumably met from the 1950–1951 term through the 1956–1957 term, when its functions were absorbed by existing divisions of the ALA, there are no published minutes of or references to its activities.[73]

Ironically, Phillips, in her zeal to transform the ALA CWFB into an organization more in tune with the issues and trends of post–World War II American society, succeeded in administering the deathblow. The ALA CWFB, which had been engendered during the Americanization crusade following World War I, ceased during the movement toward internationalism following World War II. Spanning the era of America's two most cataclysmic events, the ALA CWFB began and ended with the proverbial bang and whimper.

Final Years as Norwood's Librarian

From 1948 until her forced retirement in 1962 at the age of seventy-two, Phillips continued to serve as Norwood's librarian. She maintained an active membership in the Massachusetts Library Association in her adopted state of Massachusetts and continued to write and lecture in the broad field of adult education through the library.[74] When Phillips retired in 1962, the Norwood community poured forth its praises of her accomplishments in public library administration, which, in 1939, during her first year, and later in 1942, had won her citations from the ALA Public Relations Committee and the H. W. Wilson Company for "outstanding work in public relations."[75]

When Phillips died in 1968, the citizens of Norwood grieved the loss of their librarian emerita. Her peers and her library patrons remembered her as an educator who cared deeply for the needs of adults who could not read. The *Norwood (MA) Messenger*'s eulogy for Phillips was a most fitting memorial: "A person of strong convictions and high ideals, and a practicing Quaker, Miss Phillips worked toward excellence in all things and toward what she termed 'bridge-building' in reading as a means to individual growth in intercultural relations, and world peace."[76]

THE LEGACY OF PHILLIPS TO LIBRARIANSHIP

If Phillips's continued dedication to adult education and interracial library service had ever been doubted, one would need only to turn back the clock to that moment, in July 1958, four years before her retirement and ten years before her death, when she attended the Mid-Pacific Library Conference in Honolulu. Phillips shared her experiences in Hawaii with her colleagues in Massachusetts in an article entitled "Four Days at the Midway Point of East and West," which was published in the autumn 1958 issue of the *Bay State Librarian*, the official publication of the Massachusetts Library Association.

Phillips's comments on the conference revealed her lifelong quest for cultural understanding and adult education through the public library. Ironically, she was not cognizant of the fact that Hawaii had then and continues to have racial wounds to heal. Nevertheless, she surmised that "[t]he most arresting thing to me about Hawaii is its reputation for creative integration of many racial groups. This is brought about by no restrictive legislation and a demonstrated ability for races to live and work together. A high literacy rate and access to a fine library system might be among the factors. Where else have so many races done it so well?"[77]

Whether Phillips was aware of it or not, the answer to her rhetorical question was then and continues to be: throughout the 1920s during her tenure with the Massachusetts Division of Public Libraries. During that heady time, Phillips set the standard for public library service to immigrants through education, a standard emulated throughout the United States wherever immigrant clienteles who yearned to be Americanized came into contact with librarians who were willing to accept the challenge.

NOTES

1. Harrison Hylas Wheaton was chief of the Division of Immigrant Education, U.S. Bureau of Education. See his publications, "Survey of Adult Immigrant Education," *Immigrants in America Review* 1 (June 1915): 42–65 passim; "United States Bureau of Education and the Immigrant," *Annals of the American Academy of Political and Social Science* 67 (Sept. 1916): 273–83; and, especially, "Libraries and the 'America First' Campaign," *LJ* 42 (Jan. 1917): 21–22. See also John F. McClymer, "The Federal Government and the Americanization Movement, 1915–24," *Prologue: The Journal of the National Archives* 10 (Spring 1978): 22–41.

2. McClymer, "The Federal Government and the Americanization Movement," 26.

3. Alice M. Cahill, "19th Century Library Innovation: The Division [i.e., MA Division of Library Extension] from 1890 to 1940," *Bay State Librarian* 55 (Oct. 1965): 7–12, 15; Sigrid Robinson Reddy, "Massachusetts Library Association," in *Encyclopedia of Library and Information Science*, vol. 17, ed. Allen Kent (New York: Marcel Dekker, 1976), 261; and *MLCB* 21 (June 1931): 41–42.

4. MFPLC AR 1922/23, 1, 5.

5. Ibid.; *MLCB* 13 (Jan. 1923): 18; Resume of Edna Phillips, typescript on Commonwealth of Massachusetts, Department of Education, Division of Public Libraries, stationery, [1930?], Elizabeth (Lowell) Putnam Papers, Arthur and Elizabeth Schlesinger Library on the History of Women in America, Radcliffe College, Cambridge, MA; Resume of Phillips, undated typescript, personnel file, Morrill Memorial Library, Norwood, MA; Betty Ann Fisher, "Portraits in Print," *Norwood (MA) Messenger*, [1960?], personnel file for Phillips, Morrill Memorial Library; "Miss Phillips Will Retire Tuesday as Head Librarian," unidentified newspaper, 18 Oct. 1962, personnel file of Phillips, Morrill Memorial Library; "Town Loses a Gracious Lady . . . Miss Edna Phillips, Librarian Emeritus, Passes Away at 78," *Norwood (MA) Messenger*, 6 Nov. 1968, personnel file for Phillips, Morrill Memorial

Library; and C. C. Williamson and Alice L. Jewett, eds., *Who's Who in Library Science*, 2d ed. (New York: H. W. Wilson, 1943), s.v. "Phillips, Edna," 429.

6. Edna Phillips, "Library Work with the Foreign-Born," *Bulletin of the New Hampshire Public Library Commission* 25 (Dec. 1929): 6–8.

7. Ibid., 6.

8. Ibid., 7.

9. Ibid.

10. Ibid., 8.

11. National Education Association of the United States, *Addresses and Proceedings. . . June 29–July 4, 1924* (Washington, DC: NEA, 1924), 565, *Addresses and Proceedings. . . June 28–July 3, 1925* (Washington, DC: NEA, 1925), 337; Charles M. Herlihy, *Adult Education for Foreign-Born and Native Illiterates*, U.S. Bureau of Education Bulletin no. 36 (Washington, DC: GPO, 1925); and Charles M. Herlihy, *Elementary Instruction of Adults*, U.S. Bureau of Education Bulletin no. 8 (Washington, DC: GPO, 1925).

12. Herlihy, *Adult Education for Foreign-Born and Native Illiterates*, 3–7. See also Charles M. Herlihy, "Outstanding Accomplishments in the Field of Adult Education Since the War," in National Education Association of the United States, *Addresses and Proceedings . . . June 28–July 3, 1925*, 340–42.

13. Phillips, "Encouraging the Foreign Reader: An Account of State Encouragement for the Reading of the Foreign-Born Laborer in Massachusetts," *LJ* 49 (15 Nov. 1924): 974–76.

14. Ibid., 976.

15. Ibid.

16. Ibid.; MFPLC AR 1923/24, 4, AR 1924/25, 2, AR 1925/26, 6–7, AR 1926/27, 6-7; *MLCB* 14 (Mar. 1924): 14; *MLCB* 15 (Jan. 1925): 1, (June 1925): 41–44, (Oct. 1925): 54; *MLCB* 16 (Jan. 1926): 5, (Mar. 1926): 26, 28, (June 1926): 50, (Oct. 1926): 73; *MLCB* 17 (Jan. 1927): 9, (Mar. 1927): 19, (Oct. 1927): 56, 62; *MLCB* 18 (Jan. 1928): 2, (Mar. 1928): 26, 28, (Oct. 1928): 71–73; *MLCB* 19 (Jan. 1929): 5, (Oct. 1929): 60, 64–66; *MLCB* 20 (Jan. 1930): 2, 12, (Mar. 1930): 17–18, 39–41, (Oct. 1930): 83, 85; *MLCB* 21 (Oct. 1931): 51; *MLCB* 22 (Jan. 1932): 14–15, (Oct. 1932): 58–59; and Phillips, "Contribution of the Public Library to Adult Education," *School Life* 11 (Nov. 1925): 52.

17. Phillips, "Contribution of the Public Library to Adult Education," 52–53.

18. Ibid., 53.

19. *ALA Bulletin* 19 (Sept. 1925): 444; *ALA Bulletin* 21 (Nov. 1927): 513; *ALA Bulletin* 22 (Nov. 1928): 546; *ALA Bulletin* 23 (Nov. 1929): 464; *ALA Bulletin* 24 (Nov. 1930): H-20; *ALA Bulletin* 25 (Nov. 1931): H-22; *ALA Bulletin* 26 (Nov. 1932): H-24; *Libraries* 31 (Nov. 1926): 468; ALA CWFB Minutes, *ALA Bulletin* 20 (Oct. 1926): 399–400, *ALA Bulletin* 22 (Sept. 1928): 473–75, *ALA Bulletin* 23 (Aug. 1929): 370–71, *ALA Bulletin* 24 (Sept. 1930): 511–13, *ALA Bulletin* 25 (May 1931): 302, *ALA Bulletin* 26 (Apr. 1932): 288, and *ALA Bulletin* 27 (15 Dec. 1933): 819–20.

20. MFPLC AR 1922/23, 5–6.

21. Phillips, "Encouraging the Foreign Reader," 974.

22. Ibid., 975.

23. MFPLC AR 1922/23, 5–6, AR 1923/24, 4.

24. MFPLC AR 1922/23, 5, AR 1924/25, 2, AR 1925/26, 6, AR 1929/30, 8; Massachusetts Department of Education, Division of Public Libraries, "Important Italian Books Published within the Last Five Years," compiled by Leonilda I. Sansone, Italian Librarian, Aguilar Branch, New York Public Library, for the Round Table on Modern Literature, Northeastern Library Conference, Swampscott, MA, typescript, [1930], Putnam Papers; and "Recent German Books," selected by Dr. John A. Walz, Professor of the German Language and Literature, Harvard University, typescript, [1930], Putnam Papers.

25. MFPLC AR 1922/23, 5, AR 1923/24, 3, AR 1926/27, 6–7; Phillips, comp., "Library Aids in Naturalization (Revised, 1924)," *WLB* 2 (Sept. 1924): 262–65; Phillips, *Easy Books for New Americans, with a Reading List for Americanization Workers*, 2d ed. rev. (Chicago: ALA, 1926), 3d ed. rev. (Chicago: ALA, 1927); *MLCB* 16 (June 1926): 53; and ALA CWFB Minutes, *ALA Bulletin* 20 (Oct. 1926): 400.

26. MFPLC AR 1924/25, 3; Phillips, "Children's Picture Books from Other Lands," *Publishers' Weekly* 108 (19 Sept. 1925): 860–61; *MLCB* 15 (Oct. 1925): 67; *MLCB* 16 (Mar. 1926): 24; ALA CWFB Minutes, *ALA Bulletin* 20 (Oct. 1926): 400; Fisher, "Portraits in Print"; "Miss Edna Phillips Retires as Librarian on Tuesday," *Norwood (MA) Tribune*, 18 Oct. 1962, personnel file for Phillips, Morrill Memorial Library; and "Town Loses A Gracious Lady . . . Miss Edna Phillips, Librarian Emeritus, Passes Away at 78."

27. MFPLC AR 1926/27, 7; *MLCB* 17 (June 1927): 45; *MLCB* 18 (Jan. 1928): 2, 11; and Phillips, "American Book Service in Greece and Turkey," *LJ* 53 (1 Mar. 1928): 219–20.

28. "Book Selection on Foreign Countries: What Other Nations Regard as the Best Books in English about Their Countries," *LJ* 54 (15 Nov. 1929): 947–48.

29. MFPLC AR 1923/24, 4; Phillips, "Encouraging the Foreign Reader," 976; Phillips, "Contribution of the Public Library to Adult Education," 52; *MLCB* 15 (Oct. 1925): 54; *MLCB* 16 (Mar. 1926): 28, (June 1926): 50; and *MLCB* 18 (Mar. 1928): 28.

30. Massachusetts Library Club, Committee on Work with New Americans, "Bilingual Dictionaries and Histories of the United States in Foreign Languages," *MLCB* 15 (June 1925): 42–43, reprinted as "Bilingual Dictionaries and United States Histories in Foreign Languages," *LJ* 50 (15 Dec. 1925): 1037–38; *MLCB* 15 (Oct. 1925): 54; *MLCB* 16 (Mar. 1926): 28, (June 1926): 51; and *MLCB* 18 (Mar. 1928): 28.

31. Massachusetts Library Club, Committee on Work with New Americans, "Dealers in Foreign Books," *MLCB* 18 (Mar. 1928): 20–21, 28; and MFPLC AR 1927/28, 5.

32. *MLCB* 16 (June 1926): 52; *MLCB* 17 (Jan. 1927): 9, (June 1927): 44, (Oct. 1927): 62; *MLCB* 18 (Mar. 1928): 28, (Oct. 1928): 73, (Jan. 1929): 5; *MLCB* 19 (Oct. 1929): 65; *MLCB* 20 (Mar. 1930): 41, (Oct. 1930): 83; *MLCB* 21 (Oct. 1931): 51; *MLCB* 22 (Oct. 1932): 59; Phillips to Mrs. William Lowell Putnam, 21 Nov. 1930, Putnam Papers; and MFPLC AR 1930/31, 8. For an example of the bibliographies of French books, see "Some Recent French Books," *LJ* 57 (15 June 1932): 586–87.

33. Phillips, "Cooperative Reading," *Survey* 58 (15 May 1927): 217. See also *MLCB* 16 (June 1926): 50, 52; *MLCB* 17 (Jan. 1927): 9, (Oct. 1927): 62; *MLCB* 18 (Mar. 1928): 28, (Oct. 1928): 72–73; *MLCB* 19 (Jan. 1929): 5, (Oct. 1929): 64; Elisabeth Hardman Furst, "An Experiment in Cooperative Reading: Workers with the Foreign Born in Massachusetts," *Libraries* 33 (June 1928): 313–14; and MFPLC AR 1926/27, 6–7.

34. Phillips to Mrs. William Lowell Putnam, 21 Nov. 1930, Putnam Papers; MFPLC AR 1930/31, 8; ALA CWFB Minutes, *ALA Bulletin* 25 (May 1931): 302, *ALA Bulletin* 26 (Apr. 1932): 288; and *LJ* 56 (Aug. 1931): 664–65. For an example of the bibliographies compiled by these book review subcommittees, see ALA Committee on Work with the Foreign Born, Scandinavian Book Review Committee, "Danish Books for Libraries," *LJ* 58 (15 Feb. 1933): 173–74, which was reprinted by permission from the *American Scandinavian Review* for Jan. 1933.

35. MFPLC AR 1922/23, 5, AR 1923/24, 3–4.

36. MFPLC AR 1924/25, 2, AR 1930/31, 7; *MLCB* 15 (Jan. 1925): 3, 8; Phillips, "Contribution of the Public Library to Adult Education," 52; Phillips, "Program to Coordinate Work in Adult Education by Libraries and Schools," in *Reading Service to the Foreign Born*, compiled by the Committee on Work with the Foreign Born of the American Library Association (Chicago: ALA, 1929), 36–39; and Phillips, "A Plan for Cooperation in Work with Racial Groups," *ALA Bulletin* 26 (Jan. 1932): 29–30.

Edna Phillips, 1890–1968 191

37. MFPLC AR 1925–26, 6–7, AR 1926–27, 6–7; *MLCB* 16 (June 1926): 50; *MLCB* 17 (Jan. 1927): 9, (Oct. 1927): 62; *MLCB* 18 (Mar. 1928): 28, (Oct. 1928): 72–73; *MLCB* 19 (Jan. 1929): 5, (Oct. 1929): 64; *MLCB* 20 (Jan. 1930): 2, (Mar. 1930): 18, (Oct. 1930): 83; and *MLCB* 22 (Jan. 1932): 14–15.

38. Lucian E. Taylor, "Cataloging of Foreign Books: Report of a Round Table Meeting of the Massachusetts Library Club," *LJ* 52 (1 Mar. 1927): 237–38; *MLCB* 17 (Mar. 1927): 19, (Oct. 1927): 62; and *MLCB* 18 (Mar. 1928): 20.

39. *Reading Service to the Foreign Born*, 3, 29–35, 36–39, 56–60.

40. Phillips, "A Plan for Cooperation in Work with Racial Groups," 29–30.

41. *Reading Service to the Foreign Born*, 7–19, 20–28, 40–47, 48–55.

42. *MLCB* 20 (Jan. 1930): 12, (Mar. 1930): 40, (Oct. 1930): 83; and *MLCB* 21 (Oct. 1931): 51.

43. *MLCB* 20 (Jan. 1930): 12.

44. The Elizabeth (Lowell) Putnam Papers are administered by the Arthur and Elizabeth Schlesinger Library on the History of Women in America at Radcliffe College, Cambridge, MA. Putnam's correspondence with Phillips during and just after the Tercentenary Celebration is preserved in this collection. See, Martha Hodes "Elizabeth (Lowell) Putnam, 1862-1935. Papers, 1887–1935," [Accession List, Schlesinger Library, Radcliffe College], 1985, [1–4, 7].

45. MFPLC AR 1929/30, 8–9; and Phillips to Mrs. William Lowell Putnam, 31 May 1930, Putnam Papers; Phillips to Putnam, 31 May 1930, Putnam Papers; and Phillips to Charles F. D. Belden, 2 June 1930, Putnam Papers.

46. Charles F. D. Belden to Mrs. William Lowell Putnam, 6 June 1930, Putnam Papers; MFPLC AR 1929/30, 8–9; and *Historical Review: Contributions to Civilization of the Armenians, French, Germans, Greeks, Italians, Letts, Lithuanians, Poles, Russians, Swedes, Syrians, Ukrainians* ([Boston, MA]: Issued by the Committee on Racial Groups of the Mass. Bay Tercentenary, 1630:1930, [1930]).

47. *MLCB* 21 (Oct. 1931): 57. See also Charles F. D. Belden, "The Reading of the Foreign-Born in Massachusetts Libraries," *MLCB* 19 (Mar. 1929): 33.

48. MFPLC AR 1931/32, 3–4.

49. Ibid.

50. *MLCB* 24 (Jan. 1934): 8.

51. Galen W. Hill, [Book Review Club of Greater Boston], "Edna Phillips," *LJ* 57 (1 Dec. 1932): 1010.

52. Phillips to Mrs. William Lowell Putnam, 3 Oct. 1932, Putnam Papers.

53. Phillips to Putnam, 13 Aug. [1933], Putnam Papers.

54. See, for example, MFPLC AR 1930/31, 8.

55. Elizabeth C. Morriss, Marion V. Morse, and Edna Phillips, *An Experimental Reading Study in the Joint Library–Adult Elementary Education Field* (New York: Bureau of Publications, Teachers College, Columbia University, 1935), 1, 16–17.

56. Ibid., 2–3.

57. Edna Phillips, "The Use of Books," *LJ* 59 (1 Nov. 1934): 847–49; *LJ* 59 (15 Nov. 1934): 896; and LJ 64 (15 Feb. 1939): 158.

58. *LJ* 64 (15 Feb. 1939): 158; and *ALA Bulletin* 35 (Mar. 1941): 189.

59. *MLCB* 31 (June 1941): 55.

60. ALA CWFB Minutes, *ALA Bulletin* 34 (Aug. 1940): 224–25; and *LJ* 65 (Aug. 1940): 634.

61. Phillips, "Staff Progress Measurement," *WLB* 17 (Dec. 1942): 330; and *ALA Bulletin* 35 (Mar. 1941): 189. See also Phillips, "Time-Saver," *Massachusetts Library Association Bulletin* 33 (Apr. 1943): 29–30.

62. ALA CWFB Minutes, *ALA Bulletin* 39 (15 Oct. 1945): 401, *ALA Bulletin* 40 (15 Oct. 1946): 386, *ALA Bulletin* 41 (15 Oct. 1947): 401–2, *ALA Bulletin* 42 (15 Sept. 1948): 69–70, *ALA Bulletin* 42 (15 Oct. 1948): 464; Florence L. Simmons, Assistant to the Executive Secretary, ALA, to Phillips, 19 Dec. 1944, ALA Archives, University of Illinois, Urbana, IL; and Phillips to Florence L. Simmons, 22 Dec. 1944, ALA Archives.

63. Maldwyn Allen Jones, *American Immigration* (Chicago: University of Chicago Press, 1960), 276–79, 289–92.

64. Phillips to Miss [Julia Wright] Merrill, ALA, 27 June 1945, ALA Archives; Carl H. Milam, Executive Secretary, ALA, to Phillips, 28 June 1945, ALA Archives; and ALA CWFB Minutes, *ALA Bulletin* 39 (15 Oct. 1945): 401.

65. Phillips, "Reading Service to Migrant Mexican Laborers in the United States," Morrill Memorial Library, Norwood, MA, two-page typescript, June 1945, ALA Archives; and Milam to Phillips, 28 June 1945, ALA Archives.

66. ALA CWFB Minutes, *ALA Bulletin* 40 (15 Oct. 1946): 386.

67. ALA CWFB Minutes, *ALA Bulletin* 39 (15 Oct. 1945): 401.

68. ALA CWFB Minutes, *ALA Bulletin* 40 (15 Oct. 1946): 386.

69. *ALA Bulletin* 41 (Nov. 1947): 458.

70. Phillips to Carl H. Milam, Executive Secretary, ALA, 31 Mar. 1947, ALA Archives; Milam to Phillips, 7 Apr. 1947, ALA Archives; ALA CWFB Minutes, *ALA Bulletin* 41 (15 Oct. 1947): 401–2; and Milam to Phillips, 29 Mar. 1948, ALA Archives.

71. ALA CWFB Minutes, *ALA Bulletin* 42 (15 Sept. 1948): 69–70, (15 Oct. 1948): 464.

72. *LJ* 75 (15 Sept. 1950): 1430.

73. *ALA Bulletin* 44 (May 1950): 168, (June 1950): 221, (Nov. 1950): 406; *ALA Bulletin* 45 (Dec. 1951): 384; *ALA Bulletin* 46 (Dec. 1952): 384; *ALA Bulletin* 47 (Dec. 1953): 544; *ALA Bulletin* 48 (Dec. 1954): 619; *ALA Bulletin* 49 (Dec. 1955): 627; and *ALA Bulletin* 50 (Dec. 1956): 711, 717.

74. Phillips, "Problems in Book Selection for Physical and Mental Balance," *Public Libraries* 2 (Jan. 1948): 28–31.

75. Fisher, "Portraits in Print"; "Miss Edna Phillips Retires as Librarian on Tuesday"; "Miss Phillips Will Retire Tuesday as Head Librarian"; and Resume on Phillips, personnel file, Morrill Memorial Library, Norwood, MA.

76. "Town Loses A Gracious Lady . . . Miss Edna Phillips, Librarian Emeritus, Passes Away at 78."

77. Phillips, "Four Days at the Midway Point of East and West," *Bay State Librarian* 48 (Autumn 1958): 1–2.

8

Conclusion

Historians of American immigration agree that immigration has been and continues to be the single most important factor that has determined the nation's identity and destiny. Immigration historians differ, however, in the models they have employed to explain how the various immigrant groups have adjusted to life in the United States, including the models of change, continuity, and pragmatism. Although each of these three models is valid and relevant for explaining the patterns of adjustment of particular immigrant groups, the model of pragmatism, by cutting across all arbitrary classifications, holds true for all immigrant groups.

MODEL OF PRAGMATISM

The model of pragmatism takes into account that, although each immigrant group grappled with the immediate concerns of securing housing and employment and providing for the general welfare of families and, frequently, fellow countrymen, the groups developed divergent strategies for accomplishing these common goals. Indeed, the pragmatism model emphasizes the inescapable truth that the immigrant community was not unified, but fragmented along national and ethnic as well as socioeconomic and religious lines.

The implication of the pragmatism model as the basis for the integrative history of libraries, immigrants, and the American experience is that the public library was most successful when it offered resources, services, and programs that the immigrants themselves considered useful, if not essential. As manifested by its cooperation with a wide array of organizations all devoted to the welfare of immigrants, the public library was not the sole agent for change within the immigrant community. Although it was more useful to some immigrants and immigrant groups than others, the public library was a consistent provider of information and

Immigrant children using the Broadway Branch, circa 1915, when Eleanor (Edwards) Ledbetter was librarian. Photo courtesy Cleveland Public Library Archives.

personal attention, which empowered many immigrants to lead productive, fulfill-ing lives and to enter into the mainstream of American life.

Evidence gleaned from the annual reports of public library systems that served significantly large foreign-born populations throughout the continental United States confirms not only the centrality but also the continuity of library service to immigrant clienteles within the overall mission of the American public library. This centrality and continuity, albeit with differing intensities and emphases, has been apparent from1876, when the American Library Association was founded, through 1948, when the ALA Committee on Work with the Foreign Born ceased its activity.

PROGRESSIVE AND REVISIONIST VIEWPOINTS

Library historians who have documented, analyzed, and interpreted the in-teraction between the public library and the immigrant community have divided themselves into two camps, which represent either the progressive or revisionist viewpoints. Progressive historians view libraries and librarians who worked with immigrant clienteles as being motivated by egalitarian principles and the ideal of public education. Revisionist historians view the same libraries and librarians as being motivated by authoritarian principles and the ideal of social control by an intellectual elite. Both the revisionist and progressive interpretations assume that public libraries reflected, sometimes more, sometimes less, the attitudes of the nation as a whole with regard to immigrants and immigration.

The experiences of representative American public libraries as chronicled in their annual reports provide fuel to stoke the fires of both camps. The prepon-derance of evidence supports the progressive viewpoint. For example, during periods of political and social unrest associated with the hotly debated issue of immigration in general and, more specifically, the movement toward immigration restriction, there was a tendency for libraries to be more conservative in stance and in rhetoric. This behavior provided the foundation for a revisionist perspective of library history. During times of relative normalcy, on the other hand, when a laissez-faire attitude toward immigration prevailed, there was a tendency toward liberalism in words and deeds. This behavior provided the foundation for a contrastingly progressive perspective.

Ironically, librarians were most liberal and least reactionary during the Red Scare, which followed in the wake of World War I. The fact that during this extremely conservative period libraries developed some of the most creative programs in response to the needs of immigrants is indisputable proof of their reforming zeal. Librarians who dedicated themselves to the amelioration of immigrants' socioeconomic and educational conditions through access to the public library found themselves liberals in a conservative milieu.

If there has been any point on which consensus has been achieved among library historians, it is that the leadership within the movement for library work with immigrants derived almost exclusively from, at the local level, branch

Anglo-conformists & pluralists
its

librarians and foreign language department heads. The ALA CWFB provided national coordination during the period 1918 through 1948.

Librarians actively involved in library work with immigrant clienteles were both Anglo-conformists and cultural pluralists. The leaders in library work with immigrants, Jane Maud Campbell, John Foster Carr, Eleanor (Edwards) Ledbetter, and Edna Phillips, together represented the diversity of opinion with regard to both assimilation and immigration. Of these leaders, none gave any indication, either in speech or writing, of being motivated by racism or nativism. Carr was an Anglo-conformist in favor of free immigration, while Phillips was an Anglo-conformist in favor of restricted immigration. Campbell and Ledbetter were cultural pluralists in favor of free immigration.

Campbell, Carr, Ledbetter, and Phillips were united in their support of and belief in the Americanization process. For the Anglo-conformists, Carr and Phillips, however, Americanization provided only the means for the behavioral as-similation of immigrants, while for the cultural pluralists, Campbell and Ledbetter, it provided the means for their full structural assimilation as well.

THE MOVEMENT FOR LIBRARY WORK WITH IMMIGRANTS

The history of immigrants, libraries, and the American experience is divided into two distinct periods. The pre–1924 years represented a period of free immigration, predominantly from Europe. The post–1924 years, after the passage of the National Origins Act, represented a period of restricted immigration from outside of the Western Hemisphere and relatively free immigration within its confines.

Libraries and Free Immigration

The period from 1876, the founding year of the American Library Association, until 1924, the year the National Origins Act was passed, was a period of free immigration, when over 26 million immigrants came to America. The United States was transformed during this period from a rural and agricultural society to an urban and industrial one. A laissez-faire attitude toward immigration, which supported the ideals of America as the asylum for the oppressed and land of opportunity for the industrious, made this transformation possible.

In the first decade of the twentieth century, nativists, who had lobbied for restrictions primarily to control immigration from Asia, now targeted for exclusion immigrants from southern and eastern Europe. These "new" immigrants were, according to the congressionally appointed Dillingham Commission of 1907, inferior to the "old" immigrants from northern and western Europe, who had arrived during the early and middle nineteenth century. Armed with the biased and unsubstantiated evidence provided by the Dillingham Commission, Congress enacted the National Origins Act of 1924. With its passage, the concept of America as the asylum for all was replaced by the concept of America as the haven for a selected few.

Americanization

Surprisingly, while nativists clamored for immigration restrictions, librarians did not question immigration policy per se. Rather, they concentrated on the Americanization of immigrants already resident in the United States as their sole goal and responsibility toward the immigrant community. Reflecting to a certain degree the general attitudes among the American populace toward immigrants, librarians viewed Americanization as a service to the immigrant community during periods of relative calm, while during periods of heated debate and agitation, notably during World War I and the Red Scare that followed, librarians shouldered Americanization as a patriotic duty.

Librarians who cooperated with a host of cultural, religious, philanthropic, patriotic, and labor organizations to promote Americanization viewed it as an appropriate social and educational mission of the public library. Organizations with which libraries cooperated in the Americanization process represented all segments of the political spectrum, from conservative, including the Sons and Daughters of the American Revolution, to mainstream, including the Young Men's and Women's Christian Associations, to liberal, including the Foreign Language Information Service.

Public libraries that were founded during the pre–1924 period frequently incorporated the collections of former immigrant social libraries and eagerly sought gifts of foreign language materials from immigrants, individual scholars, and foreign societies. Foreign language books were collected for scholars as well as for library users who wanted to maintain a cultural identity with a particular national or ethnic group and for older immigrants who would never learn English well enough to exist outside the environs of the immigrant community.

The pre–1924 period witnessed the development of distinctive immigrant branches and foreign language departments at the central library headquarters within local systems as well as the coordination of services to immigrant clienteles on a statewide basis through traveling library collections administered by state library commissions. At the local level in particular, librarians surveyed their communities regularly to make certain that programs, collections, and services were provided to meet the needs of often diverse and highly mobile foreign-born populations.

International recognition was forthcoming from foreign visitors to the major public libraries of the United States. Visitors were particularly impressed by the fact that immigrants who spoke foreign languages were hired as assistants and librarians, particularly in immigrant branches. Children's services, including cooperation with public and parochial schools, and adult services, including cooperation with evening schools and Americanization classes under various auspices, notably the offices of the U.S. Naturalization Bureau and local citizenship agencies, provided impressive examples of the coordination between the public library and the public school. Library work with children was usually more extensive and more fully developed, since librarians believed firmly that the way to lure immigrant adults to the library was through their children.

Home visits; the distribution of circulars, flyers, placards, and leaflets in various languages explaining library service; and extensive cooperation with the foreign language newspaper press were the principal means of publicizing library services for the immigrant community. Special events and lecture series were sponsored to promote among the American-born community a tolerant attitude toward immigrant cultures. Librarians working with primarily immigrant clienteles participated in continuing education and self-education programs in their respective library systems.

Throughout the period of free immigration, librarians as a profession viewed immigrants as Americans-in-the-making and themselves as active agents in the Americanization process. Librarians called for a progressive laissez-faire attitude toward immigrants, including not only a tolerance for but also an encouragement of cultural differences. Succumbing to the prevailing mood of xenophobia and to the edicts of state legislatures and local library boards during World War I, some libraries withdrew German materials from their collections.

In 1920, the ALA geared up for a major campaign to raise funds for the continuance of successful programs begun during World War I and for the initiation of new programs, including those for library work with immigrant groups. Notwithstanding the subsequently demoralizing failure of the ALA Enlarged Program, the ALA CWFB continued to serve as a clearinghouse for information on library work with immigrant groups. The committee provided national coordination principally through consultation and publications, and encouraged publishers to publish books on American history and life in immigrant languages as well as in easy English. The Carnegie Corporation study on Americanization activities in the early 1920s applauded public libraries as being the most effective agencies in reaching the immigrant community.

Two transformations thus occurred simultaneously from 1876 to 1924. The first, which involved American society as a whole, was manifested in a movement from a relatively laissez-faire attitude toward immigration to a decidedly restrictionist stance. The second transformation, which involved the American public library community, was manifested in a movement from Americanization as being the only goal of library work with immigrants to Americanization as a process of building mutual respect and tolerance for foreign cultures among the foreign born and the native born alike.

Librarians, in their crusade to Americanize the immigrant, found justification within the immigrant community itself. Since Americanization was, in many ways, their ticket to economic and social success in American society, immigrants sought to be Americanized; they did not shun it. Americanization became for librarians not an end in itself, but the means to allow immigrants to enter into the mainstream of American life. Librarians evolved into sovereign alchemists who instilled Americanization into eager immigrants and, as mediators and conciliators, justified the needs and rights of immigrants to the native-born community. During this evolutionary process, librarians were transformed into more tolerant Americanizers and more responsive professionals.

Leadership during Free Immigration

Jane Maud Campbell, the only immigrant among the four leaders in library work with immigrants, was the prototypical advocate for immigrants' rights. Throughout her varied career in service to immigrants, which spanned the period from 1903 to 1922, Campbell consistently defended the policy of free immigration and the rights of immigrants as taxpayers.

Campbell, a staunch proponent of cultural pluralism, viewed American culture as a conglomeration of cultures, each representing a unique gift and each worthy of preservation. She believed in the philosophy that library work with immigrants involved an intellectual exchange between librarians and immigrants and that librarians, as much as the immigrants themselves, benefited from this mutual learning experience.

Beginning her career as a public librarian in New Jersey, Campbell was the first woman to be appointed to a New Jersey State commission, the 1906 Commission on Immigration. This commission was, in turn, the first state commission to survey and offer recommendations for the amelioration of immigrants' conditions on a statewide basis. Campbell's role as advocate was later reinforced by her service outside of librarianship, but within the field of immigrant education, with the New York–New Jersey Committee of the North American Civic League for Immigrants.

Campbell ended her career of advocacy for immigrants' rights as the first librarian to be appointed by a state library commission to serve the library needs of the foreign-born population on a statewide basis. From 1913 to 1922, Campbell, as Secretary of Work with Foreigners of the Massachusetts Free Public Library Commission, the first state library commission, organized an extensive system of traveling libraries and provided consultation throughout the state of Massachusetts, in the Northeast, and even in the Midwest. Campbell served briefly on the ALA CWFB in the early 1920s.

John Foster Carr, founder and director of the Immigrant Publication Society, was a propagandist for free immigration. Throughout his career as a publisher, which spanned the period from 1910 to 1930, Carr chose the American public library as the appropriate agency for carrying out his mission to Americanize the immigrant. Given Carr's mission and his choice of the public library as the means for public education and the perpetuation of Anglo-Saxon ideals, it is not surprising that Carr's propaganda was of two types: guidebooks for Italian-, Yiddish-, and Polish-speaking immigrants, and handbooks for librarians working with immigrant clienteles.

Carr's publications for immigrants were designed to modify or eliminate all of the attributes of immigrants that hindered their Americanization, including the predilection for living in segregated neighborhoods and maintaining or continuing Old World habits in New World communities. The king of Italy decorated Carr in recognition of his particular concern for the social adjustment of Italian immigrants as well as his service as an agent of the Dante Alighieri Society. Carr felt justified in his quest to Americanize immigrants as quickly as possible, since he viewed Americanization as a process that was mutually beneficial to both the immigrant and American society.

Imbued with a passionate sense of patriotism and dedication to maintaining the glory of American traditions and accomplishments, Carr was the archetypal Anglo-conformist. For Carr, immigrants had a three-pronged commitment to the country of their adoption: to reside permanently in the United States, to learn English, and to become naturalized citizens as quickly as possible. He was convinced that all immigrants could be and, indeed, desired to be Americanized.

Through his work with the ALA to collect books for servicemen during World War I, Carr brought himself and his publishing enterprise to the attention of the ALA Executive Board. The board, in turn, appointed Carr as the first chair of the ALA CWFB in 1918 and delegated him the major responsibility for fund-raising for the citizenship component of the ALA Enlarged Program. Carr served as chair of the ALA CWFB from 1918 to 1920.

Unfortunately for Carr, the ALA Enlarged Program failed due to lack of support from a divided ALA membership. If it had been successful, the ALA Enlarged Program would have provided funds for the expansion of library services for the immigrant community and the extensive coordination of the work of Carr's Immigrant Publication Society and the ALA CWFB.

The failure of the Enlarged Program not only signified the lack of support for coordination of library services at the national level, but also precipitated the eventual demise of Carr's publishing ventures. Nevertheless, for the span of twenty years, librarians deferred to Carr and his publications, which together set the tone for librarians' attitudes toward immigrants and immigration.

Libraries and Restricted Immigration

The passage of the National Origins Act of 1924 was a watershed event in the history of American immigration as well as the history of American public library service to the immigrant community. Designed to limit the immigration of the "new" immigrants from southern and eastern Europe, the quota system imposed by the National Origins Act limited immigration to the United States from outside the Western Hemisphere to 150,000 per year.

During the late 1920s and into the 1930s, many forces were at play, both in the United States and in Europe, to slow the tide of European immigration. In the United States, these forces were the strict enforcement of the quota system and the economic deprivations associated with the Great Depression. In Europe, the forces were the decline of birthrate, the loss of lives during World War I, the rise of totalitarian regimes, and the economic prosperity brought about by industrialization and social reforms.

For whatever reason or combination of reasons, the majority of immigrants from 1924 onward would be from countries of the Western Hemisphere, primarily Canada, Mexico, and the West Indies, with limited immigration from the Philippines. Other significant immigrant groups entering the United States during this period included pre–World War II refugees from Hitler's atrocities in Europe and post–World War II displaced persons and war brides.

The quota system imposed by the National Origins Act, coupled with the Great Depression, World War II, and the postwar boom not only changed the composition and quantity of American immigration, but also worked to dissolve ethnic and national ties within the immigrant community. The depression, by drawing renewed attention to class divisions among Americans in general, thus tended to override cultural differences of workers, which had heretofore kept various ethnic elements apart in the workplace. Especially for the second generation, the ethnic tie became increasingly meaningless, while religious affiliation; occupational and residential mobility; political clout, particularly within the Democratic Party; and structural assimilation within American society gained ascendancy in immigrants' priorities.

From the mid- to late 1920s, librarians began to view Americanization increasingly as an integral part of the more all-encompassing adult education movement, which was attuned to the needs of illiterate American-born adults, including blacks and whites from the rural South. The once distinctly separate and narrowly focused goals of American public libraries, to educate the general populace and to Americanize immigrants, were merging. The overarching goal became to build a literate citizenry composed of both foreign- and native-born Americans who were imbued with a spirit of tolerance and internationalism.

The American Library Association's study on adult education activities in American public libraries and the survey of American public libraries, both funded and supported by the Carnegie Corporation, documented a wide array of library resources and services for immigrants. Researchers using the data compiled for these studies found, however, that the quantity and quality of resources in foreign languages were not up to the standard of resources available in the English language.

Throughout the 1930s, the decrease in the foreign-born population and the depression worked together to curtail services that had grown to be considered traditional. Both the creation and continuation of library programs were often contingent upon the labor provided by the federal human resources programs of Franklin Delano Roosevelt's New Deal.

Libraries continued to work to find solutions for providing foreign language materials to shifting foreign populations. Many libraries consolidated collections to form a central reserve from which loan collections were dispatched. Others instituted foreign departments, while still others discontinued them in favor of emphasizing branch and interlibrary loan services. The designation of certain public library branches as immigrant branches became more and more meaningless as immigrants originally served by a particular branch moved to other neighborhoods to find better housing and occupational opportunities.

Resources collected originally for burgeoning foreign-born populations were now used to provide reference service for the community at large. The emphasis of children's services shifted from Americanization to internationalism. Summer reading programs, lecture and educational forum series, book fairs, and film festivals encouraged internationalism through the social mingling of native- and foreign-born citizens. By the late 1930s, libraries began to report the trend toward cultural, rather than recreational, use of foreign language books.

At the national level, the ALA CWFB continued its work with publications that were designed to acquaint librarians with various immigrant groups and their reading habits as well as to aid in the acquisition of foreign language materials. Publicity strategies that incorporated both print and nonprint media, including the foreign language press, radio, and moving picture shows, were encouraged. Cooperation within library systems and between local libraries working with immigrant clienteles was commonly reported, and statewide cooperation, particularly in Massachusetts, New Jersey, New York, and Pennsylvania, was laudably extolled.

Libraries during World War II coordinated the dissemination and distribution of information released by the various government organizations. Censorship attempts were reported with less frequency than during World War I. The ALA CWFB was, however, ambivalent and subsequently ineffectual in providing for the needs of the Japanese, who were confined to internment camps during World War II.

After World War II, the ALA CWFB began to address the needs of Filipino and Mexican immigrants as well as European refugees and displaced persons. It became particularly evident that a fundamental transformation had occurred. The movement to Americanize the immigrant community, which had been subsumed initially by the movement to educate the adult community, was now subsumed by the movement to internationalize the American citizenry. Ultimately, the mission of the American public library was to empower people, citizens and aliens alike, to become full participants in the dynamics of a pluralistic society.

Leadership during Restricted Immigration

Throughout her distinguished career in library work with immigrants from 1910 to 1938, Eleanor (Edwards) Ledbetter guided and directed the movement from her station as librarian of the Broadway Branch of the Cleveland Public Library. A cultural pluralist and advocate for free immigration, Ledbetter served a brief tenure just after World War I as a member of the Mayor's Advisory War Board of the Cleveland Americanization Committee. This committee produced publications and sponsored activities designed to bring the foreign- and native-born populations of Cleveland together.

Ledbetter patterned her career after that of the social worker. Adapting the techniques of the marketing agent, she sought to sell the library to the immigrant community, particularly the Polish and Czech tenants of the Broadway neighborhood in Cleveland, rather than to wait for the immigrants themselves to discover the library. In addition to the home and the workplace, Ledbetter's targets were the church, public and parochial schools, and the foreign language press. Home visits and regular community surveys were standard tools of her trade.

Ledbetter's pamphlet, *Winning Friends and Citizens for America*, became almost the credo for library work with immigrants. Published by Carr's Immigrant

Publication Society, this pamphlet as well as the trust and admiration that existed between Carr and Ledbetter were responsible for her appointment to succeed Carr as second chair of the ALA CWFB. During her tenure as chair from 1920 through 1926, Ledbetter worked to give direction to library work with immigrants on a nationwide basis, particularly in the area of publicizing library service for the immigrant community.

Her philosophy of library service was epitomized in the conviction that the public library should be a truly democratic, community-centered institution that gave preference when funds were limited to those portions of the community having least opportunity at their own command. Immigrants, who paid taxes, deserved books and periodicals in easy English and in foreign languages as well as qualified librarians to assist them in using these foreign language materials. Ledbetter also encouraged the development and implementation of courses in library schools and special training programs for librarians working with immigrant clienteles.

Ledbetter's progressivism and liberalism were revealed in the close cooperation in educational publishing efforts between the ALA CWFB and the Foreign Language Information Service. Her devotion to her immigrant patrons carried over into her religious life as well as her scholarly pursuits. Tangible evidence of this involvement included her participation in immigrant education programs of the Episcopal Church, her translation of Czech fairy tales and folklore, and her compilation of bibliographies of Polish literature. She was decorated by the governments of Poland and Czechoslovakia for her work with the Polish and Czech communities of Cleveland.

The selection of Edna Phillips as secretary for Library Work with Foreigners marked a significant shift in philosophy of the Massachusetts Free Public Library Commission. Hiring Phillips, an Anglo-conformist who favored restricted immigration for economic rather than racial reasons, represented a conscious move on the part of the commissioners toward a more conservative stance in keeping with the restrictive national immigration policy.

Throughout her leadership as chair of the ALA CWFB from 1927 to 1933, Phillips had a clear vision for library work with immigrants. The goals of public library service to the foreign-born were (1) to facilitate the learning of English, (2) to prepare immigrants for citizenship, and (3) to preserve immigrant cultures while instilling American values. All three goals were viewed within the context of a central, overarching mission to eradicate illiteracy.

Phillips's years at the MFPLC were characterized by a deft coordination of work among four distinct but related agencies seeking to serve the immigrant community. By her involvement with all four agencies, Phillips balanced the Americanization efforts of the Division of Public Libraries and the Division of University Extension as well as the Massachusetts Library Club Committee on Work with New Americans and the ALA CWFB. Her workshops on bibliographic instruction for Americanization teachers and conferences on cooperative reading for Americanization personnel from various organizations received national recognition.

Phillips's contributions to the movement for library work with immigrants included the writing, editing, and compiling of numerous bibliographies, handbooks, and articles on adult education for immigrants through the public library. Like her colleague Ledbetter, Phillips traveled extensively abroad to find sources for foreign language books, which she then publicized and made available to the American immigrant community. For her work with Italian immigrants, Phillips was decorated by the Italian city of Ravenna.

When her position with the MFPLC was eliminated in 1932 due to financial exigency, Phillips pursued graduate work in adult education at Columbia University, where she did research and published in the area of improving the reading skills of foreign- and native-born adults. From this point onward through 1948, Phillips concentrated all of her energies on literacy training and increasing reading skill for the adult American.

From 1944 through 1948, during her second tenure as chair of the ALA CWFB, Phillips was instrumental in improving educational opportunities for Mexican migrants. Phillips, in her commitment to improve the education of adults, whether foreign- or native-born, brought about not only the redirecting of the mission of the ALA CWFB but also, ironically, its demise in 1948.

THE LIBRARY AS SOVEREIGN ALCHEMIST

From 1876 to 1948, the American public library and the library profession consistently provided the information, the personal attention, and the guidance that immigrants needed to adjust, survive, and advance. Thus the American public library empowered many immigrants to transform their individual dreams and potentialities into American realities.[1]

American immigration historian John W. Briggs affirms that "it is in the study of the educational function of the institutions which shape, perpetuate, and transfer culture that we may hope to find the means to expand our understanding of ethnic influences in America."[2] Truly, the American public library, through its educational mission with the immigrant community, shaped, perpetuated, and transferred culture from one generation to another. American librarians, in their collective role as sovereign alchemists, raised our national consciousness to the point where ethnic differences were not just tolerated, but more fully understood and respected.

NOTES

1. Eric Frederick Goldman, "Century of the American Dream," *Saturday Review* 3 (13 Dec. 1975): 20–22.

2. John W. Briggs, *An Italian Passage: Immigrants to Three American Cities, 1890–1930* (New Haven, CT: Yale University Press, 1978), 278.

Where are his sources on what the immigrants thought, did & wanted? (a small # on p. 29)

Selected Bibliography

PRIMARY SOURCES (Mainly Pre-1948)

Archival Materials

American Library Association. Committee on Work with the Foreign Born. File. ALA Archives, University of Illinois, Urbana, IL.

Campbell, Jane Maud. Papers. Arthur and Elizabeth Schlesinger Library on the History of Women in America, Radcliffe College, Cambridge, MA.

Carr, John Foster. Papers. Manuscript Division, New York Public Library.

Ledbetter, Eleanor (Edwards). Papers. Archives, Cleveland Public Library.

Phillips, Edna. Personnel and clipping files. Morrill Memorial Library, Norwood, MA.

Putnam, Elizabeth (Lowell). Papers. Arthur and Elizabeth Schlesinger Library on the History of Women in America, Radcliffe College, Cambridge, MA.

Stokes, Edward Casper (Governor). Papers. New Jersey State Archives, Trenton, NJ.

Interviews

Kaynor, Fay Campbell (Reed), Amherst, MA, 11–12 August 1987.

Reed, Georgia (Waterman), East Longmeadow, MA, 12 August 1987.

Library Annual Reports

Boston Public Library. 1876–1948.

Brooklyn Public Library. 1876–1948.

Buffalo Public Library. 1897–1948.

Carnegie Library of Pittsburgh. 1896–1948.

Chicago Public Library. 1876–1948.

Cleveland Public Library. 1876–1948.
Denver Public Library. 1889–1948.
Detroit Public Library. 1886–1948.
Enoch Pratt Free Library (Baltimore). 1887–1948.
Free Library of Philadelphia. 1897–1948.
Jersey City Public Library. 1892–1948.
Los Angeles Public Library. 1889-1948.
Louisville Free Public Library. 1905–1948.
Milwaukee Public Library. 1879–1948.
New Orleans Public Library. 1897–1948.
New York Public Library. 1896–1948.
Newark (NJ) Public Library. 1891-1948.
Passaic Public Library. 1903–1909/10.
Providence Public Library. 1879–1948.
Queens Borough Public Library. 1902–1948.
St. Louis Public Library. 1894–1948.
San Francisco Public Library. 1880–1948.

Other Annual Reports

Massachusetts Free Public Library Commission (later, Massachusetts Board of Library
    Commissioners). 1890–1932.
National Education Association of the United States. 1876–1948.
North American Civic League for Immigrants. 1910/11.

Periodicals

ALA Booklist. Vol. 1 (Jan. 1905)–Vol. 13, no. 10 (July 1917). Superceded by *Booklist.*
    Vol. 14 (Oct. 1917)–Vol. 52, no. 3 (Aug. 1956). Cited as *Booklist.*
American Library Annual. 1911/12–1917/18.
American Library Association. *Bulletin.* Vol. 1 (Jan. 1907)–Vol. 32, no. 11 (15 Oct.
    1938). Superceded by *ALA Bulletin.* Vol. 33 (Jan. 1939)–Vol. 63, no. 11 (Oct. 1969).
    Cited as *ALA Bulletin.* Superceded by *American Libraries.* Vol. 1 (Jan. 1970-
    present).
Cleveland Americanization Bulletin. Vol. 1, no. 1 (15 Oct. 1919)–no. 8 (18 June 1920).
    Cited as *CAB.* Only issues published.
Committee for Immigrants in America. *Immigrants in America Review.* Vol. 1 (Mar.
    1915)–Vol. 2 (July 1916). Only issues published.
Foreign Language Information Service. *Interpreter.* Vol. 1 (1922)-Vol. 9 (Nov.–Dec.
    1930). (Includes *Interpreter Release Clip Sheets.*) Only issues published.
Library Journal. Vol. 2 (1877–present). Cited as *LJ.* Formerly *American Library Jour-
    nal.* Vol. 1 (1876).
Massachusetts Library Club Bulletin. Vol. 1 (1911)–Vol. 26, no. 1 (Jan. 1936). Cited as
    MLCB. Superceded by Massachusetts Library Association. *Bulletin.* Vol. 26, no. 2
    (Apr. 1936)–Vol. 37, no. 3 (1946). Superceded by *MLA Bulletin.* Vol. 37, no. 4 (Jan.
    1947)–Vol. 45, no. 4 (Oct. 1955). Superceded by *Bay State Librarian.* Vol. 46, no. 1
    (Winter 1956–present).
New York Libraries. Vol. 1 (Oct. 1907)–Vol. 16, no. 8 (Aug. 1939). Only issues pub-
    lished.

North American Civic League for Immigrants. New York–New Jersey Committee. *Bulletin.* 1910–1911. Only issues published.

Public Libraries. Vol. 1 (May 1896)–Vol. 30, no. 10 (Dec. 1925). Superceded by *Libraries.* Vol. 31 (Jan. 1926)–Vol. 36, no. 10 (Dec. 1931). Only issues published.

U.S. Department of the Interior. Bureau of Education. Americanization Division. *Americanization.* Vol. 1 (15 Sept. 1918)–Vol. 2, no. 3 (1 Nov. 1919). Only issues published.

Wilson Bulletin. Vol. 1 (Nov. 1914)–Vol. 13, no. 10 (June 1939). Superceded by *Wilson Library Bulletin.* Vol. 14, no. 1 (Sept. 1939)-Vol. 69, no. 10 (June 1995). Cited as *WLB.* Only issues published.

Books, Pamphlets, and Government Documents

Alessios, Alison B. *The Greek Immigrant and His Reading.* Library Work with the Foreign Born. Chicago: ALA, 1926.

American Library Association. *A Survey of Libraries in the United States.* 4 vols. Chicago: ALA, 1926–1927.

Americanization Conference. *Proceedings [of the] Americanization Conference, Held under the Auspices of the Americanization Division, Bureau of Education, Department of the Interior, Washington, May 12, 13, 14, 15, 1919.* Washington, DC: GPO, 1919.

Campbell, Jane Maud. *Immigrant Women; Paper read at the New Jersey Conference of Charities and Correction, Princeton, NJ, April 3, 1911.* New York: New York–New Jersey Committee, North American Civic League for Immigrants, [1911?].

———. *Selected List of Hungarian Books.* Compiled for the New Jersey Library Commission. Adapted for use by the League of Library Commissions. Foreign Book List no. 2. Boston: ALA Publishing Board, 1907.

———. *Selected List of Russian Books.* Compiled for the Free Public Library Commission of Massachusetts. Foreign Book List no. 7. Chicago: ALA, 1916.

Carr, John Foster. *The Coming of the Italian.* New York: Liberal Immigration League, 1906. Reprint from *Outlook,* 24 Feb. 1906.

———. *The Declaration of Independence and the Colonies, with a Literal Reprint of the Declaration of Independence.* New York: Immigrant Publication Society, 1924. Reprinted in 1926.

———. *Guida degli Stati Uniti per l'Immigrante Italiano.* Pubblicata a cura della Societa delle Figlie della Rivoluzione Americana, Sezione di Connecticut. New York: Doubleday, Page and Company, 1910.

———. *Guide to the United States for the Immigrant Italian; A Nearly Literal Translation of the Italian Version.* Published under the auspices of the Connecticut Daughters of the American Revolution. Garden City, NY: Doubleday, Page and Company, 1911.

———. *Guide to the United States for the Jewish Immigrant; A Nearly Literal Translation of the Second Yiddish Edition.* Published under the Auspices of the Connecticut Daughters of the American Revolution. New York: John Foster Carr, 1912.

———. *Immigrant and Library: Italian Helps, with Lists of Selected Books.* New York: Immigrant Education Society, 1914. Issued in cooperation with the ALA Publishing Board.

———. *Przewodnik po Stanach Zjednoczonych do Uzytku Polskich Imigrantow*. Opracowal John Foster Carr. [Bristol, CT]: Wydawnictwo Stowarzyszenia Corek Amerykanskiej Rewolucyi Stanu Connecticut, 1912.

———. *Some of the People We Work For; Address Delivered before the American Library Association, Asbury Park, New Jersey*. New York: Immigrant Publication Society, 1916.

———. *War's End: The Italian Immigrant Speaks of the Future*. New York: Immigrant Publication Society, 1918.

———. *Wegweiser von die Vereinigte Staaten fur des Yiddishen Imigrant*. [Bristol, CT]: Connecticut Daughters of the American Revolution, 1912.

Cleveland Americanization Committee. *Americanization in Cleveland; An Account of the Work which Has Been Done in Cleveland to Develop and Maintain a City Morale*. Issued by the Cleveland Americanization Committee of the Mayor's Advisory War Board. Cleveland: Economy Printing, 1919.

———. *Report of the Work of the Cleveland Americanization Committee of the Mayor's Advisory War Board, July 1917–July 1918*. Cleveland: The Committee, 1918.

Cleveland Mayor's Advisory War Committee. *Cleveland in the War: A Review of Work Accomplished by the Mayor's Advisory War Committee and Work Proposed during the Great Period of Reconstruction*. Cleveland: Harris Printing and Engraving, 1919.

Daniels, John. *America via the Neighborhood*. With a new introduction by Florence G. Cassidy. Americanization Studies: The Acculturation of Immigrant Groups into American Society, republished under the general editorship of William S. Bernard. New York: Harper and Brothers, 1920. Reprint, Montclair, NJ: Patterson Smith, 1971.

Farrar, Ida F. *Books about America for New Americans*. Boston: Distributed by the Massachusetts Free Public Library Commission, 1914.

Frank, Mary. *Exploring a Neighborhood; Our Jewish People from Eastern Europe and the Orient*. Edited and with additional notes on Jewish immigrant life by John Foster Carr. New York: Immigrant Publication Society, 1919.

Hand Book of Library Organization. Compiled by the Library Commissions of Minnesota, Iowa and Wisconsin. Minneapolis: Minnesota State Library Commission, 1902. S.v. "Books in Foreign Languages," "Library Commissions," "Traveling Libraries."

Herlihy, Charles M. *Adult Education for Foreign-Born and Native Illiterates*. U.S. Bureau of Education Bulletin no. 36. Washington, DC: GPO, 1925.

———. *Elementary Instruction of Adults*. U.S. Bureau of Education Bulletin no. 8. Washington, DC: GPO, 1925.

Historical Review: Contributions to Civilization of the Armenians, French, Germans, Greeks, Italians, Letts, Lithuanians, Poles, Russians, Swedes, Syrians, Ukrainians. [Boston]: Issued by the Committee on Racial Groups of the Mass. Bay Tercentenary, 1630:1930 [1930].

Kallen, Horace M. *Culture and Democracy in the United States: Studies in the Group Psychology of the American Peoples*. New York: Boni and Liveright, 1924. Reprint, New York: Arno Press and the New York Times, 1970.

Ledbetter, Eleanor (Edwards). *The Czechs of Cleveland*. Cleveland: Cleveland Americanization Committee, Mayor's Advisory War Committee, 1919.

———. *The Jugoslavs of Cleveland, with a Brief Sketch of Their Historical and Political Backgrounds*. Cleveland: Cleveland Americanization Committee, Mayor's Advisory War Committee, 1918.

———. *The Polish Immigrant and His Reading*. Library Work with the Foreign Born. Chicago: ALA, 1924.

———. *Polish Literature in English Translation; A Bibliography with a List of Books about Poland and the Poles*. With a foreword by Tadeusz Mitana. Published under the Auspices of the Polish National Alliance. New York: H. W. Wilson, 1932.

———. *The Slovaks of Cleveland, with Some General Information on the Race*. Cleveland: Cleveland Americanization Committee, Mayor's Advisory War Committee, 1918.

———. *Winning Friends and Citizens for America; Work with Poles, Bohemians, and Others*. Library Work with the Foreign Born, edited by John Foster Carr. New York: Immigrant Publication Society, 1918.

Libraries and Adult Education: Report of a Study Made by the American Library Association. Chicago: ALA, 1926.

Mahoney, John J. *Training Teachers for Americanization; A Course of Study for Normal Schools and Teachers' Institutes*. U.S. Bureau of Education Bulletin no. 12. Washington, DC: GPO, 1920.

Mahoney, John J., and Charles M. Herlihy. *First Steps in Americanization: A Handbook for Teachers*. Boston: Houghton Mifflin, 1918.

Massachusetts Commission on Immigration. *Report of the Commission on Immigration on the Problem of Immigration in Massachusetts*. Boston: Wright and Potter, State Printers, 1914.

Miller, Herbert Adolphus. *The School and the Immigrant*. Cleveland Education Survey. Cleveland: The Survey Committee of the Cleveland Foundation, 1916. Reprint, New York: Arno Press and the New York Times, 1970.

Morriss, Elizabeth C., Marian V. Morse, and Edna Phillips. *Experimental Reading Study in the Joint Library–Adult Elementary Education Field*. New York: Bureau of Publications, Teachers College, Columbia University, 1935.

Nemcova, Bozena. *The Shepherd and the Dragon; Fairy Tales from the Czech of Bozena Nemcova*. Translated by Eleanor E. Ledbetter. Illustrated by William Siegel. New York: Robert M. McBride & Company, 1930.

New Jersey Commission of Immigration. *Report of the Commission of Immigration of the State of New Jersey Appointed Pursuant to the Provisions of Chapter 362 of the Laws of 1911*. Trenton, NJ: MacCrellish and Quigley, State Printers, 1914.

North American Civic League for Immigrants. New York-New Jersey Committee. *Education of the Immigrant; Abstracts of Papers Read at a Public Conference Under the Auspices of the New York-New Jersey Committee of the North American Civic League for Immigrants, Held at New York City, May 16 and 17, 1913*. Washington, DC: GPO, 1913.

———. *New York-New Jersey Committee of the North American Civic League for Immigrants, December, 1909–March, 1911*. New York: The Committee, 1911.

———. *New York-New Jersey Committee of the North American Civic League for Immigrants, December 1, 1909–February 1, 1913*. New York: The Committee, 1913.

Pecorini, Alberto. *The Story of America*. Prepared for the Massachusetts Society of the Colonial Dames. Boston: Marshall Jones, 1920.

Peschke, Melitta D. *The German Immigrant and His Reading*. Library Work with the Foreign Born. Chicago: ALA, 1929.

Phillips, Edna. *Easy Books for New Americans, with a Reading List for Americanization Workers*. 2d ed. rev. Chicago: ALA, 1926; 3d ed. rev. , Chicago: ALA, 1927.

Reading Service to the Foreign Born. Compiled by the Committee on Work with the Foreign Born of the American Library Association. Chicago: ALA, 1929.

Rose, Ernestine. *Bridging the Gulf; Work with the Russian Jews and Other Newcomers.* Library Work with the Foreign Born, ed. by John Foster Carr. New York: Immigrant Publication Society, 1917.

Soltes, Mordecai. *The Yiddish Press, an Americanizing Agency.* New York: Teachers College, Columbia University, 1925, copr. 1924. Reprint, New York: Arno Press and the New York Times, 1969.

Sweet, May M. *The Italian Immigrant and His Reading.* Library Work with the Foreign Born. Chicago: ALA, 1925.

Thompson, Frank Victor. *Schooling of the Immigrant.* Americanization Studies: The Acculturation of Immigrant Groups into American Society, republished under the general editorship of William S. Bernard. New York: Harper and Brothers, 1920. Reprint, Montclair, NJ: Patterson Smith, 1971.

U.S. Immigration Commission. *Report of the Immigration Commission.* Submitted to 61st Congress, 2d and 3rd Sessions. 41 vols. Washington, DC: GPO, 1911.

U.S. Library of Congress. Division of Bibliography. *List of References on American Immigration Including Americanization, Effect of European War, Etc.* Select List of References no. 268. Washington, DC: GPO, 1918.

Articles and Essays

Ackerman, Carl W. "The Book-worms of New York: How the Public Libraries Satisfy the Immigrant's Thirst for Knowledge." *Independent* 74 (Jan. 1913): 199–201.

Addams, Jane. "The Public School and the Immigrant Child." In National Education Association of the United States, Addresses *and Proceedings . . . June 29–July 3, 1908.* Washington, DC: NEA, 1908.

ALA Committee on Work with the Foreign Born. "Dealers in Foreign Books." *LJ* 47 (Aug. 1922): 647–48.

Allen, Faith L. "Children and Patriotism." *Wisconsin Library Bulletin* 14 (Feb. 1918): 46–47.

"Americanization." *Maine Library Bulletin* 8 (Jan. 1919): 86.

"Americanization by the Public Library." *Survey* 41 (18 Jan. 1919): 537–38.

"Americanization of Foreigners." *Maine Library Bulletin* 8 (Jan. 1919): 75.

"Americanization Work in Seattle Public Library." *Public Libraries* 25 (Oct. 1920): 448–49.

Antin, Mary. "The Immigrant in the Library." *ALA Bulletin* 7 (July 1913): 145–50.

Arnold, John J. "Americanization and Libraries." *Illinois Libraries* 1 (Apr. 1919): 15–19.

Aronovici, Carol. "Americanization, Its Meaning and Function." *Minnesota Public Library Commission Notes* 5 (Dec. 1918): 181–82.

Bailey, Louis J. "Standards and Tests in Evaluating Easy English Books for Adults." *ALA Bulletin* 22 (Sept. 1928): 473–74.

Belden, Charles F. D. "Library Commission Work in Massachusetts." *LJ* 42 (Jan. 1917): 5–10.

———. "The Reading of the Foreign-Born in Massachusetts Libraries," *MLCB* 19 (Mar. 1929): 33.

Bernhard, Josephine Butkowska. "Suitable Books for Foreign-Born Readers." *Booklist* 31 (Jan. 1935): 149–52.

Blake, Katherine Evans. "Americanization." *Minnesota Public Library Commission Notes* 5 (June 1918): 150–51.

Bogardus, Emory S. "Mexicans and Filipinos in the United States." *ALA Bulletin* 24 (Sept. 1930): 511–12.

"Book Selection on Foreign Countries: What Other Nations Regard as the Best Books in English about Their Countries." *LJ* 54 (15 Nov. 1929): 947–48.

"Books for and Concerning Foreign-Born People." *Maine Library Bulletin* 8 (Jan. 1919): 75–79.

"Books for Immigrants." *New York Libraries* 1 (July 1908): 98.

"Books for the Foreigners." *Pennsylvania Library Notes* 8 (Jan. 1916): 7–10.

"Books in Foreign Languages." *New York Libraries* 1 (Oct. 1908): 129.

Bostwick, Arthur E. "Books for the Foreign Population—II." *LJ* 31 (Aug. 1906): 67–70.

"Branch Libraries Make Friends with Their Community." *The Library* 4 (June 1932): 95–96.

Briggs, Elizabeth V. "Service to Foreign Readers in the Small Library." *Michigan Library Bulletin* 21 (Dec. 1930): 315–17. Reprinted in *LJ* 57 (1 Apr. 1932): 324–27.

Britton, Jasmine. "The Library's Share in Americanization." *LJ* 43 (Oct. 1918): 723–27.

Bry, Ilse. "Reading for Refugees." *LJ* 65 (1 Nov. 1940): 903–6.

Campbell, Jane Maud. "Americanizing Books and Periodicals for Immigrants." *ALA Bulletin* 10 (July 1916): 269–72.

———. "Books for the Foreign Population—III." *LJ* 31(Aug. 1906): 70–72.

———. "An Educational Opportunity and the Library." *LJ* 32 (Apr. 1907): 157–58.

———. "Foreign Periodicals." *MLCB* 4 (Mar.–May 1914): 67–69.

———. "The Library and the Immigrant: Part II." *New York Libraries* 1 (Oct. 1908): 132–36.

———. "The Public Library and the Immigrant: [Part I]." *New York Libraries* 1 (July 1908): 100–105.

———. "The Small City Library." *LJ* 28 (July 1903): 50–52.

———. "Supplying Books in Foreign Languages in Public Libraries." *LJ* 29 (Feb. 1904): 65–67.

———. "What the Foreigner Has Done for One Library." *MLCB* 3 (July 1913): 100–106. Reprinted in *LJ* 38 (Nov. 1913): 610–15.

Canfield, James Hulme. "The Library in Relation to Special Classes of Readers: Books for the Foreign Population—I." *LJ* 31 (Aug. 1906): 65–67.

"Carnegie Corporation to Study Americanization." *LJ* 43 (May 1918): 339.

Carr, John Foster. "Anglo-American Unity Fast Coming." *World's Work* 6 (Oct. 1903): 4016–17.

———. "Books in Foreign Languages and Americanization." *LJ* 44 (Apr. 1919): 245–46.

———. "Campaign Funds and Campaign Scandals." *Outlook* 81 (4 Nov. 1905): 549–54.

———. "The Coming of the Italian." *Outlook* 82 (24 Feb. 1906): 418–31.

———. "Fighting the Fire." *Outlook* 88 (28 Mar. 1908): 681–93.

———. "A Fire in the Country." *Suburban Life* 6 (Apr. 1908): 206–7.

———. "The Great Northwest." *Outlook* 86 (22 June 1907): 363–77.

———. "A Great Railway Builder [James Jerome Hill]." *Outlook* 87 (26 Oct. 1907): 390–98.

———. "A Greater ALA—A Letter to the President." *LJ* 45 (1 Dec. 1920): 979.

———. "A Greater American Library Association." *LJ* 45 (1 Oct. 120): 775–78.

———. "The Immigrant Problem in the United States; Pertinent Clippings with Speeches by John Foster Carr, 1910–1917." [Scrapbook of clippings, mounted and bound at the New York Public Library, 1941.]

———. "An Immigrant's Baedeker." *Outlook* 106 (7 Feb. 1914): 287–88.

———. "Is English Supremacy Worth a War." *World's Work* 18 (June 1909): 11684–88.

———. "The Italian in the United States." *World's Work* 8 (Oct. 1904): 5393–5404.

———. "John Ireland, Bishop of St. Paul." *Outlook* 91 (24 Apr. 1909): 970–2.

———. "The Library and the Immigrant." *ALA Bulletin* 8 (July 1914): 140–7.

———. "The Library in Americanization Work." *Illinois Libraries* 1 (Oct. 1919): 60–61.

———. "The Library, the Friend of the Foreign Born." In *Proceedings [of the] Americanization Conference Held under the Auspices of the Americanization Division, Bureau of Education, Department of the Interior, Washington, May 12, 13, 14, 15, 1919.* Washington, DC: GPO, 1919.

———. "Library Work for Immigrants." *ALA Bulletin* 10 (July 1916): 273–76.

———. "'Making Americans': A Preliminary and Tentative List of Books." *LJ* 45 (1 Mar. 1920): 209–12.

———. "The Nation's Need and the Library's Opportunity." *New York Libraries* 5 (Feb. 1917): 192–94.

———. "The New Northwest and the Railways." *Outlook* 86 (24 Aug. 1907): 869–83.

———. "The Panama Canal [Seven-Part Series]." *Outlook* 82 (28 Apr. 1906): 947–63; 83 (5 May 1906): 21–24; (12 May 1906): 69–72; (19 May 1906): 117–20; (2 June 1906): 265–70; (23 June 1906): 435–45; 84 (29 Sept. 1906): 263–68.

———. "The Plight of Russia." *World's Work* 9 (Nov. 1904): 5531–34.

———. "A School with a Clear Aim." *World's Work* 19 (Dec. 1909): 12362–65.

———. "Some of the People We Work For." *LJ* 41 (Aug. 1916): 552–57.

———. "What the Library Can Do for Our Foreign-Born." *LJ* 38 (Oct. 1913): 566–68.

"Cataloging Foreign Books, Seattle Plan." *Libraries* 32 (May 1927): 240-41.

Cleve, Edna G. "Our Foreign-Born Americans." *WLB* 9 (Dec. 1934): 181–87.

Cohen, Henry. "The Immigrant Publication Society." *Jewish Charities* 6 (Aug. 1915): 3–5.

Comstock, Sarah. "Eight Million Books a Year: How the New York Public Library Distributes Them through Forty-One Branch Libraries to More Than Three Million People—The Service It Performs for the Blind, for Foreigners Who Cannot Read English, and for the Children Who Are Just Learning to Love Books." *World's Work* 26 (May 1913): 100–108.

Countryman, Gratia. "Shall Public Libraries Buy Foreign Literature for the Benefit of the Foreign Population?" *LJ* 23 (June 1898): 229–31.

Cowgill, Ruth. "Tendencies Today in Some of the European Literatures." *ALA Bulletin* 22 (Sept. 1928): 473.

Crane, Frank. "The Ten Points of Americanism." *LJ* 45 (1 Mar. 1920): 214–15.

[Crawford, Ruth]. "The Library and the Immigrant in St. Louis." *LJ* 41 (July 1916): 478–79.

Daggett, Mabel Potter. "The Library's Part in Making Americans: Free Books Are Helping Our Foreign-Born Citizens to a Bigger and Better Patriotism." *Delineator* 77 (Jan. 1911): 17–18.

Daniels, John. "Americanization by Indirection." *LJ* 45 (1 Nov. 1920): 871–76.

"Dealers in Foreign Books." *Pennsylvania Library Notes* 14 (July 1934): 438–41.

"Developing Americanism." *New York Libraries* 5 (May 1916): 74–75.

Dunning, Mrs. James G. "Educational Work of the Daughters of the American Revolution." *Immigrants in America Review* 1 (Sept. 1915): 51–53.

Eastman, Linda A. "The Library and the Children: An Account of the Children's Work in the Cleveland Public Library." *LJ* 23 (Apr. 1898): 142–44.

Fiske, Anna J. "The Human Interest in Library Work in a Mining District." *Public Libraries* 13 (Mar. 1908): 78–81.

Flexner, Jennie M. "Readers' Advisory Work with the New Émigré." *LJ* 66 (July 1941): 593–95.

"The Foreign Language Information Service." *LJ* 49 (15 Nov. 1924): 981.

"Foreign Language Press Publicity." *LJ* 52 (1 June 1927): 603.

Frank, Mary, and John Foster Carr. "Exploring a Neighborhood." *Century* 98 (July 1919): 375–90.

Furst, Elisabeth Hardman. "An Experiment in Cooperative Reading: Workers with the Foreign Born in Massachusetts." *Libraries* 33 (June 1928): 313–14.

Gaillard, Edwin White. "Why Public Libraries Should Supply Books in Foreign Languages." *LJ* 28 (Feb. 1903): 67.

Gavit, John Palmer. "Through Neighbors' Doorways." *Survey Graphic* 29 (Sept. 1940): 471–72.

Gratiaa, Josephine. "Making Americans: How the Library Helps." *LJ* 44 (Nov. 1919): 729–30. Excerpt from St. Louis Public Library, AR 1918/19.

———. "Roumanians in the United States and Their Relations to Public Libraries." *LJ* 47 (1 May 1922): 400–404.

Guhin, M. M. "Americanization in South Dakota." *South Dakota Library Bulletin* 6 (Sept. 1920): 46–49.

H., M. R. "Some Work of the Library with Bohemians." *LJ* 35 (June 1910): 265.

Hall, Anna G. "Work with Foreigners in a Small Factory Town." *New York Libraries* 5 (Nov. 1916): 159–61. Summarized in *LJ* 42 (May 1917): 410.

Hansen, Agnes Camilla. "Books to Cultivate Tolerance." *LJ* 64 (1 Oct. 1939): 729–31.

———. "Work with Foreigners." *ALA Bulletin* 9 (July 1915): 196–98.

"Helps in Government and Language for Immigrants." *Public Libraries* 16 (Mar. 1911): 111–12.

Herlihy, Charles M. "Outstanding Accomplishments in the Field of Adult Education since the War." In National Education Association of the United States, *Addresses and Proceedings . . . June 28–July 3, 1925.* Washington, DC: NEA, 1925.

Hickman, Margaret Gabriel. "Why a Foreign Department in an American Public Library." *LJ* 57 (1 Apr. 1932): 327–29.

Himmelwright, Susan. "Work with the Foreign-Born: Pennsylvania Libraries." *Pennsylvania Library Notes* 14 (July 1934): 433–38.

Hirsch, Rudolf. "The Foreigner in Library Service." *WLB* 14 (Sept. 1939): 50–51, 56.

"Holiday Receptions for Foreigners." *LJ* 40 (June 1915): 450.

Horton, Marion. "Here in the Land of Promise." *LJ* 44 (Mar. 1919): 139–42.

———. "Library Work with the Japanese." *LJ* 47 (15 Feb. 1922): 157–60.

Howard, C. E. "The Carnegie Library of Pittsburgh, and the Foreigner." *Pennsylvania Library Notes* 3 (Oct. 1910): 12–16.

Hrbek [i.e., Hrbkova], Sarka. "The Library and the Foreign-Born Citizen." *Public Libraries* 15 (Mar. 1910): 98–104.

"The Immigrant Publication Society." *LJ* 45 (1 Mar. 1920): 213–14.

Jacobson, Karen M. "What Minnesota Does for Its Foreign Citizens." *Minnesota Public Library Commission Notes* 9 (Dec. 1906): 31–32.

Johnston, Esther. "Report of the New York Library Association—Committee on Work with the Foreign Born." *ALA Bulletin* 16 (July 1922): 371–74.

Josephson, Aksel G. S. "Books for the Immigrants: I. Swedish." *LJ* 33 (Dec. 1908): 505.

———. "Foreign Books in American Libraries." *LJ* 19 (Nov. 1894): 364.

Kallen, Horace M. "Democracy versus the Melting-Pot." *Nation* 100 (18 Feb. 1915): 190–94; (25 Feb. 1915): 217–20.

———. "The Meaning of Americanism." *Immigrants in America Review* 1 (Jan. 1916): 12–19.

"King Oscar's Traveling Library." *Minnesota Public Library Commission Notes* 2 (Jan. 1908): 101–2.

Kirkwood, Elizabeth T. "Life and the Librarian." *Scribner's Magazine* 71 (June 1922): 737–38, 740.

Kudlicka, Josepha. "Library Work Among Foreigners." *Public Libraries* 15 (Nov. 1910): 375–76.

Ledbetter, Eleanor E. "Books in Foreign Language." *Public Libraries* 27 (Dec. 1922): 599.

———. "Books in Immigrant Languages." *LJ* 50 (15 Jan. 1925): 73–75.

———. "Channels of Foreign Language Publicity." *Christian Science Monitor*, 23 Mar. 1927.

———. "Czech Literature in American Libraries." *Christian Science Monitor*, 25 Jan. 1928.

———. "The Czechoslovak Immigrant and the Library." *LJ* 48 (1 Nov. 1923): 911–15.

———. "Easter in the Karpathians." *Spirit of Missions* 85 (Apr. 1920): 209–15.

———. "Factors that Should Determine the Proportion of a Library's Book Fund to Be Spent for Reading of the Foreign Born." *ALA Bulletin* 22 (Sept. 1928): 475. Summarized in *LJ* 53 (Aug. 1928): 670, and *Libraries* 33 (Nov. 1928): 476–77.

———. "A Gallant Institution: The Warsaw Public Library." *Poland* (Jan. 1924): 28–29, 52, 54.

———. "The Girl Queen." *Poland* (Nov. 1926): 681–82, 708, 710–11, 714–15.

———. "Group Service to Immigrants." *Christian Science Monitor*, 29 June 1927.

———. "Group Service to Immigrants—II." *Christian Science Monitor*, 3 July 1927.

———. "Helpful Magazines for Workers with Foreign-Born." *Christian Science Monitor*, 26 Jan. 1927.

———. "The Human Touch and the Librarian." *Scribner's Magazine* 72 (Oct. 1922): 450–55.

———. "Immigrant Parents and Their American Children." *Christian Science Monitor*, 25 May 1927.

———. "Is the Public Library Democratic?" *ALA Bulletin* 16 (July 1922): 366–70.

———. "June in Czechoslovakia." *Survey Graphic* 52 (1 June 1924): 301–3.

———. "Libraries and the Attitude of Tolerance." *Christian Science Monitor*, 24 Nov. 1926.

———. "A Library for Bohemians." *Czechoslovak Review* (Sept. 1919): 258-60. Also appeared in *LJ* 44 (Dec. 1919): 792–93.

———. "The Lobkovic Library at Roudnice, Czechoslovakia." *Christian Science Monitor*, 27 Apr. 1927.

———. "My Serbian Christmas." *Survey Graphic* 49 (1 Dec. 1922): 306–9.

———. "The Polish Immigrant and the Library." *LJ* 47 (15 Jan. 1922): 67–70; *LJ* 47 (1 June 1922): 496–98.

———. "Polish Literature in English." *Poland* (Apr. 1924): 229–33, 249. Summarized in *LJ* 49 (1 Sept. 1924): 738–39.

———. "Recent Development in Library Work with Immigrants." In *Proceedings of the National Conference of Social Work (Formerly National Conference of Charities and Correction) at the Fifty-First Annual Session.* Chicago: University of Chicago Press, 1924.

———. "The Religion of the Rusins: The Greek Catholic Church in America." *Czechoslovak Review* (Jan. 1920): 14–19.

———, comp. "Slav Literatures: A List of Bibliographies." *LJ* 49 (1 June 1924): 553.

————. "Some Immigrant Readers Considered." *Christian Science Monitor*, 2 Mar. 1927.

————. "Types of Immigrant Readers Studied." *Christian Science Monitor*, 9 Mar. 1927.

Lee, Ettie. "Social Value in Studying English." *ALA Bulletin* 24 (Sept. 1930): 512.

Lescohier, Don D. "The Library in Americanization." *Wisconsin Library Bulletin* 16 (Jan. 1920): 3–6.

"Libraries and the Adult Foreign Born." *Interpreter Release Clip Sheet* no. 13 (18 Oct. 1926): 1–3.

"Libraries as Americanizers." *Minnesota Public Library Commission Notes* 5 (Sept. 1918): 174.

"Libraries for Schools." In U.S. Bureau of Education. *Report of the Commissioner of Education for the Year 1887–88.* Washington, DC: GPO, 1889.

"The Library's Part in Americanizing Foreigners." *New York Libraries* 6 (Aug. 1918): 88-89. Reprinted in *LJ* 43 (Nov. 1918): 848.

"The Library's Part in Making Americans." *New York Libraries* 4 (Aug. 1915): 235–36.

Lyman, Jean. "The Library Needs of the Foreign Child." *WLB* 5 (May 1931): 581–83.

MacLean, Helen Hirt. "Library Aid for Refugees." *WLB* 13 (June 1939): 683, 685.

McLellan, Mary B. "Babel and the Loan Assistant." *WLB* 7(Feb. 1933): 363–65.

————. "Recent Aids to Inter-Racial Service." *LJ* 59 (1 Apr. 1934): 303–5.

————. "There's Still Work to Be Done with the Foreign Born." *LJ* 70 (Aug. 1945): 676–77.

McPike, Josephine M. "The Foreign Child at a St. Louis Branch." *LJ* 40 (Dec. 1915): 851–55.

Maltby, Adelaide B. "Immigrants as Contributors to Library Progress." *ALA Bulletin* 7 (July 1913): 150–54.

Martin, Arabel. "Buying of Foreign Books for Small Libraries." *Minnesota Public Library Commission Notes* 9 (Dec. 1906): 30–31.

Massachusetts Library Club. Committee on Inter-Racial Service. "New Americans and Americanization Workers." *LJ* 60 (15 Oct. 1935): 808–9.

————. Committee on Work with New Americans. "Bilingual Dictionaries and Histories of the United States in Foreign Languages." *MLCB* 15 (June 1925): 42–43. Reprinted as "Bilingual Dictionaries and United States Histories in Foreign Languages" *LJ* 50 (15 Dec. 1925): 1037–38.

————. "Dealers in Foreign Books." *MLCB* 18 (Mar. 1928): 20–21.

Milam, Carl H. "What's Left of Library War Service." *LJ* 44 (Dec. 1919): 755–56.

Miller, Herbert Adolphus. "The Oppression Psychosis and the Immigrant." *Annals of the American Academy of Political and Social Science* 93 (Jan. 1921): 139–44.

————. "The True Americanization of the Foreign Child." *ALA Bulletin* 13 (July 1919): 130–32.

Moore, John H. "The Sons of the American Revolution and Better Citizenship." *Immigrants in America Review* 1 (Sept. 1915): 40–41.

Morgan, Vera. "Expanding the Small Library's Contact with New Americans." *ALA Bulletin* 22 (Sept. 1928): 474–75.

"New Americans and the Tacoma Public Library." *LJ* 45 (1 Mar. 1920): 218.

Palmer, Margaret. "The Library and the Immigrant." *Minnesota Public Library Commission Notes* 2 (Dec. 1909): 192–95.

Panunzio, Constantine. "The Immigrant and the Library." *LJ* 49 (15 Nov. 1924): 969–73.

Parsons, Mary Prescott. "Libraries and Foreign Born Readers, 1942." *ALA Bulletin* 36 (15 Sept. 1942): 28–31.

"Personnel of Americanization Survey." *LJ* 43 (July 1918): 505.

Peters, Orpha Maud. "Libraries in Relation to Citizenship and Americanization." *LJ* 44 (Dec. 1919): 759.

Phillips, Edna. "American Book Service in Greece and Turkey." *LJ* 53 (1 Mar. 1928): 219–20.

———. "Children's Picture Books from Other Lands." *Publishers Weekly* 108 (19 Sept. 1925): 860–61.

———. "Contribution of the Public Library to Adult Education." *School Life* 11 (Nov. 1925): 52–53.

———. "Cooperative Reading." *Survey* 58 (15 May 1927): 217.

———. "Encouraging the Foreign Reader: An Account of State Encouragement for the Reading of the Foreign-Born Laborer in Massachusetts." *LJ* 49 (15 Nov. 1924): 974–76.

———. "Four Days at the Midway Point of East and West." *Bay State Librarian* 48 (Autumn 1958): 1–2.

———. "Library Aids in Naturalization (Revised, 1924)." *WLB* 2 (September 1924): 262–65.

———. "A Library Commission's Work for the Foreign Born." *ALA Bulletin* 23 (Aug. 1929): 370–71. Summarized in *LJ* 54 (July 1929): 622; *Libraries* 34 (July 1929): 326–27.

———. "Library Work with the Foreign-Born." *Bulletin of the New Hampshire Public Library Commission* 25 (Dec. 1929): 6–8.

———. "A Plan for Cooperation in Work with Racial Groups." *ALA Bulletin* 26 (Jan. 1932): 29–30.

———. "Problems in Book Selection for Physical and Mental Balance." *Public Libraries* 2 (Jan. 1948): 28–31.

———. "Reading Service to Migrant Mexican Laborers in the United States." Typescript dated June 1945. ALA Archives.

———. "Staff Progress Measurement." *WLB* 17 (Dec. 1942): 330.

———. "Time-Saver." *Massachusetts Library Association Bulletin* 33 (Apr. 1943): 29–30.

———. "Use of Books." *LJ* 59 (1 Nov. 1934): 847–49.

Poɾay, Aniela. "The Foreign Child and the Book." *LJ* 40 (Apr. 1915): 233–39.

Posell, Elsa Z. "The Librarian Works with the Foreign Born." *ALA Bulletin* 35 (July 1941): 424–30.

Prescott, Della R. "Americanization thru Foreign Print." *LJ* 43 (Dec. 1918): 884–85.

———. "What Americanization Is Not." *LJ* 45 (1 Mar. 1920): 218.

———. "Work with Foreign Newspapers in Newark Free Public Library." *LJ* 44 (Feb. 1919): 77–78.

"The Public Library and Allied Agencies." In *The Library without the Walls*, Reprints of Papers and Addresses, selected and annotated by Laura M. Janzow (New York: H. W. Wilson, 1927), 323–49.

"The Public Library and Patriotism." *Minnesota Public Library Commission Notes* 5 (June 1917): 81–83.

Quigley, Margery. "Encouraging Use of Foreign Books." *WLB* 14 (Jan. 1940): 392.

———. "The Greek Immigrant and the Library." *LJ* 47 (15 Oct. 1922): 863–65.

Randall, William M. "What Can the Foreigner Find to Read in the Public Library?" *Library Quarterly* 1 (Jan. 1931): 79–88.

Reid, Marguerite. "Our New Americans." *MLCB* 2 (Mar. 1912): 29–36.

Reid, Marguerite, and John G. Moulton. "Aids in Work with Foreigners." *MLCB* 2 (Mar. 1912): 37–56.

"Report of the Committee of an Enlarged Program for American Library Service." *ALA Bulletin* 14 (July 1920): 297–309.

Robbins, Jane E. "Schools in Temporary Construction Camps." *Immigrants in America Review* 1 (June 1915): 28–30.

Roberts, Flora B. "The Library and the Foreign Citizen." *Public Libraries* 17 (May 1912): 166–69.

Roberts, Peter. "The Library and the Foreign-Speaking Man." *LJ* 36 (Oct. 1911): 496–99.

———. "What Can Libraries Do to Aid the Foreign Speaking Peoples in America?" *Pennsylvania Library Notes* 3 (Oct. 1910): 16–23.

———. "The YMCA Teaching Foreign-Speaking Men." *Immigrants in American Review* 1 (June 1915): 18–23.

Rosche, Bertha Morse. "Strangers in a Strange Land." *Illinois Libraries* 26 (May 1944): 163–65.

Rose, Ernestine. "How the Public Library Helps the Foreigner Make His American Contribution." In National Education Association of the United States, *Addresses and Proceedings of the Sixtieth Annual Meeting.* Washington, DC: National Education Association, 1922.

Sanders, Minerva. "The Possibilities of Public Libraries in Manufacturing Communities." *LJ* 12 (Sept.–Oct. 1887): 395–400.

Schretter, Natalie. "What Books for the Newcomer?" *WLB* 15 (Sept. 1940): 24–27.

Sergio, Lisa. "The Importance of Interpreting America." *ALA Bulletin* 35 (1 Oct. 1941): 486–89.

Shiels, Albert. "The Immigrant, the School and the Library." *ALA Bulletin* 10 (July 1916): 257–63.

Smith, Irene. "Human Side of Library Work with Foreign-Born Children." *LJ* 58 (1 Nov. 1933): 865–68.

Solis-Cohen, Leon M. "Library Work in the Brooklyn Ghetto." *LJ* 33 (Dec. 1908): 485–88.

Sommer, F. E. "Books in Foreign Script in the Public Library." *LJ* 59 (15 Nov. 1934): 892–93.

"The Status of the 'Books for Everybody' Campaign as Reported by the Regional Directors on July 15th." *LJ* 45 (1 Oct. 1920): 798–800.

Stevens, W. F. "Use of the Library by Foreigners as Shown by the Carnegie Library of Homestead, Pa." *LJ* 35 (Apr. 1910): 161–62.

Stull, Maud I. "Inter-Racial Services Needed by Libraries." *LJ* 58 (1 Sept. 1933): 707.

Sutliff, Mary L. "The Spirit of America." *Wisconsin Library Bulletin* 16 (Mar. 1920): 34–36.

Sweet, May M. "Italians and the Public Library." *LJ* 49 (15 Nov. 1924): 977–81.

Tafuris, Marguerite. "The Immigrant: A Composite Portrait." *WLB* 1 (June 1919): 349.

Taylor, Lucian E. "Cataloging of Foreign Books: Report of a Round Table Meeting of the Massachusetts Library Club." *LJ* 52 (1 Mar. 1927): 237–38.

Taylor, Zada. "War Children on the Pacific: A Symposium Article." *LJ* 67 (15 June 1942): 558–62.

Tracey, Catharine S. "Bibliography on Library Work with Foreigners, 1911–1916." *ALA Bulletin* 10 (July 1916): 263–64.

"Translation Service from the Business Men's League of St. Louis." *LJ* 42 (July 1917): 519.

"Traveling Libraries of Foreign Books." *Wisconsin Library Bulletin* 1 (Sept. 1905): 74–75.

Utley, George B. "Shall a Permanent Endowment Be Undertaken for Peace Time Work of the ALA?" *ALA Bulletin* 13 (May 1919): 92–93.

Varley, Harry. "Gauging the Sentiment Appeal in Selling Charity to the Crowd: The New York Library Book Campaign, a Study in Mob Psychology." *Printers' Ink* 107 (19 June 1919): 65–68.

"Visitors from Many Lands." *The Library* 4 (Mar. 1932): 67–68.

Webster, Caroline F. "Library Work with Foreigners." *ALA Bulletin* 9 (July 1915): 192–95.

Wendel, F. C. H. "The Stranger within Our Gates; What Can the Library Do for Him?" *Public Libraries* 19 (Mar. 1911): 89–92.

Wetmore, Francis. "Library Work with Foreign Born." *Illinois Libraries* 25 (Jan. 1943): 49–50.

"What One Library Is Doing in the Making of Americans." *New York Libraries* 5 (May 1916): 110.

Wheaton, H[arrison] H[ylas]. "An Americanization Program for Libraries." *ALA Bulletin* 10 (July 1916): 265–69.

———. "Libraries and the 'America First' Campaign." *LJ* 42 (Jan. 1917): 21–22.

———. "Survey of Adult Immigrant Education." *Immigrants in America Review* 1 (June 1915): 42–65.

———. "United States Bureau of Education and the Immigrant." *Annals of the American Academy of Political and Social Science* 67 (Sept. 1916): 273–83.

Willcox, Mary Alice. "The American Baedeker." *Journal of Education* 78 (4 Dec. 1913): 571–72.

———. "The Little Green Book: How It Is Used in the Schools." *Journal of Education* 78 (18 Dec. 1913): 631–33.

———. "The Use of the Immigrant's Guide in the Library." *MLCB* 4 (Mar.-May 1914): 69–73.

Wirt, Edith. "English Speaking Readers in the Foreign Literature Division, Cleveland Public Library." *Libraries* 36 (July 1931): 305–6.

[Wolcott, J. D.]. "Library Service to Immigrants." In U.S. Bureau of Education, *Report of the Commissioner of Education for the Year Ended June 30, 1915.* Vol. 1. Washington, DC: GPO, 1915.

Wong, Vi-Lien. "Chinese Collections in American Libraries." *LJ* 60 (15 June 1935): 527–28.

Wood, Grace W. "Autobiographies of Foreign-Born Americans." *LJ* 49 (1 May 1924): 420.

"Work with Foreigners." *LJ* 40 (Apr. 1915): 292–93; (Aug. 1915): 621; (Sept. 1915): 684.

"Work with Greeks." *LJ* 40 (Aug. 1915): 621.

"Work with the Foreign Born and Preparation for Citizenship." *ALA Bulletin* 14 (July 1920): 299–300.

Wright, Ida Faye. "The Gifts of the Nations." *LJ* 45 (1 Mar. 1920): 215–16.

Yust, William F. "What of the Black and Yellow Races?" *ALA Bulletin* 7 (July 1913): 159–67.

SECONDARY SOURCES (Post-1948)

Books and Pamphlets

Barton, Josef J. *Peasants and Strangers: Italians, Rumanians and Slovaks in an American City, 1890–1950.* Cambridge, MA: Harvard University Press, 1975.

Bodnar, John. *The Transplanted: A History of Immigrants in Urban America.* Bloomington: Indiana University Press, 1985.

Briggs, John W. *An Italian Passage: Immigrants to Three American Cities, 1890-1930.* New Haven, CT: Yale University Press, 1978.

Cinel, Dino. *From Italy to San Francisco: The Immigrant Experience.* Stanford, CA: Stanford University Press, 1982.

Coleman, Marion (Moore), comp. *Polish Literature in English Translation: A Bibliography.* Cheshire, CT: Cherry Hill Books, 1963.

Cordasco, Francesco. *The Immigrant Woman in North America: An Annotated Bibliography of Selected References.* Metuchen, NJ: Scarecrow Press, 1985.

Cramer, C[larence] H[enley]. *Open Shelves and Open Minds; A History of the Cleveland Public Library.* Cleveland: Press of Case Western Reserve University, 1972.

Dain, Phyllis. *The New York Public Library: A History of Its Founding and Early Years.* New York: New York Public Library, Astor, Lenox and Tilden Foundations, 1972.

Ditzion, Sidney. *Arsenals of a Democratic Culture: A Social History of the American Public Library Movement in New England and the Middle States from 1850 to 1900.* Chicago: ALA, 1947.

DuMont, Rosemary Ruhig. *Reform and Reaction: The Big City Public Library in American Life.* Westport, CT: Greenwood Press, 1977.

Garrison, Dee. *Apostles of Culture: The Public Librarian and American Society, 1876–1920.* New York: The Free Press, 1979.

Geller, Evelyn. *Forbidden Books in American Public Libraries, 1876–1939: A Study in Cultural Change.* Westport, CT: Greenwood Press, 1984.

Gordon, Milton Myron. *Assimilation in American Life: The Role of Race, Religion, and National Origins.* New York: Oxford University Press, 1964.

Handlin, Oscar. *Race and Nationality in American Life.* Boston: Little, Brown, 1957.

————. *The Uprooted: The Epic Story of the Great Migrations that Made the American People.* Boston: Little, Brown, 1951; 2d ed., 1973.

Hansen, Marcus Lee. *The Immigrant in American History.* Edited with a foreword by Arthur M. Schlesinger. New York: Harper and Row, 1964, copr. 1940.

Harris, Michael H. *The Purpose of the American Public Library in Historical Perspective: A Revisionist Interpretation.* ERIC Reports, ED 071 668; LI 004 063. Washington, DC: ERIC Clearinghouse on Library and Information Sciences, 1972.

————. *The Role of the Public Library in American Life: A Speculative Essay.* University of Illinois, Graduate School of Library Science, Occasional Paper no. 117. Champaign: University of Illinois, Graduate School of Library Science, 1975.

Hartmann, Edward George. *The Movement to Americanize the Immigrant.* New York: Columbia University Press, 1948.

Herberg, Will. *Protestant, Catholic, Jew; An Essay in American Religious Sociology.* Garden City, NY: Doubleday, 1955.

Higham, John. *Send These to Me: Immigrants in Urban America.* Rev. ed. Baltimore: Johns Hopkins University Press, 1984.

————. *Send These to Me: Jews and Other Immigrants in Urban America.* New York: Atheneum, 1975.

————. *Strangers in the Land; Patterns of American Nativism, 1860–1925*. Corrected and with a new preface. New York: Atheneum, 1965, copr. 1963.

Howe, Irving. *World of Our Fathers*. New York: Harcourt, Brace, Jovanovich, 1976.

Jones, Maldwyn Allen. *American Immigration*. Chicago: University of Chicago Press, 1960.

Kalisch, Philip Arthur. *The Enoch Pratt Free Library: A Social History*. Metuchen, NJ: Scarecrow Press, 1969.

Kessner, Thomas. *The Golden Door: Italian and Jewish Immigrant Mobility in New York City, 1880–1915*. New York: Oxford University Press, 1977.

Lee, Robert Ellis. *Continuing Education for Adults through the American Public Library, 1833–1964*. Chicago: ALA, 1966.

Monroe, Margaret E. *Library Adult Education: The Biography of An Idea*. New York: Scarecrow Press, 1963.

Moore, Deborah Dash. *At Home in America: Second Generation New York Jews*. New York: Columbia University Press, 1981.

Rischin, Moses. *The Promised City: New York's Jews, 1870-1914*. Cambridge, MA: Harvard University Press, 1977, copr. 1962.

Seller, Maxine. *To Seek America: A History of Ethnic Life in the United States*. Englewood, NJ: Jerome S. Ozer, 1977.

Thomison, Dennis. *A History of the American Library Association, 1876–1972*. Chicago: ALA, 1980, copr. 1978.

U.S. Department of Commerce, Bureau of the Census. *Historical Statistics of the United States: Colonial Times to 1970*. Bicentennial ed. Washington, DC: GPO, 1975.

Van Tassel, David D., and John J. Grabowski, eds. *The Encyclopedia of Cleveland History*. Published in Association with Case Western Reserve University. Bloomington: Indiana University Press, 1987. S.v. "Americanization," by Edward M. Miggins; "Horvath, Helen"; "Immigration and Migration," by John J. Grabowski; "Ledbetter, Eleanor Edwards"; "Mayor's Advisory War Committee."

Whitehill, Walter Muir. *Boston Public Library: A Centennial History*. Cambridge, MA: Harvard University Press, 1956.

Wiegand, Wayne A. *"An Active Instrument for Propaganda": The American Public Library during World War I*. Foreword by Edward G. Holley. Beta Phi Mu Monograph no. 1. Westport, CT: Greenwood Press, 1989.

Woodford, Frank B. *Parnassus on Main Street: A History of the Detroit Public Library*. Detroit: Wayne State University Press, 1965.

Yans-McLaughlin, Virginia. *Family and Community: Italian Immigrants in Buffalo, 1880–1930*. Urbana: University of Illinois Press, 1982, copr. 1977.

Articles and Essays

Beck, Nelson R. "The Use of Library and Educational Facilities by Russian-Jewish Immigrants in New York City, 1880–1914: The Impact of Culture." *Journal of Library History* 12 (Spring 1977): 128–49.

Bodnar, John. "Schooling and the Slavic American Family." In *American Education and the European Immigrant: 1840–1940*, ed. by Bernard J. Weiss. Urbana: University of Illinois Press, 1982.

Cahill, Alice M. "19th Century Library Innovation: The Division [i. e., MA Division of Library Extension] from 1890 to 1940." *Bay State Librarian* 55 (Oct. 1965): 7–12, 15.

Coleman, Marion (Moore). "Eleanor E. Ledbetter: Bibliographer of Polonica." *Polish-American Studies* 19 (Jan.–June 1962): 36–41.

Dain, Phyllis. "Ambivalence and Paradox: The Social Bonds of the Public Library." *LJ* 100 (1 Feb. 1975): 261–66.

———. "Outreach Programs in Public Libraries—How New? With Specific Reference to the New York Public Library." In Library History Seminar, 5th, Philadelphia, PA, 1976, *Milestones to the Present*, ed. by Harold Goldstein. Syracuse, NY: Gaylord Professional Publications, 1978.

Drzewieniecki, Walter M., and Joanna E. Drzewieniecki-Abugattas. "Public Library Service to American Ethnics: The Polish Community on the Niagara Frontier, New York." *Journal of Library History* 9 (Apr. 1974): 120–37.

Fain, Elaine. "Books for New Citizens: Public Libraries and Americanization Programs, 1900–1925." In *The Quest for Social Justice; The Morris Fromkin Memorial Lectures, 1970–1980*, ed. by Ralph M. Aderman. Madison: University of Wisconsin Press, 1983. Published for the Golda Meir Library of the University of Wisconsin-Milwaukee.

Goldman, Eric Frederick. "Century of the American Dream." *Saturday Review* 3 (13 Dec. 1975): 20–22.

Gordon, Milton M. "Assimilation in America: Theory and Reality." In *The Shaping of Twentieth-Century America: Interpretive Essays*, selected and with commentary by Richard M. Abrams and Lawrence W. Levine. 2d ed. Boston: Little, Brown, 1971.

Harris, Michael H. "Externalist or Internalist Frameworks for the Interpretation of American Library History—The Continuing Debate." *Journal of Library History* 10 (1975): 106–10.

———. "Portrait in Paradox: Commitment and Ambivalence in American Librarianship, 1876–1976." *Libri* 26 (Dec. 1976): 281–301.

———. "The Public Libraries and the Decline of the Democratic Dogma." *LJ* 101 (1 Nov. 1976): 2225–30.

———. "The Purpose of the American Public Library: A Revisionist Interpretation of History." *LJ* 98 (15 Sept. 1973): 2509–14.

Jones, Plummer Alston, Jr. "The Odyssey of the Immigrant in American History: From the Changed to the Changer; A Bibliographic Essay." *Immigrants and Minorities* 7 (Nov. 1988): 314–23.

Kalisch, Philip Arthur. "A Parable of Three Branch Libraries: A Social and Historical Analysis of the Waterfront Branches of the Enoch Pratt Free Library, Baltimore, Maryland." In Library History Seminar, 4th, 1971, Florida State University, *Proceedings*, ed. by Harold Goldstein and John M. Goudeau. Tallahassee, FL: Journal of Library History, 1972. Microfiche.

Kaynor, Fay Campbell (Reed). "'A Most Progressive Woman': Lynchburg's Librarian, Jane Maud Campbell (1869-1947)." *Randolph-Macon Woman's College Alumnae Bulletin* 80 (Dec. 1986): 16–19, 50–51.

Kennedy, Ruby Jo (Reeves). "Single or Triple Melting Pot? Intermarriage in New Haven, 1870–1950." *American Journal of Sociology* 58 (July 1952): 56–59.

McClymer, John F. "The Americanization Movement and the Education of the Foreign-Born Adult, 1914–25." In *American Education and the European Immigrant: 1840–1940*, ed. by Bernard J. Weiss. Urbana: University of Illinois Press, 1982.

———. "The Federal Government and the Americanization Movement, 1915-24." *Prologue: The Journal of the National Archives* 10 (Spring 1978): 22–41.

McMullen, Haynes. "Services to Ethnic Minorities Other than Afro-Americans and American Indians." In *A Century of Service: Librarianship in the United States and*

Canada, ed. by Sidney L. Jackson, Eleanor B. Herling, and E. J. Josey. Chicago: ALA, 1976.
"Massachusetts Division of Library Extension, Executive Staff, 1890–1965" [Chart]. *Bay State Librarian* 55 (Oct. 1965): 15.
Vecoli, Rudolph J. "The Resurgence of American Immigration History." *American Studies International* 17 (Winter 1979): 46–66.

Dissertations and Theses

Butrick, May Wendellene. "History of the Foreign Literature Department of Cleveland Public Library, 1925–72." Master's thesis, Kent State University, 1974.
Elmquist, Ruth A. "The Education of the Immigrant in American Society: 1880–1915." Master's thesis, Drew University, 1982.
Freeman, Margaret B. "The Brownsville Children's Branch of the Brooklyn Public Library, Its Origin and Development." Master's thesis, Brooklyn Public Library, 1940.
Heimanson, Rudolf H. "The Library in the Americanization of the Immigrant." Master's thesis, Pratt Institute, 1953.
Jones, Plummer Alston, Jr. "American Public Library Service to the Immigrant Community, 1876–1948; A Biographical History of the Movement and Its Leaders: Jane Maud Campbell (1869–1947), John Foster Carr (1869–1939), Eleanor (Edwards) Ledbetter (1870–1954), and Edna Phillips (1890–1968). Ph.D. dissertation, University of North Carolina at Chapel Hill, 1991.
Murray, Mary Elizabeth. "The Branch Library: A Mirror of Its Community, with Case Histories of Several Branches of the Cleveland Public Library." Master's thesis, Western Reserve University, 1951.
Nagy, Mary Catherine. "History and Relationship of the Rice Branch Library to Its Hungarian Patrons." Master's thesis, Western Reserve University, 1952.
Phillips, Virginia. "Fifty-Six Years of Service to the Foreign-Born by the Cleveland Public Library." Master's thesis, Western Reserve University, 1957.
Rodstein, Frances M. "The East 79th Street Branch of the Cleveland Public Library: An Historical Overview 1909–1970." Master's thesis, Kent State University, 1971.
Silver, Robert Alan. "A Description and History of the Foreign Literature Division of the Cleveland Public Library." Master's thesis, Western Reserve University, 1953.
Weinberg, Daniel Erwin. "The Foreign Language Information Service and the Foreign Born, 1918–1939: A Case Study of Cultural Assimilation Viewed as a Problem in Social Technology." Ph.D. dissertation, University of Minnesota, 1973.
Wong, Rita. "History of the Chatham Square Branch of the New York Public Library." Master's thesis, Pratt Institute, 1955.

Index

see Cleveland, St. Louis NYPL,

About the Author

PLUMMER ALSTON JONES, JR. is Director of Library Services and Professor of Library Science at Catawba College, Salisbury, North Carolina. He is currently Vice President, President-Elect of the North Carolina Library Association. He is a Visiting Lecturer for the Department of Library and Information Studies, School of Education, at the University of North Carolina-Greensboro.

4* bio's (not on the immi's)

ALA's CWFB

1901–

*2 end in eva's of free &
of restricted immi.

Nat'l Origins Act of 1924

p.150 the librarian as social worker is
a constant, even as the goal
of that social work evolves

adult education as a means

p.194 the model of pragmatism: library
service defined by what is useful
[but what data on low immigrants themselves viewed it

No foreign-language
sources cited, though he
reports them (p.134)—
that remains to
be studied.